criminals

VALERIE TRUEBLOOD

criminals

LOVE STORIES

COUNTERPOINT | BERKELEY, CALIFORNIA

Copyright © 2016 Valerie Trueblood

"His Rank" was previously published in *Southword* (Ireland).

Library of Congress Cataloging-in-Publication Data
Names: Trueblood, Valerie.
Title: Criminals : love stories / Valerie Trueblood.
Description: Berkeley : Counterpoint, 2016. | 2015
Identifiers: LCCN 2015035616 | ISBN 9781619026186 (softcover)
Subjects: | BISAC: FICTION / Literary.
Classification: LCC PS3620.R84 A6 2016 | DDC 813/.6—dc23
LC record available at http://lccn.loc.gov/2015035616

Cover design by Faceout Studios
Interior design by Neuwirth & Associates

ISBN 978-1-61902-618-6
Counterpoint Press
2560 Ninth Street, Suite 318
Berkeley, CA 94710
www.counterpointpress.com

Printed in the United States of America
Distributed by Publishers Group West

10 9 8 7 6 5 4 3 2 1

contents

bride of the black duck   1

his rank   13

skylab   17

astride   45

kisses   59

you would be good   81

da capo   89

the war poem   111

lightning   123

aiken   135

americans love dogs   163

sleepover   167

the ivy field   203

novel of rose   225

criminals   231

bride of the black duck

It was my husband, not me, who had the binoculars and the bird books. He closed his heavy Audubon on his chest and died with a finger marking a page. The nurse moved the book, so I don't know which bird his eyes saw last. I didn't want to look at them. I never wanted to know all about birds. What Walt Whitman told us in poems, of his little canary greater than books, his frigate bird that "rested on the sky": that was enough. His gray-brown thrush. His mockingbird. Not symbols but animals with souls, like himself. One his sad brother.

My husband would have been glad when the black duck appeared, glad to see me take an interest in it. In the first months, I would hear his voice in the house. "Take an interest!" "Go ahead and cry, I'm honored. Cry, but not all day." "Go to the doctor." "Just give the bird books to the library." He had loved birds, put time and thought into them, but they were a hobby. He would not have stayed up at night worrying about a particular one. Yet if you were to do that, he was a man who would have tried to console you.

The year he died, the year the duck appeared, I got involved with a family in the neighborhood, the Lesages.

Raya, the mother, would not settle for anything halfhearted once you crossed into her house and she into yours. That was a troth. People were always breaking it, though. Half the friends she had made had lost patience with her drinking and her high-handed, possessive affection. Of a defector she would say, "I don't know what it is, I've known her forever, she's someone I love."

"That's probably it," her son would say. He could say it kindly.

The one I would have wanted when I was young was her son, for his beauty. He, Randy, was a twenty-one-year-old boy with a perfect good nature—the only good-natured one in the family. It was hard to say how an ordinary liking for people could have sprung up in that family. But Randy would single you out, invite you. "Connie, come upstairs. You can see my stuffed animals! Mom kept them all." He would take the stairs two at a time: to him you were not somebody having to grab the banister and catch up. In his old room, stuffed animals by the dozen were flopped on the comforter and sitting up on the shelves. Looking out of the black eyes at us was Time itself. I lost my breath. Did I have sons in their fifties, living in cities of their own? Where had I put the donkey, the elephant without ears? Quickly Randy gave me his arm.

Randy was a sharer; he stood ready to share your moment of panic. He had long-lashed blue eyes, a child's eyes. He could disarm and flatter you with a beautiful, intimate, predatory smile, for along with his sweetness went a streak of something less than cruelty but more than mischief.

He lived with his lover, Hans. Hans was in his forties, a fit, handsome, unsmiling man with hair cut so close you could see the curl only as a silver ripple. "You're going to love Hans," Raya said, and she was right. I would love him for his resemblance to my husband, in his austerity, his ardent, unshareable, preoccupying interests, but would he love me? I didn't say that of course. At this age we are thought to have left off longing to be anyone's favorite, while coming ourselves into a manageable and harmless general fondness, as for books we finally have time to read.

"I know he's a lot older than Randy," Raya went on, "but I think of it this way: Randy's safe there. He's safe with Hans."

Hans was a professor of anthropology and had a name in his field; he was Hans Klaas, author of books about the original peoples of the Northwest. Once he knew you he would let fall facts about them here and there, in his withdrawn but precise way. What happened to these people to eradicate all they lived to do was too serious for conversation. You had to go out onto the balcony of his condo in winter and stand in the cold rain at night, hold the wet railing with him in a stiff homage to the lost. You had to look down at the Sound, cross out the freighters and tugs, the ferries with their lights, and place on the black waters one high-prowed dugout canoe as long as a semi.

Hans never touched on the subjects Randy chattered about away from him—the two-spirit, once known as *berdache,* who dressed and lived as the opposite sex, or the "manly-hearted woman." "Don't ask him about that stuff," Randy said. "No no no."

That first night, on being told that I had taught English and even written a book in my younger days, Hans said, "Indeed!" The cold smile he gave me was the opposite of Randy's.

"It's about Walt Whitman," Randy said. "I'm halfway." People are always halfway through your book. Zeno was right; they will never reach the end. I'm thankful not to have written another. "It's good!" Randy added.

"I would have assumed no less," said Hans. That was our meeting. It didn't matter; we would be friends. A midnight would come when, overcoming his hatred of the phone, he would call me and say lightly, "You don't happen to remember where Randy's class was meeting, do you, dear?"

Randy was attending the community college where he could get night classes, though moving in with Hans had taken him far from the campus and the cruising areas of Capitol Hill.

The rooms were huge, spare. There was an elaborate sound system, and once Hans knew I was losing my hearing he would invite me over to listen with the volume up. He planned carefully so as not to do this when his neighbors were at home. The music open on the rack of the piano was the *Diabelli Variations,* but he had an intention tremor that had put a stop to his playing. "He won't shake hands,"

Randy told me in the elevator, the first night. With someone my age, however, politeness compelled Hans to offer the hand with its slow tremble.

"I'm his only friend," Randy said in the elevator going down. "People come over because of his cooking. I'm the one who talks to them. If they touch the piano they can't come back. I tell him he's just like my mother—he doesn't like anybody." This he said with some pride.

"They both love you."

"Oh, love." Randy waved his hand.

The strength of Hans's feeling for Randy was such that when you were in the room with them the air felt close, as in a dedicated enclosure like an ICU or an indoor pool. He wanted Randy home; he disapproved of his day job as a transporter at the hospital. "I couldn't possibly quit. The nurses bring me cookies!"

"Ah," I said. "But now half the nurses are guys. And the doctors are women." This I had noticed in my recent stay in the hospital, but what made me say it?

"Guys can make cookies now, it's the law. Hans makes the best macaroons."

• • •

The day I met the Lesages I was halfway through my cardio circuit with the pedometer when I heard shouts coming from one of the big houses. I didn't know who lived there. Even without my hearing aids I could hear the words. Never! Never! Liar! A man and a woman. It was ten in the morning, an hour when most people are not home to scream and weep, but safe in the office or school. A third voice, young and shrill, joined in. I had stopped walking anyway, short of breath and lightheaded, but I listened until a silence fell and one of them opened the door and let the dog out. The dog was a golden retriever, so I put out my hand as he—or as it turned out, she—tore down the steps and ran at me. She was whining rather than barking. She bit me on the hand. After the bite she hung her head, curled her tail under, and retreated. A tall woman stepped onto the porch. "What are you doing here?" she said. Her face was white.

"I'm walking," I said. "Your dog bit me."

"You're trespassing."

"I'm standing on the sidewalk."

"You're spying."

"I am not. I'm having a heart attack." I squatted down to rest my palms on the sidewalk, which tilted and became a gray slope. A phrase I had read came into my mind: desert of sidewalk. Something from the paper, about a suburb. Desert of sidewalk, I said to myself as I got down on my side. I reclined like Whitman. I felt I could begin on a poem.

"Oh God! Nathan! Call 911! Morgan bit her! Jesus, she's having a heart attack!" The woman ran back into the house, where, as she would tell it later, her stepdaughter stopped crying to say, "And if you say Jesus in my presence one more time I will call the police," and she, Raya, the stepmother with two DUIs, in therapy for failing this girl, Caitlin, and all the other members of her family, screamed, "Do that, they'll love it, they'll lock you up and shock your little shit brain. Jesus! Jesus! Jesus!" Raya was to confess this, and many worse things screamed at this praying girl entrusted to her as a daughter. "But I love her!" And she did, faithful as Caitlin was at that time to a group of kids who stood passing out leaflets about the Rapture. "Convicted Christian! Convicted! That's the word they use!"

Meanwhile a man had crouched and rolled me onto my back. He had his arm under my neck and he was cramming an aspirin past my teeth. "Chew it." I swallowed and whispered, "You're a doctor, I bet."

"I am," he said with that proud sternness they have. Of course he was, as my husband had been, along with the owners of a good number of these houses. He picked up my bitten hand, looked at the tooth marks. He must have been thinking, they put your dog down for this.

"For God's sake, Nathan, start CPR!"

"She's breathing, Raya, and she has a pulse." The aid car pulled up.

The next day was the first of our friendship. I was going to have a bypass in an hour. The Lesages walked into the CCU holding hands. "I'm so sorry I said you were trespassing," Raya said, starting to cry as she raised my hand with the IV in it and kissed my fingers and her own. "Oh, if you'll just believe me."

"About what?"

"Just please believe that Morgan is a gentle dog. She was worked up. She can't take screaming. She starts racing back and forth, up and down the stairs. . . . Oh Jesus, what's wrong with me?"

To this her husband had no answer, but while we were waiting they filled me in: Nathan was an orthopedist and this was the hospital where he admitted. They had a son, Randy, who had a part-time job there; Raya volunteered there. "Actually, it's community service. Court-ordered. My real work is at home," Raya said. "Destruction and repair."

From the CCU you go in your own bed instead of a gurney. Everybody said hello to Nathan as I was rolled along half hearing—now my hearing aids were out—and looking up at the soundproof tiles. I thought of his shouts the day before. What if the OR techs putting on their soft booties had heard him? What if a patient knew the surgeon had been at home screaming, "Because you're a bitch!" before gentle hands gowned him in the OR?

They both walked me all the way to the elevator, where the doors opened for my bed and Raya laid her hand on her heart.

At the bus shelter near my house we have a round lily pond with turtles and ducks. That's the kind of neighborhood it is. At least there's a bus. The people waiting at the river-rock shelter, with its shake roof and benches and pleasantly leaf-strewn floor, carry briefcases.

Across the way is a low ivy-covered church whose bells clang out a hymn at noon. "Joyful, Joyful, We Adore Thee," a hymn I sang as a child. "Wellspring of the joy of living, ocean depth of happy rest!" The bells are so out of tune the newspaper ran a letter of complaint. It said you should not do that to Beethoven, and who would disagree? In deference to a life of such mad certainty and exaltation, re-erupting out of every misery, you must not play the music except perfectly. That's what Hans would say, did say. The tragedy of Beethoven's life went far beyond the deafness. No one would love him, let alone marry him.

Were his last words really "The comedy is over," in Latin? I wish I had asked Hans. He would have known.

You must start right now memorizing music, Hans advised me. Where my hearing was concerned he was almost tender.

I know without needing to hear it that ducks quack to each other in little snaps, sotto voce. It's an intimate voice, not after a response from anything but a duck.

The dog walker goes by with six dogs, who do not bother the ducks or fight among themselves or even cross leashes, no matter that they did not choose each other. He lets them off the leash in the empty parking lot of the church, where there's a fence and they're safe to play like children. Before she moved away with Nathan and Caitlin, the dog Morgan, who bit me, was sometimes among them. She would recognize me, but quickly look away.

All spring, nannies and a few mothers come to the pond wheeling the new giant strollers, bringing toddlers to feed the ducks. They squat with their bags of crumbs, unconcerned about avian viruses or anything else disorderly or malign, like the SUV that jumped the curb and landed in the middle of the pond among the lily pads. It was nighttime and no one was hurt, not even a duck. These are calm wide streets where you might buy a house and move in imagining you had reached a kind of resolution.

Yet things happen here. In this same long year an old man's wife died under suspicious circumstances, drowned in the bathtub. The same day, their son disappeared. The old man was cleared; the son was the person of interest—over forty and back living at home. He was odd, of course. That's what was being said. Odd to do that, come home at his age as if you had given up, and yet dye your hair black and wear the haircut of a Beatle. Odd to go mad like that—if he did go mad—and commit such a crime for the sake of the old man, his father, yet never to have walked with him as he went around the block every day stamping his cane or eventually his walker and sometimes having to be steered back by a neighbor.

I would see the old man but I didn't know he was searching for his house. He didn't know I had a husband who had died. I would look the other way so he wouldn't see tears on my face. Maybe he had them on his, too. One day he was standing under a tree looking up with an awful concentration and I almost said, "Are you a birder?" The wife stared balefully out from the newsprint. The article said she had been in the habit of beating him with his own cane, a revelation forced on him when the investigators made him take off his shirt.

The ducks hide their eggs on little islands in the pond or among the bushes and tree roots on the banks. In the spring they swim forth, each pulling a filmy banner of puffs. One mother could have as many as ten or twelve ducklings. The line grows shorter; one spring will not leave her so many. The males swim along behind, or fly off together in a rush, and once the ducklings have grown too big to get entirely under the fluffed-out feathers of the mother, too big to be crow or raccoon bait, all of them sun together and groom their feathers on the banks of the little pond.

One day the black duck and his mate appeared among the mallards. They joined the flock, although without any friendliness, and stayed on. They were not wild ducks; someone must have left them there. Such ducks exist in a city, pets, or pedigreed animals from gardens with water features. "Ornamentals." Unlike the mallards, who rise up as one and disappear over the rooftops, these birds do not fly. They are runner ducks, I found when I looked them up, though I never saw them run.

The black pair stood apart, bigger than the mallards. At times the male would lower his head and snake his neck at them. They weren't interested in his mate but he could not seem to help it. Soon after their arrival, the female was hit by a car. No one from the neighborhood would hit a duck. Even the buses come to a stop so the ducks can parade to the big lawns across the street. But people from elsewhere don't know, they just barrel through. They killed the black duck's mate. I didn't see it, the city park people told me.

The duck went into an ugly mourning. He interrupted the shaking of his torso and stabbing at his breast only to snake his head at any duck who came near him, male or female. The green-shining black of his feathers went dull.

I got out my husband's books, trying to see what the future might hold for such an animal. I started a sheet in one of his notepads: "Interbreeding: wild w/ domestic. More males—'oversupply.' Female offspring of hybridization often infertile, take on male plumage. ???"

After Nathan left Raya and went to live with his girlfriend, Randy would sometimes spend the weekend with his mother, and when he did that he would meet me at the park bench to watch the ducks. Sometimes he would have a friend with him.

The black duck would not come to our bench with the others. He didn't have a look to spare for our kind, so occupied was he with tearing at his body in a ritual to which the others paid no heed. He drove his beak into his breastbone or rooted in his wings, or spread his flat tail and worked it up and down in spasms as if to rid his body of it.

"Poor baby, he needs a new wife." This was one of the boys Randy brought with him. He and Randy were in a poetry class together. It was the second time I had met this particular one, Reed, who wanted to be a poet. He was the only one who accompanied Randy more than once on these weekends. Randy had given him my book about Whitman and he was halfway through.

"I don't think they can have more than one wife," Randy said. "I think it's all over for them after one."

"Can't we find him a bride?" Reed persisted.

That's when I said, "'Out of the Cradle Endlessly Rocking.' Do you know that poem? Stay here. I'll get it."

"Oh, you don't need to go all the way home," Randy said.

"I want to see it," Reed said.

"Her house is blocks away."

"Please," Reed said, turning to him.

When I got back with the book, they took turns reading to themselves. The off-key bells started in and Reed looked up and laughed, but when he got to the end of the poem he sat in silence. He asked if he could read it aloud. I wasn't sure about that, because he had laughed, and there we were at the duck pond, after all, with the toddlers. But he read gravely. He was studying acting as well as poetry. Randy said so before he started. Not everyone can read this poem, with its terrible sincerity, the extremes of its romantic lament and final ecstasy. All these things amuse some readers, some students in particular, as I remember. From a bird in a nest the poem moves skyward and seaward to the immeasurable—and to Whitman, relieving—subject of death.

"Loved! Loved! Loved! Loved! Loved!" That's the chant of the remembering bird in his nest close to the ocean. There the narrator listens to him and to the sound of the waves, which at first, before the sea makes clear its true word, comes to his ears as "soothe, soothe."

The mate called to, coaxed, beseeched, never comes. The true mate is death, and that is the word from the sea. "Death, death, death, death, death," the boy read. When he had finished, even the toddlers were watching him, dribbling crumbs from their bags. Finally he turned and he and Randy looked into each other's eyes.

By Sunday evening of these weekends, whatever boy Randy had brought with him would be gone and Hans would come to dinner at Raya's and he and Randy would go back home together.

A few weeks after Nathan left to be with his girlfriend, he came to get his daughter and the dog. All that time Caitlin had been living in a new peace with Raya. Nathan said to me, "I know how it looks, I know what Raya's told you, but this time I've got it right. But Connie, I want you to watch over Raya because she's capable of anything. Anything."

I had been spending time with Raya as she gathered his things and Caitlin's into boxes, saying nothing against either of them for the first time since I had known her. A trance of mildness had come over her. Caitlin too was as she had never been, free of accusation, packing up her room without stopping to pray. "Capable of anything," I said. "Like what?"

"OK, fine," Nathan said. "Fine. So we all are."

It wasn't Raya who was capable of anything, or Randy with his secrets and the strange absence, in one so amorous and kind, of what we use the words "a heart" to mean. It wasn't Nathan, who stayed behind when his girlfriend vanished into California. It wasn't Caitlin, who, within a week of going with her father, had taken his car and driven without a license back to Raya's. It wasn't the dog Morgan, who had consorted with strange dogs in obedience to a stranger, and once in her life given in to the longing to bite. It wasn't even the black duck, who stayed behind alone when the mallards deserted the pond, lost his feathers, and did not know his bride when she came.

It was Hans. Caitlin was at my door, ringing the bell and banging. "Connie, Connie!" When I opened the door she sagged into my arms. "Can you come? Come. Hans died."

"Died" is better than "is dead." "Died" is a word for an act; it contains a bit of time, it contains for the briefest moment the idea that the person can somehow go back on it. When the doctor told me about my husband, I asked her, "Are you sure?" "Yes, he has died."

Hans jumped off the balcony where we had stood when he cleared the Sound of ships to show me the great canoe.

Before he jumped, he tried to strangle Randy, but in the middle of the attempt, he let go. He gave up. He walked to the balcony doors— we do know he walked, maybe resuming his stiff manner on the way, so Randy didn't know to hold him back—and drew them apart.

As a witness to the act, Randy got into the crowded elevator with the police and descended to the sidewalk. Desert of sidewalk. "I witness the corpse with its dabbled hair." That's Whitman. What Randy said, we don't know. The police had no trouble getting him to admit to the struggle between himself and Hans, and the questioning satisfied them. They photographed the bruises on his neck, measured the distance from bedroom to balcony and the height of the rail.

Raya told me several times about a thumbprint the size of a tablespoon on Randy's trachea, the whole neck purple where Hans's unmatched hands had grasped and released before he jumped. She got into describing it again the day I went over to say bon voyage. "Don't think I'm excusing my son for driving that poor man mad," she said. I was afraid she was going to say something like, "We all loved Hans," but she did not.

"Oh God, speaking of the mad, Nathan's already threatening to join us in Mexico," she said. She and Caitlin were going. Caitlin had the suitcases out on the sidewalk ready for the airport van. "Here's where I met you," Raya said, pointing to the spot on the pavement. "And Connie, look at this." Around her neck she had a gold chain with a six-month AA medallion on it, from Caitlin. "Yeah, check out the 'Recovery Gifts' site," Caitlin said. She was going down to join a group of Catholic students who were building an orphanage. Raya was going to visit a famous well nearby, where people came with bottles and the farmer let them pump the curative waters. "I want to be a different person. Daria says that's possible for me." Daria was the social worker assigned her by the court. "Oh Connie. How I long for things to just simply somehow someday be normal."

When we say "normal" I think we must mean "good." Is that right? How widely Whitman opened his eyes, his arms, to find death normal.

My own feeling is that we never change. Not by choice, not on purpose. I didn't say that to Raya. For one thing I had just been noticing the new attitude in her daughter now that she was sixteen. "This will be good. She can just drink the water or pour it on herself or whatever," Caitlin told me, getting into the front seat of the van with the driver. "Take care, Connie."

Raya opened her window in the back. "Oh, I'm leaving you here all by yourself."

"I'm fine," I said. Because she wanted to be the only friend you had, you didn't say to Raya that there were people who would look in on you, or that you didn't care whether they did or not, because you didn't want the helpful, oh, never, never. For yourself, you wanted the ones who would not answer, the obsessed, the ardent, the lost.

As for Randy, in the summer he was driving across the country with Reed. They were going to explore Long Island, called by the native peoples Paumanok, where Walt Whitman heard the sea speak to a bird to console it.

his rank

Knox had a favorite bar, because of the bartender, a woman he was preparing to get to know. It was on a block where the university ran up against a changing neighborhood, close enough to the campus to bring in the grounds crew and campus security. It was small and dark, with nothing except neon beer signs in the window to set it apart from the outbuildings of the university.

The bartender had hair cut as close as Obama's. Her eyes were so large they took time to complete a blink. When Knox first started coming in they had had a happy hour menu; now a guy in the back washing glasses would make you a plate of nachos, but that was it. The bartender was on her own, no servers.

Knox decided beautiful was a word thrown around—he had employed it a good deal himself—when it should be reserved for examples of indifferent power like that in the curve of the bartender's eyelids as she worked the taps. When she gave you your beer she looked straight at you and that was like being wanded at the airport. Even if you were white, the eyes could say you were a man. Then something nice with the lips though not a smile. Then the luxurious blink, as if you, and the whole arrangement—time of day, frosted glass, work, play, men, women—had made her sleepy. Yes, he was going to make his move.

His feet were stiff from being hooked over a rung of the high wooden stool by the window. He had been sitting for an hour breaking up with his girlfriend, who kept saying, "It's because I gained the weight."

"That has nothing to do with it."

"I weigh more than you do. You think I'll get that big." In a booth two hefty women in the black uniforms of campus security were sharing a plate of nachos. "Right back." She stumbled getting down off the stool; she couldn't hold her beer.

A man held the front door open and allowed a pit bull to precede him into the room. Big guy, already spotted by Knox in the crosswalk with his dog, with a funny look on his face that made Knox say casually to himself, Don't come in here, dude. The man had on a green tank though it was not really warm enough for that, and he was handsome in a flaring way Knox had to admit made him uneasy even in some sports figures.

"Dog can't come in here," said the bartender.

"She can't, huh?" The man advanced into the room with the dog, snubbed up tight on the leash so its front paws had to scrabble for the floor.

"You tie him up." The bartender stretched out her whole arm and pointed her long finger.

"Bus stop. Can't tie this kind of a dog up in a bus stop."

"What you want to come in here for?" said the bartender, not unkindly, filling a schooner and setting it on the empty bar. "This that new dog? He nice?"

"She." The dog sat, facing the table of the two guards eating nachos. "You did it," the man said to the bartender. The way he said it made the dog look up and emit a growl. "You goddamn married him."

"I did. Last Friday. I said I was."

"You did it. OK. All right. Where is he?"

"He can't sit around in here. He's at work."

"He knew you were with me."

"I wasn't with you, baby."

The man reached in his pants and pulled out a gun, small as a phone. People set down their drinks in the quiet. He scanned the room with the gun, like a flashlight. The bathroom door opened and Knox's girlfriend came out. Knox held perfectly still, praying the man's attention onto her. But one of those girl guards was sure to pull a weapon. Everybody in the place was going to get shot. He, Knox, was going to die.

Somehow, his girlfriend took in the situation. Moving slowly, she sank into the booth with the two women. One of them put a fat arm around her. The other one had a walkie-talkie.

"Don't nobody go on your cell or nothing," said the bartender. "This is Jerome. I know Jerome."

"You think you know me." He pointed the gun at her.

"Come on, Jerome. Don't do that. You don't want to do that." And she came out from behind the bar and put her hand up in front of the little stump of gun. She took hold of the barrel with two long fingers and thumb as if it were a straw she was going to drop into a drink. "Come on, now." She raised the flap and went behind the bar. Jerome got up on a stool, and instead of putting the gun out of sight the bartender laid it down on the bar. Jesus God, are you kidding me? Knox screamed in his head.

"Sit," Jerome said to the dog. Then he put his forehead down on the bar and his shoulders began to shake. "Baby boy," the bartender said, spreading her fingers, with the gold ring on one, around his head and holding it while he shook.

At one table a man got to his feet. "Hey, don't you forget the check," the bartender called. Then Knox's girlfriend stood up, hugged the big security guard, and started across the room to Knox. Her face shone with tears. He stared at her outstretched arms. So people loved, even many of them, and his rank among them was not high.

skylab

There it was: the blue bee. Off the clothesline and down into the flowerpots, weighing down orchids with its thumb-size abdomen. It made Amy think of fat women she had washed in nursing school. A panniculus might hang to the thighs; you lifted it on the back of your hand and wrist, swabbed carefully because of yeasts. In this country the patient's family gave the baths, women carrying basin and washcloth from home. And here you wouldn't see a swag of fat on a patient. As if it were new itself, this was a country of young, slim people.

Amy sat on the amah's terrace at the back of the house, letting her hair dry in the sun. *Skylab.* It was on every page of the newspaper. Skylab was going to fall on Asia.

Next door the shirts on the line began to jig as the amah snatched them, with an unsmiling glance at Amy. She was a Malay girl, not an Indian like most of the amahs in this circle of houses built for foreigners, and wore the snowy headscarf. She was known to have gone down on her knees, after the Australian couple stir-fried pork on her day off, to wash everything with red mud as the Koran decreed—cupboards, drawers, refrigerator, the blackened little gas stove these houses all had.

"Wholesome dust," the Koran said. "Pure earth." When there was no water, pure earth could be used for bathing, for purification.

Amy and John had no amah. Eleanor, the Englishwoman who ran the Koran study group, said why not hire one simply to avoid flouting custom, but Amy knew they would not, even if her own work permit finally came through and she went to work in the hospital, they would not have somebody in the house with them, in on their life, which was too frail and groggy after the labor and shame of all that had tumbled them down here, and at the same time too full of a hot, irresistible pride in their being here alone, their having left everything behind.

The blue bee challenged her whenever she hung something on the clothesline. She could see where it had been chewing the clothespins. A bee that ate wood? It was solitary, territorial, more like a shrunken comical dog than an insect.

She was starting to miss dogs, the easygoing, confident dogs of home. In contrast to the thin and craven animals here, they seemed, those golden retrievers with waving tails, to have been the kindly guards of everything untroubled and ordinary.

The bee had a routine: it would zigzag in front of her face like a bulldog on a chain, flexing its iridescent hind parts in midair. Did it have a sting? But it was cowardly, it dodged out of sight.

"You *are* eating those clothespins," she said aloud. It ate everything. She had seen it squeeze out from under the lid of the garbage can, going at a drunken sideways crawl. Now, just like a dog giving up on barking, it had blundered downward and zeroed in on something at her feet.

An eviscerated bird. That was the smell. A bird with empty eye sockets. Yes, the beak pointed at their door. She thought without surprise, *They* left it. For us, for the infidel.

Here you saw the word in the paper every day, ever since the Shah had fallen in Iran. *Infidel.* The Shah had been spat out, he could find no harbor, now he was in Mexico trying to get to the US. In the shade of every building young men stood talking, striking their palms. *US.* You heard it, a hiss among the soft syllables. Amy wore skirts and long sleeves but eyes followed her. It didn't matter that she freely borrowed the code for virtue, keeping her eyes down and her step narrow.

Among the white scarves on the campus a black fin, too, rose now and then, the chador. The chador had to do with men as well as God. Inside it moved women like the nuns of her childhood, but more complex in their loyalties and more secret. The eyes, though, were just embarrassed young eyes, the eyes of girls, students, sending skittish glances.

Inside, blinking from the sun, she saw a cellophane wrapper on the floor of the amah's little pantry, where she never went except to trip the hot water heater after a thunderstorm. She reached for it and stood up fast. The pale crinkled thing was the skin of a snake. Along the wall lay eight or ten inches of it, silver and empty, and somewhere behind the water heater the rest of it. However long it was. Its head.

John would know what to do. He had lived here before. He remembered many things: he knew the plague of frogs in the drain would end, he could predict the first yap of the hungry house lizards, the cicaks, coming out from behind calendars and picture frames at the cocktail hour, when the air would fill with mosquitoes for them to catch. He would tell her what to do about the snake. He would say a cat had left the bird. "If it were for us"—she could hear him—"they would have put it at the front door."

Despite the white hair John didn't look his age, but bit by bit she recognized the time hidden on him, brought in with them like contraband. It was the old-fashioned obviousness of his teasing, his careful fingers bringing up the knot of his tie. His way of waving, his saying "Drink up" and "Right-o." She had seen it in movies. His flick to alertness if she casually said "fuck," his inability to hear it as anything but sexual. While she, whose lust for him had been legendary among the nurses, had entered a state of quietness and caution, and become watchful, as a bird might watch its nest from another tree.

His calling certain songs "her" music. His discreet awe of pill and tampon. His wife had finished with all that. First wife.

"Oh, John, look!" While they were having breakfast one of the tribe of feral cats had come into the yard, stepping sideways with little hops. He knew what the trouble was. He said, "Somebody put boiling water down the drain. They scald their paws." The house sinks emptied directly into a concrete drain surrounding every house like a little moat, running into the great V-shaped monsoon gutters along the streets and roads. Strays fed in the drains, cats and the hairless raw-skinned dogs. The cats had eye infections but kept their hair. *Cats are like women*, Amy thought. *We are not as pitiful as the men.*

That liquid song was an oriole, John said. That swipe of yellow paint in the profuse white flowers of the frangipani tree planted all over the *lorong*, the little circular lane where the university housed visiting faculty. And was it the tree of graveyards, as someone said? Closer to the house was a row of lime trees, the fruit like bottle caps among the leaves. Sometimes a lime flinched, blinked, became the pouch of a green lizard.

John stood up, stretched and shook himself, ran his hands through his hair already darkened with sweat. "Don't forget the Barneses are coming for a beer. I think that's still on. And the fellow from New Zealand. Carruthers. His wife's gone home without him. Don't you do that." There was a faint tremble in the hand that tipped up Amy's chin. She sank against him.

"Let's not do anything special," he said against her hair. "Just put out beer, they'll leave before dinner. Do we have any napkins?"

Napkins. How could he think of that? An invisible life reared up in back of him. A woman. Napkins. Silver.

"We have some paper ones. I wish . . . I wish they didn't have to come." With her thumb she wiped the sweat from under his eyes. She would have liked to press the dark lids restfully down.

"I don't care much for the idea either," he said. "But let's get it over with. It will satisfy everybody for a while." He sighed and tapped his breastbone. She didn't like that, the scar there with his heart under it.

One day not long after they arrived, the students who played handball with him had made him stop. They had sat him down, fanned him. They weren't medical students but he was short of breath and they called the hospital.

The doctor who saw him had a wife in the Koran study group, who mentioned it the next day. Amy pretended she knew. When she asked John, he said they had made him sit down not because of his breathing, as the wife reported, but because of twisting his ankle on the court. And indeed he was limping.

He waved from the gate and disappeared on the back path to the hospital. This whole slope of the city was recently cleared jungle. Part of it was cultivated, rubber trees being grown in slim-trunked orderly rows, but old stands of jungle remained here and there, little zones of furious life. Monkeys came out to rob the trash cans. Once when John took the back way at night with his flashlight there was a thrashing in the bushes and a huge lizard wagged across his path.

She could picture him, alone under the thick trees, hand on his chest. He wouldn't be looking out for anything. He thought everything was behind them.

Spiders swung against his cheek when he was hurrying to Accident & Emergency to operate on the boys who wrecked their motorbikes on the Federal Highway or flipped into the drains scattering tanks of cooking gas, baskets of pottery, plate glass.

"He died?" she would say. She was a nurse, used to the ones who died. But no, they didn't die. If she was meeting him in the hospital she would see these boys of his, shrouded in gauze and elastic burn mask, hobbling between nurses. She repeated the Malay she heard them croak, "*Perlahan-lahan.*"

"Slow-slow," John said.

She shut her mind and began to work on her theory of suffering. The insistence on countries might be wrong, but it was no better to think of the world as one, one organism with a saline of wrongs dripping in regularly and impartially. Wrongs didn't go steadily, fairly, into solution. They went into lumps and clots. It was all right if all suffered, but some escaped.

"No one escapes," John said, smiling because he knew the story of the spell on Amy, cast by her mother and witnessed by her brothers, that kept her from harm. She was the youngest. Her father had begun to drink, leaving things in the hands of four brothers already obliged by a decree from their dying mother, binding and irreversible: *Take care of your sister.*

When she got away from her brothers the spell continued on its own. In one of her tests of it, she forded a Guatemalan stream where flies carrying *Onchocerca* were known to breed. She unloaded a jeep and carried supplies, one bundle after another, across the waist-deep water into a village full of river blindness, and the worm in the stream did not settle in her.

Pouring out of a hole in the floor, the ants filed up past the medicine cabinet to a hole in the ceiling. No, some of them were coming down, the line was double. Sometimes they came down carrying some of their own. What drew them inside and up? Did they live up there, or were they fighting an invader? What was up there? Did they die working on it? Did they weaken and fall out of the line when the time came? What was age, what was natural death for an ant? She can walk on ants, the Malays said. It meant that lightness of step the women had no matter how much they had in their arms along with the babies proudly turned to show you if you smiled.

She could sit for a long time in the bathroom studying the ants. On the way up, huge loads, shouldered and pushed. Once a dozen of them had maneuvered a peanut up the wall. And the forearm jaws around a corpse: that carrying away of the dead looked like dignity. They should learn not to squander themselves on these crusades! But each one on the wall today might never have been there before, pushing with a head like a shiny seed. But a seed with sense organs— able to find a grain of palm sugar on the kitchen counter.

The medicine cabinet had a gap behind it where cicaks lived in the cracked plaster. Sometimes an unusually large one, gray and pink, came out when she was shaving her legs in the bathtub. Once it fell into the tub and swam, lunging to and fro like a little shark. The warm water must have dazed it; it let her lift it out by the tail.

You must leave, everybody said, if the cicaks ever leave.

One day a baby one, tiny, popped out of the ants' hole and raced down the wall. The big gray-pink one snatched it back. Look at that, she thought. Saved.

For a moment, crosswise in the adult's mouth, the baby cocked its head, flicked its black eyes. "Oh, God," Amy said aloud, as it was deftly flipped and swallowed.

. . .

Someone said, "At this point, all religions are cultural treasure."

It was an older woman in a batik halter dress, with skin tanned dark as that of the waiters, if not silky and luminous like theirs. This was a party in a garden with lanterns. She was English, maybe she was the hostess.

She gave Amy's hand a downward yank when they were introduced and turned to John. She was saying that before she came she had sat herself down to do her reading, and made her husband do the same. Some of the new arrivals, the wives in particular, had no idea. They were surprised to get off the plane and find themselves in a Muslim culture. Though there was more to it, of course, than Islam. "I drove myself here tonight! I drove the Federal Highway in that awful car!" So she was not the hostess. "Our driver is sick. Why? He saw the Penanggalan and it put him to bed."

The Penanggalan was a ghost, a head that flew, trailing intestines. "I have no doubt he saw it!" the suntanned woman said, shaking her finger at Amy, who had started to laugh without any feeling of amusement. She was doing that here, in the heat, if she had anything to drink. That was when the woman, curving one shoulder toward John in a way that excused Amy from having to speak, said to John, "All religions are cultural treasure."

Why are there so many people now I can't stand? Amy thought.

Allah, the Koran said, "imposed mercy on himself as a law."

The half dozen women in the Koran study group wanted to do without a guide, to be under no obligation, as Eleanor said—she was the one emerging as the leader—except to consider just what the meaning of the sacred book might be.

Amy would imitate Eleanor. "I say, this may do the trick." If John was tired she did various women in the group to make him laugh: the know-it-all doctor, the timid Japanese woman Eleanor bullied, the nice Australian—that was their neighbor who had fried the pork. "'Yehs, the attitude to animals . . . yehs . . .'" That was Eleanor, with her sprayed gray permanent and her maddening "yes" on the intake of breath, listening intently, especially beforehand when they were all drinking tea, or after an hour or so when the planned topic would wilt of its own accord like a parachute that had made it to earth. Almost as soon as she met you Eleanor found something in her big embroidered bag for you and whisked it out. The second time Amy was there Eleanor said, "A member of the royal family has made animals her cause," and she slipped Amy a little pamphlet and patted her hand closed on it.

The newest member of the group, the doctor, had arrived some months after Amy had, but she already knew how everything worked. She knew all about the place, she knew it was not going to be her favorite stint overseas. "It's the religion," the doctor said briskly, whenever anyone in the group complained about anything. She said the female medical students were not permitted to touch a patient. Because they were women they had to reach out of their deep sleeves and touch with a pencil. A pencil! If she felt that way, why was this doctor attending the Koran study group? "I have to do something with my mind," she said.

This woman knew how to drive in the flying traffic to a particular kampong for batik, and to the Batu Caves outside the city to take pictures. She was a photographer as well as a doctor. She showed her slides at the meeting, lingering over one of a monkey on the stone steps to the Hindu temple, taken with a wide-angle lens so the eyes in the monkey's lined face bugged with weary comment at a pilgrim carrying up a tray of fruit. Another was of a fantastically wrinkled trishaw driver smoking a cigarette. "You've captured him, dear!" Eleanor said. The driver's eyes were abnormally bright yet full of calm. Amy looked away from them.

The women in the study group knew how to choose a live chicken, and behind which cement wall in the open market the sellers of pork were sequestered, and where the veterinary hospital was, and which teacher at the International School belonged to which religion. All of this tired Amy, made her balk.

She had always been efficient. Why in this country was she going in circles in the heat, when all the vendors had the same red chilies, the same sheaves of long beans, to find the vendor who had smiled at her? She didn't want to choose a live chicken swung by the legs with straw between its toes; she went in secret to the new super-market to get chicken in a package. Quite suddenly she was not practical, not enterprising. She wouldn't have a car. They took the cheap taxis when they had to go somewhere. If she had to go out she scraped her hair back or wore a scarf. They could say foreign women, too, had to veil themselves, as a faction was proposing, and she would do it gladly.

In a storm, blue lightning flew through the house along the wiring and spat out of the outlets. She would sit on the floor with her back to the inner wall of flagstone, at the farthest point from any outlet, and plug up her ears. If John was home to see it he said, "Is this the girl who saved Guatemala?" He liked to be reminded of how long he had actually known her, as if years held the power of gradual sanction.

She had always been one of the calm ones who could be put to work with the dog handlers. Hours after the Guatemala earthquake she had been on the plane. They worked through the aftershocks, twenty-hour stretches in the rubble with dogs. For a surprising number of days they could dig out bodies that were alive; she had seen a slab of concrete act as a perfect tourniquet.

By the time she was in her mid-twenties she had stepped out of floatplanes and cargo jets all over the world. Sometimes on her return she could hardly say what country she had been in. A place of crum-pled awnings, statues lifted off their bases, roads heaved into ditches, where her team had sat on sand, seen eels and bright fish in a new lagoon where houses had been standing a few days before. The dazed figures lining up to get out were not the men and women they had been previously, any more than she was the same person who had been pacing with her coffee in an airport hours before. Once you felt your teeth bite down on ash, or used your hands to gouge out mudbanks, once you herded the mesmerized, all airports, all normal sleeping and eating, were set aside. Rescuer and rescued were indistinguishable, like heads bobbing in the water in a lifesaving class.

Her boyfriend Tommy had put this choice of hers down to being raised with no mother, raised with brothers. Raised *by* brothers, to strap on a catcher's pad, gap the spark plugs, go for the two-year EMT course after graduation. Though she knew her brothers had expected her to go to college, even to medical school. She was smart enough for that, they thought. But she wasn't and she didn't want to.

She couldn't brag that she was a natural, that nothing suited her better than to grab a duffel and pass through terminal doors into the smoke and tears of whatever place had been flooded or crushed or quickly rigged up as shelter.

After a few years of that she went to nursing school. She nursed. She got married.

Always, Amy had boyfriends to spare. But except for the one prolonged, impossible crush on a married man, once she met Tommy she settled in, waited years to marry him. His mother, with five sons grown, had been waiting, too. So had Amy's brothers: the wedding swarmed with brothers, hers and his, nearly a dozen of them.

Tommy was not the baby, as she was in her family, though he was the last to marry. In the receiving line his mother, who had four daughters-in-law, whispered, "Now I've got my daughter." "And I've got you," Amy answered.

But she had managed without a mother since she was six. It might not be lucky for her to take someone else, even this mother-in-law who kept hugging her, for a mother. It might remove the umbrella that traveled over her, of her mother's blessing.

After she had been lifted away from the hospital bed, where she had been allowed to lie beside her mother, words had been spoken to her brothers: the spell that kept her safe.

In the receiving line Tommy's mother kept saying, "Aren't I lucky? Now Amy can do all the worrying about this guy." In reality no one worried about Tommy, who said every day, "I'm a happy man."

They were both lucky. By the time Tommy started his peds residency they could afford the down payment on a house. On the day they were to sign the papers, she was reading the chart as she followed a bed out of the recovery room when Dr. Woods appeared, blocking her way. He had something to speak to her about; could she have lunch? She stuttered. "Today? Today? Oh, but I—I'm supposed to meet the realtor." In a departure from his usual courtesy he turned away with a shrug. "Well, but what about tomorrow?" she said.

"All right," he said, frowning. "Yes, all right, tomorrow. That will have to do."

She thought he was going to mention a position she ought to apply for. A promotion. If so the timing was right, because of the house and the fact that she was eight weeks pregnant.

Still, she was uneasy at the thought of having lunch with him. He was the one. John Woods. He was the one, with his looks and that shyness unusual among surgeons, on whom not just she but all of them had had crushes when they were in school. When he went in for his bypass, nurses had shed tears. It looked bad. It was bad; the nurses had kept the CCU filled with balloons for a month while he came back to life.

Seeing her friend Gail peel tape off the deep lines in his cheeks and lift out the sticky endotracheal tube, Amy had had a sweltering sensation. She had put her hand on Gail's arm and passed out.

For her the whole episode had stretched out and become, really, something far less agreeable than a crush. She had followed this man. Tears squeezed out of her shut eyes when she was on the phone with him about a post-op. Gail, who had three children, told her this kind of thing meant you needed to get pregnant.

In the elevator she clenched her thighs at the sound of his voice making polite replies about his health. It was a kindly voice, thickened and withdrawn a little now into his convalescence. Down it sank into her, while the large eyes he was known for looked straight into the interior of her where the naked encounters with him took place.

He always took pains to speak to her, asking her opinion. He went to some trouble to have the patients he was uneasy about assigned to her. In her old rosary case she kept a Polaroid of him cutting his birthday cake at the nurses' station. It was hers to be held, beseeched.

All the while she was throwing on her raincoat at the end of the day, grabbing her wedding lists, running out to meet Tommy in the parking lot.

At the end of the last quarter she gave in to it. She was that way; she decided a thing. It was a dark Friday morning. Patti Smith was singing "Because the Night" on the car radio and she crossed the wet parking lot with the song going on inside her. She took a Valium out of a cup on the pre-op cart. She didn't see him on the OR schedule. He must be in clinic. Three times she pushed the heavy door into the stairwell where she often met him coming down, and mounted the concrete stairs as lightly and slowly as if she were being carried up by water. She was going to speak. She was ready.

But he was not there; he was on a plane to Mexico. He had gone away with his wife and son. It was said that this son, much younger than his other children, who were grown now, was unstable. He had had trouble in school after his father's heart attack, he had been suspended for getting into fights in the gym. Everyone said the whole family needed a rest.

Finally Amy graduated, got out. Eventually of course she got on with things, and put him out of her mind. She washed her hands of her student self, the skimping, praying, caffeine-driven girl who had treasured a Polaroid wrinkled with tears. She got ready for her wedding.

By the time she went back to work at the university his hair had gone white, but he had lost his stoop and the paunch from the long period of inactivity. They all saw him out running in his black shorts; he was tall again, fit.

The next day? That would have to do.

She said, "So I'll see you down there at what, twelve thirty?" Then she was embarrassed at knowing the time he ate his lunch. He ate in the main cafeteria rather than the doctors' dining room.

"Not in the cafeteria," he said. "I thought somewhere outside."

. . .

The son still at home, Nicky, was a freshman in high school. He began to lose weight. As that year wore on, the coach put him on leave from the JV basketball team until he could show responsibility by getting some weight back on. The coach said his fighting was serious and his thinness and loss of skills were due to anorexia. Never mind how rare that was in a boy, never mind that a coach wasn't a doctor.

Once, from the car, just before they left the country, Amy had seen this son dribbling and shooting baskets by himself. A bony, horrible slow motion dribbling on the curved driveway of the house that had been John's. *Thud. Thud.* A sound that had nothing to do with a sport.

Behind the rolled-up car window she had sunk down and down, to a place from somewhere in grade school, a place of woe, where her head was heavy, tight in the braids she did herself, where she pretended to erase something on her paper. First grade. The Sister was speaking to her. The Sister said she should be sitting her brothers down—she was the girl in the family—and praying the rosary with them, for their mother's sake.

His son's legs, long sticks ending in buckets, the huge bright shoes they wore, that looked too heavy to lift. The ugly knot that a knee was when there was no fat: like the leg of her cadaver in Anatomy, with its petrified, scrotal skin. Her despair at the sight of those legs must have had something to do with her brothers. Years of boys, of running legs, Band-Aids, scabs, casts. That was it—more than John's wife, or his married daughter who went into a rage and stalked her, or the letter she got from his in-laws, a loyal old pair who did not believe any of it at first.

He had friends who tried to get him to change his mind; he had houses, cars, memberships. Years and years, like rings in a tree trunk, put into his work. She had the same things, really, and she had her brothers, though when the oldest said, "It's not so bad, really, if you think of it as King Lear marrying Juliet," she had to tell all four of them to back off. She had a mother-in-law who bragged about her and knitted her sweaters. She had a house; her signature was lying in an in-basket in the escrow office. And she had one more thing.

All of it had to be dismantled. To give birth to Tommy's child, Tommy who would no longer be her husband and would most certainly have to try to get the child away from her, kind as he was. Of course Tommy would do that, with everyone saying he should. It would make them *enemies*. Or worse, what if he did *not* try. If he gave up. Despaired. Let Amy and John take his child.

She didn't tell either one, the one who knew she was pregnant or the one who did not. She made the appointment. To the one who knew, she would say she had been worrying all along because she was spotting. She would say miscarriage.

"Certainly, come along this morning," said the man in Zoology, with that beautiful unhurried politeness, so unlike her own "if you have time" and "it wouldn't have to be today." "But make certain, before you pick up the skin, that the fellow is no longer associated with it."

Snakes of all kinds, said the young man who lifted the skin out of her cardboard box with tweezers, were common in the newer housing plots that had been jungle not so long ago.

"Oh dear, yes," he said. "It is a cobra we have here."

An enlarged scale near the hinge of the mouth identified it. He showed her with a magnifying glass. Cobras had adapted to junk piles, dumpsters, dark shelves where amahs stored food under straw domes, crevices behind rice bins. Anywhere there were rodents. Did she know the Japanese couple in the *lorong*, who had surprised one in a linen closet where mice had been into a baby quilt?

If the snake showed itself she must call, and most certainly his department would send someone to capture it.

Panting in the heat, carrying the box under her arm and abandoning her effort to maintain the straight back of the Malay women, she walked, reading the *Star*. *Skylab*. The satellite took up the whole front page. Satellite or space station. Crippled now. "Crippled American space station."

. . .

As she entered the *lorong* the insects of midday were shrilling. The word *lorong* gave her a feeling of safety, just as his name, Woods, sometimes made her see a place where they were concealed together.

On the amah's terrace at the back she saw a dark shape. It was a dog, sprawled on the stone. It didn't move at her approach. Was it dead? She crouched. The dog's withdrawal was a mere shifting of the hide. The tongue lay on the flagstone, the lips were pulled tight by sores. A male. When she moved closer his eyes widened in powerless alarm, but he only tightened the muscle that drew his penis up against his belly.

When she brought a piece of chicken the tongue left the stone and drew the meat in sideways, while the eyes kept their forward gaze. It rolled the meat drily in its mouth. Thirst. Water. She brought water in a pan. When the dog didn't raise its head she dribbled a little onto the gray gums. The back of the tongue arched, the water ran across the stone. As if the dog had given up most of its reality, no smell rose from its body.

Dogs here were like endless rings of a telephone you could not answer. The first day one had trotted past her, a female, nude and measled, with dragging teats, not spending the energy of a sniff on the rinds and prawn shells in the drain. Wearing that beady female look of having something to do.

At a fruit wagon among the Chinese flower stalls, they were buying a pineapple with their host, Dr. Subra. The boy pared the knots from it with a few curving strokes of his long knife.

"Parasites and malnutrition," Dr. Subra said to Amy, pointing to the dog. If he was a Hindu, it must matter to him. He could be Catholic, though, like her. Many Indians were. And about the suffering of animals, Amy thought, what is our position?

John said, "Dogs are the least of the problem."

"Actually," Dr. Subra said with his rueful smile, "this is the most prosperous country in this part of the world, next to Singapore."

"Even at home these things worry Amy," John said.

Dr. Subra said, "You have stray animals, is it? Where all the people like the dog, not as here, where some of course do not?"

"We have strays," Amy began. "People abandon dogs. It's quite a problem, they have to be killed in droves."

If you disparaged the United States, people here became uneasy for you and looked away. Amy knew that as well as John did. It didn't matter that all three papers carried the UPI article about the Chicago transient chewed by rats, and "Man Marries His Mother," and "Schoolgirl Sniper," and everybody read and enjoyed items like these about the United States every day.

Dr. Subra identified each fruit: the mangosteen, the spined rambutan hanging in red bunches, the famous durian. His pride was wonderful. She would know now to show visitors the apples and sweet onions at home, that was what they liked, not buildings. She would know to point out raccoon dens under garages. She liked the stories of fruit bats, not the stories of the Emergency. She liked to hear about the spells the *bomoh* called down on a dormitory to get rid of a demon, and the little forest-dwelling *toyol*, who stole handsome men from their beds and hid them. A husband such as hers, with that powerful hair—smiles all around, none of them had white hair—if the *toyol* took him, he would never be seen again.

A dog was unclean. Here a good Muslim would not touch a dog, and yet the Koran was kinder than the religion of St. Francis: all the animals would stand before God in the last judgment. Although perhaps this was not kind. Would they be judged for killing and eating each other?

After their hundred lashes, the Koran said, the adulterers must marry no one but other adulterers or each other.

It was John who had made the confession, not she. He had been waiting from the day he first saw her. The lengths to which he had gone to drag her out of his mind! One day he looked up as she came down the ward, back from some disaster freckled and strong, her hair bleached white, and as he looked at her his angina started in. *It's no use*, he told himself. *Let her be. Leave her alone.*

But then one day when he was lying on the hot sand in Mexico after his surgery—telling her this his face darkened as if he were holding his breath—he had come to a decision, suddenly, that he would, when he got back he would do this, he would simply go up to her and ask her if it had been his imagination, what he had seen in her eyes once years before.

Of course the real decision had been that he must live. Did she understand? He must live. He must.

There was a promise, that was all, in a restaurant. A terrible promise, chaste in the first days, that set everything in motion. Then things went so fast there was almost no time for adultery. Writs, stamped documents, licenses, immunizations, supplies. In one two-week period at the end, the visas arrived, he had his contract. She had a day to be stretched open, an hour to put her legs up and give up what she contained of the past. A day to rest, they had their chloroquine, they were ready to go, they were gone.

Next door the amah stopped sweeping the walk with her soft broom, turned her face up and scanned the sky. Amy looked, too. *Skylab.* But there was nothing against the white.

The Voice of America was going to give a precise latitude. Amy meant to get ready—at least put out napkins and make sure there was enough beer—but all she did was carry out a kitchen chair and drape a sheet up to the bush to create a patch of shade over the dog. The blue bee zoomed in as she dribbled water and offered shreds of chicken, went in to wash her hands, and came back out and did it again.

She watched the sky. She tried to decide whether they were saying "Indian Ocean" more frequently on the radio. Once, in the morning, they had said "South China Sea." The waves of space the satellite was riding could be mapped, up to a point. Alaska would be best for the burnup, or Australia, and probably what was best would happen, as it sometimes did with technology just when you were most bitterly accusing it.

When the news came on there was a loud snap and the electricity went off. The refrigerator chugged once, the ceiling fans drifted to a stop. *Skylab*. Had it fallen on a power line?

She went to check on the dog, which was lying in the same thrown-down position except that it had crossed its front paws. The blue bee zigzagged above it. "Get away," she told it. "You little hyena! Get over there on your clothespin."

They were talking about John. "He's not well, you know," Amy said, flattening her bare feet against the tile to cool them and taking care to group her words in manageable phrases because she had had three beers in rapid succession. "Not for the pace they keep. They're so young, the doctors here."

"Your age," said Carruthers. Both men had leaned forward at the same time, though, with concern. But this was something triggered easily in men.

"And then—and then that monitor lizard back in there leaps out at night and scares him half to death."

"Dear girl, that's not a monitor," Barnes said with chuckle. "And it's a fixture around here, practically a pet." She was not going to argue with Barnes because she had seen that he was sick. He was yellowish and thin, and newly, rapidly thin, to judge by the pleated skin on his yellow arms and the fit of his pants in the rear, hollow as windsocks, with gathers at the belt and no sign of a separation of buttocks.

Eleanor was chattering from the kitchen. "Oh dear, I do hope it wasn't bad news on the phone, just as the poor man goes off to save life and limb." John had gone back to Accident & Emergency on the careening ambulance they sent into the lane to get him there in a hurry. "I'm just rinsing bottles in here, dear. I know our Lakshmi forgets and we've got ants. Shall I refill the treats? Oh! Charles, do tell Amy about Hari Raya! My goodness, the feast they laid out! I don't know quite how we managed to be in on the religious festivities!"

The infidel, Amy thought.

"I'd need a court language to describe it," Barnes said tiredly.

Amy didn't answer, trailing her beer bottle against her neck. *Everything you say is in a court language. So shut up.* The electricity had been off so long there was no ice and the beer was only cool. She was starting her fourth. The others were on their second, at most. She didn't look up when Eleanor came in carrying the lone bowl, half full of the last of the chips.

The talk had gone slowly from the time they took off their shoes at the door and settled themselves under the ceiling fan. When the fans stopped the air was a medium they could not quite part with words. Then the phone rang with the staccato overseas ring, and John lunged from his chair. When he reappeared Amy saw his white lips frame the name of his son. The phone rang again and he stumbled back.

The second call was the emergency room. Already Amy could hear the siren in the *lorong*. She ran out as it wailed past the gate, missing their drive as it always did, so she could flag it down when it came back around.

Before it came to a stop John had one leg in. He called to her. "Nicky's in the ICU!" He leaned out the window as the little van spun gravel and lurched in a circle. "Messed up his potassium. They're calling back, get hold of me in the OR!"

An hour had passed. She sat staring at the men, Barnes and Carruthers. She let something flow in on the heat of the beer, some instinct. Maybe they could help her. Somehow it worked out that it was men she helped, men who helped her. Men and boys. But what did she want? Carruthers, who flirted doggedly with her as if youth were a shared hometown, winked at her legs and said, "Amy's got the right idea." She had put on a short skirt, one she never wore here. She didn't care. It was so hot, and they were Westerners. She leaned forward and folded her hands around her crossed damp leg as if it might kick out at Carruthers. Legs are pets, she thought. The body is a pet. Stupidly doted on. Like the awful dog out in the back, blameless but unmentionable. Or not blameless. No. Not like the dog.

Eleanor Barnes had angled her calves and pressed her small ankles together, crimping her toes. She had on stockings in this heat, and a khaki skirt nipped in with a belt. She came from far back, from a time when toes were tucked in, ankles and waist meant something, maybe that you were in control of yourself. *Those little legs of yours would snap right off at the hip if a slab of concrete fell on you. You would pop like a boil.* But up and down Eleanor's legs she could see big mosquito bites.

Sweat had run along her hairline all afternoon; she could feel the hair frizzing. "The heat this month's a bit much for me," Barnes said, and she saw he was breathless and pale.

Then, as if a striped tent had gone up over them, the subject was Skylab.

Skylab was circling downward, coming nearer and nearer to the Malay Peninsula. Quite possibly it would crash here. "Jittery Asia Waits for Skylab," said the black headline. It took up the whole front page of the *Star* on the glass table. Where the point of entry would be no one could say for sure, not even in America. Eleanor flapped the paper open. "Oho—'Skylab jitters!'"

"Read on," said Carruthers.

"'Singapore, Tuesday. Skylab jitters spread across several Asian countries today,'" she read. She used a marveling voice, with which she must have read, Amy thought bitterly, to the five children she and Barnes both liked to say they had inadvertently produced, "'and the dying space station was reported to have claimed its first casualty in the Philippines. A fifty-four-year-old man died of a heart attack after shouting "Skylab Skylab" in a nightmare at four AM' Oh dear oh dear. Blah blah . . . 'In largely illiterate and superstitious rural India, people have fled their homes and begun chanting prayers . . . ,' and so on and so on, '. . . largely Buddhist Thailand . . . attitude fatalistic . . .' Oh! Oh my dears! Here we are! 'Many business-minded Singaporeans say if they find a piece of the space station they will try to sell it.'"

"There's a good chance it will fall here," Amy said loudly. "This isn't a little ticking clock coming down. One section weighs *five thousand pounds*."

"Good lord, look out!" cried Carruthers.

"It won't land on us," said Barnes. "It's a real American who thinks it will seek her out in Southeast Asia. States paranoia. All of you have a touch of it, my dear," he said, wagging his finger at her. "It's only right for it to fall on you Americans."

"What about a woman out tapping rubber trees. A child." Amy took a long, sullen pull on the bottle. "If it's going to fall on anyone, it'll be somebody who is just going about his business while we're sitting here, while it's still up there. Somebody as alive as we are, but the same as dead."

The beer was giving her the feeling of a barely delayed repetition: the same fleeting expression crossing each face like a goldfish coming round in a bowl, the same bottle closing with a little suck onto the water ring on the glass table, herself saying what she had already said, ". . . the same as dead."

She had stopped the billowing of the tent of excitement. They drank their beer becalmed. Then Carruthers started talking about a gyroscopic guidance system used in missiles, and the thing whirled again in the room with its giant film vault, its seven-meter aluminum ring, its nuclear reactor. This last had been mentioned only once, in the morning, and then had disappeared from the news coverage. She thought the film vault and the reactor might be the same thing. Why would you need two tons around *film*?

Eleanor cut Carruthers off and began to tell them about the couple who had left their cat behind when they went home. Packed up and left it in the empty house. Of course it could get in and out through the louvers and rejoin its thin sisters in the wild, but the wildness had left it, and it stayed. It was getting spoiled rice somewhere; it had the smell of the drains on it. "And the next thing, of course, was that it slunk in one morning and arranged itself on *our bed*. My dear!"

Amy said nothing.

"Then of course it was ours, it just fastened on us! We had to shut it in a back room and there it howled while we waited for the animal control people to make an appearance. You can imagine. You know these people. But Charles fed it faithfully, didn't you, Charles?"

"All but the one day."

"Shame on you, dear. Whatever day?"

"When we were off having Hari Raya. . . ." Barnes scratched his yellow arm.

"Guess what I found today!" Amy got up unsteadily. "In the house. In the amah's pantry. Look at this." She grabbed the box and tipped the snakeskin out onto the table, making loops on the glass. When she stepped back, Barnes gave a weak shout and jumped up, knocking over his chair and beer bottle.

"Oh, for pity's sake, Charles." Eleanor leaned forward to sop up the beer with napkins and scrutinize the skin. "I'd be willing to bet that's a cobra!" Barnes was over against the flagstone wall. "Charles is phobic," Eleanor said wearily. "She said, dear, that it went behind the water heater. By now it's off hunting, like Kaa. After rodents, not us. Quite gone."

"I'm just—I'm going out for just a moment to see—we have a dog here," Amy said, putting up her hands to keep them in their seats.

"Whatever is the matter? Where are you off to?" It was Carruthers, pushing aside the palm leaves and coming out with her. "Look here, a cobra doesn't swallow a dog."

"Do keep that *bee* from launching an attack!" cried Eleanor's voice from inside. "One of those pesky great bees has been assaulting poor Amy over the washing!"

"Over my dead body!" Barnes had recovered himself and came blinking out into the sun swinging his wife's big embroidered purse by the straps.

Amy grabbed for the purse, in slow motion because of the beer. "Don't! You can't *swat* it!"

But Barnes held on. "Oh no *no*. There's no need! No, my dear, this is what you do. The clothesline, is it?"

The clothesline was in the same place in all the yards. He got away from Amy while Carruthers trotted backward blocking her path and waving his arms. "Amy! Now then! A cobra won't go after a dog! Not to worry." But the dog was gone.

All day the bee had its routine, leaving its perch and returning. Over and over all day long it left and returned on some errand, until the sun went down. Then it went somewhere secret. It slept.

"I have the culprit in view," came Barnes's voice. "He's not an insect, he's a V-2!"

Amy shook Carruthers off her arm. Barnes had Eleanor's purse hairspray straight out in front of him in both hands. "Try this in the propeller!" The bee was visible in the jet of spray. It wobbled on the clothespin, shivering its wings one at a time, and dropped to the ground where it began to crawl past the bird with no eyes, which Amy had failed to wrap up and throw away. It crawled over the mess of fallen orchids, laboring now, and over the network of roots leading under the bush.

"Oh, God!" Before Amy's eyes everything went dark gold, like gasoline. She slapped the spray can out of Barnes's hands, straight up in the air, and shoved him in the chest. He staggered backward against the garbage cans, which clattered over and spilled with him between them, at the same time as Amy dropped to all fours so that she could spread the branches, so clamped to the ground they were half roots already. She couldn't see anything under the bush, but she could hear a metallic resounding from the trash cans. Then streams of words from all sides. "I'm afraid," Carruthers's voice kept saying, "I'm afraid that she was rather fond of it," while Eleanor Barnes was murmuring in a stricken way, pulling her husband up by the hands.

Carruthers insisted on stroking Amy's back and speaking very slowly to her. What was the dog's name? And what breed of dog?

"Why did you have to do that?" She stayed down on the ground while a voice came out of her, flat and mean. "Why would you hurt a bee? I bet you think you're a good person. I bet you don't know what the Prophet said. He said the man who tied up his cat and starved it would be *thrown into hell*." After she said that she had a return of dead sobriety and opened her eyes. Maybe they would not be there.

But there they were. There was an open-endedness to the scene, as if they might be in the process of rehearsing it. There was Barnes blindly cleaning his glasses. There was Eleanor wordlessly holding him by the arm, both of them looking shocked and old. Of course. And herself, below them, in the dirt with anthills and shreds of ancient plastic.

Eleanor's blouse was untucked, her nose was purple under melting powder. Her face had puffed up so that she resembled those bedraggled women who sat in the dirt outside refugee tents.

"I'm sorry," Amy said. "I'm awful. I'm awful."

"You aren't yourself," Eleanor got out finally. "I must say."

"Ready?" Carruthers said, and he hoisted Amy to her feet with so much momentum it almost threw her into his arms, but she pulled free. She bowed her head and held out her hand to Barnes, who took it weakly and smiled at her. Of course it would happen that way. He would smile at her.

"Don't forgive me," she said.

"We'll be off, and you have a rest," Eleanor said, getting back some of her authority. "Heat will combine with alcohol, you know, or . . ." She looked Amy up and down.

"I'm not pregnant, if that's what you think," Amy said. "Don't touch me," she said to Carruthers, lifting his hand off her arm. "I'm unclean." She laughed a short burst and then another, on the way to the front door. Hurriedly the three guests bent, the Barneses propping each other, and put on their shoes.

It had been Eleanor Barnes. The voice in a kitchen in the *lorong*, at a meeting of the Koran study group.

"Oh, I think in her twenties. Poor man, she just made off with him. A silly little thing. A little floor nurse, I think she was. But look at her, of course." *"Do you think they* are *married?"* *"Heaven knows, my dear. And there were children. And the wife was so involved here years ago, I'm told. Quite his equal."* Then there was silence, the silence of someone pointing, because Amy had gone in through the kitchen ahead of them, it was the amah's day off and she went into the amah's bathroom.

A silly little thing. Of course in that bathroom there was no toilet. But now she was in there. There was a pit, quite clean, and a little hose. She kept thinking of turning the hose on herself, drenching herself from head to foot.

A silly little thing.

She, who in another country had wrapped a brown leg severed at the knee in her shirt, and carried it under her arm, pressed against her and dripping down her ribs like a bloodied infant. She and her partner were in their underpants; they had taken off their jeans to make a kind of hammock. With him she was carrying the one-legged boy, shocky and grinning, who kept sighing, *"Gracias, gracias."*

A silly little thing. She, who had, at home in her own city, shriveled a boy the same age as that one to a skeleton by uttering in savage joy, as she stood with his father in a crowded place, the ordinary syllable, "Yes."

Later that day she had a different reaction to it. She warmed to the idea. *A silly little thing.* The comfort of being that.

But at the time she stayed in the amah's bathroom for a while, and when she opened the door she thought about going home, but went around to the front of the house instead and came in again, and sat down to tea as if she had merely been out finding something forgotten in the car, though she had no car, she had come on foot, and in an hour she would walk back, in the loud afternoon shrilling of that insect, whatever it was, that drowned out thought.

She could hear a mosquito under the net with her. It was late, the plush navy darkness. She was awake because the ceiling fan and the radio had suddenly come on.

She sat up and yanked the net aside with her feet: John had not come back. And the telephone had not rung. No call from his family. Nothing about his son. But Skylab had fallen. Of course it had; it had fallen in the afternoon, even before they were sitting with their beer arguing about it.

It had not landed on anyone.

Several BBC reporters were doing a sort of reprise of the day, hour by hour as Skylab lumbered down the sky, now over this city, now over that. What was it the voices reminded her of? As they had been predicting with more and more certainty all along, Skylab had come down far from any human settlement, in Australia. It had done no harm.

But something was wrong. Something had filled Amy with an awful, stifling regret while she slept.

". . . the way we expected it to. And that's a relief to a lot of people in that part of the world who have a crick in their neck. But there's work to be done to set the public's mind at rest, and I think, don't you? that NASA would be the first to agree it's their job to do it."

Charge nurses sometimes had that reined-in satisfaction when everything was going to pieces. The nuns—that was it—the nuns had had it when they rounded everyone up for an assembly after a girl had been expelled. That insistence on the hidden order that included whatever had taken place, but still required them to search their consciences, each one, to see if the punishment that had fallen on that other girl was really meant for her.

Amy got up and stood under the wobbling fan. It was too dark to see in the room. She didn't want to step on anything alive. Did the ants labor up and down the bathroom wall all night? Why did they climb the leg of the bed in the morning, when you had left? What kept them from coming while you were there, following the scent of lips, eyeballs, sticky membranes? Why didn't they eat you alive?

Often the thing the expelled girl had done was something Amy herself commonly did, though in the end she was trying to hold herself back, she had to, because of a disturbing suspicion that she had a vocation. A vocation. Acts to perform that were brave, wild, wildly brave, *heroic*.

But if you were protected, if you went under an umbrella of protection, then not heroic. Was it a blessing to be protected, to be skipped?

The tile was cool to her feet as she crossed from room to room and stepped out into the dark. The porch light had burned out but she could see the great slow-winged moths at the windows, and then a bat. In the grass by the path something stirred, but there was no moon to show it. Gradually the white frangipani blossoms melted forward out of the dark as she breathed their scent.

Mother!

Mother, if you are out there I'm asking you to leave everything alone. Don't save me. Don't let someone else get my punishment. I'm asking you.

After a while she could hear John. He was coming on foot; she could hear his step on the gravel, with the hitch from the sprained ankle. All she could see was his white shirt wavering toward the gate.

Let the snake be. She squeezed her eyes shut. *Let whatever happens happen. But not to him. Don't let him die. Or his son. His child! Don't let his son die. I'm asking you.*

She sank down and sat against the wall of the house, making the face of crying but not crying, just passing her hand over the ground at the edge of the flagstones, digging with her nails. She rubbed the dirt between her fingers, and on her leg.

Pure earth. Pure earth.

Outside the *lorong*, which had no streetlights, she knew the dark lost its surrounding softness, its hugeness, and let itself be broken up and moved back like the dark in any city. Here, in the fuller dark, John's white shirt swelled like cloth in water as he unfastened the gate. In a disconnected piece of her life she had climbed the steep streets of a coastal town after a tidal wave. She remembered being shown the jellyfish swirling along the esplanade or left glued to walls, as she walked at night exalted and calm from digging out a family alive and being kissed and blessed by them, after days of lifting and hauling and counting the dead.

astride

There was an incident, the summer I worked in the Pentagon. My supervisor vanished.

That summer I didn't know any better than to take the job offered me. I knew nothing. My father worked in the Commerce Department and raised a few Angus in Virginia, in that wide grass circle, not then covered with suburbs, that poured civil servants and in summer their college-age children into the offices of the government. I remember the commute. In the morning you would pass combines and dairy herds and girls up early schooling horses in the wet grass. I was newly appreciative of the green beauty of my state, the Old Dominion, because I had come back to it after being away at college for the first time.

I took a typing test and not long afterward I walked up the steps of the Pentagon. I did that. I have no excuse.

One morning toward the end of that summer my supervisor's door was standing wide open when I arrived, and all that was left of him was the straight-backed wooden chair he had brought from home. He never came back. He had a high security clearance, though that was downplayed because the official reason given for his disappearance was thwarted passion.

This was early in the sixties, in the days before anyone came to levitate the Pentagon. Certainly no one had attacked it. Its enchantment was internal and impervious. Whatever else has changed since then, I know the vast building must still be filled, despite the throngs inside it, with the same cathedral air, of hushed, guarded, exquisite knowledge. No photograph really shows it as the massive thing it is, a stone wheel covered with portholes, an inhabited wheel, spun down into Virginia swampland and fallen on its side, to be cordoned and protected forever.

It was a city, with sloping ramp-avenues leading to a vast city square of shops and restaurants, the Concourse. The Concourse had the feeling of a great hotel as well as that of a department store. Dignitaries were led along it, parades marched through it, shoppers crowded the aisles of pottery and books. Other countries may give their generals villas, but surely they are outdone by this bazaar of flowers and souvenirs and cosmetics, of pastries, crystal, and the scented wood of carvings, available to everyone, right in the heart of the fort.

In the seventeen miles of corridor, which radiated in spokes and revolved in concentric rings, pedestrians flowed aside for motorized carts carrying men with brooms and buckets, or sometimes tanned young lieutenants in summer uniform, calmly steering little vehicles among the civilians on foot. Little boys saluted them. There were crowds of children there, headdresses, saris floating. Regular tours came through from schools and embassies.

It was never clear which individuals were not important. Always disputable. A janitor could be going through the wastebaskets on the orders of a foreign government.

Underneath the building was an enormous depot with the green and white buses of Washington and the red buses of Virginia, and even Greyhounds, pulling up to dozens of stations and surging away with echoes and grinding of gears. In the late afternoon I descended a numbered stairway to get the bus to Commerce where I would meet my father, whose day was longer than mine. Hundreds waited with me on hot platforms with puddles steaming where the air-conditioning dripped. In the gloom you looked through open hangars to the white air of Virginia. The buses shimmered one last time as their backs crossed into the shade. Blue exhaust, islands of pink gum on the concrete, at every station people just down from the Concourse with their bags and packages. Anything could have been carried into or out of DOD, as we called it, the Department of Defense.

What really happened to my boss, Mr. Orlenko, was that he was accused of a security violation. All of us knew we stood to lose our clearances, even our jobs, if we failed to take every precaution with classified material. But we knew, too, how unlikely it was that our little errors would hurt us, we knew we were innocent.

From the secretaries—"Mr. *Orlenko*, what a pain!"—we knew he had a wife still in shock from the DP camp after years in this country. He was Ukrainian. He hated the Soviet Union with a devotion of hatred. At the mention of Khrushchev his heavy-lidded eyes would grow sinister. From his window he would scout the wide parking lots as if he could see the hammer and sickle creeping in a liquid Disney shadow across them. He hated the president, whose inauguration was still fresh in everybody's mind, mine in particular because of the raising of a *poet* to the dais, white-haired Frost, pure as his name— nobody then knew of meanness in a poet—the poet I had studied all the spring before, in my freshman year.

I was a clerk-typist. Somebody read through records and newspapers every day looking for certain references, then gave the marked passages to the typists to type into lists for Mr. Orlenko, who was able to enter each item into lists of his own.

Mr. Orlenko was an analyst. Subjects he analyzed were apt to be already classified and to move up to a higher classification because they had been worked on by him. His desk was a haystack of legal pads and folders stamped "Secret," and like all the offices his had its safe, that is, a filing cabinet—in his case two of them—with a combination lock and a steel rod dropped through the drawer handles and padlocked.

The theme of our summer was National Security.

The theme covered everything from the aims of the Soviet Union to our own missteps and oversights. At that time, one-use carbon ribbons preserved everything we typed in a readable form; although the letters jumped and skittered unevenly along the tape, a spy could unfurl the ribbon and read your whole document. Of course the college students with summer jobs were the poorest at remembering to take out their ribbons and lock them up at the end of the day.

Considering that we were there not to help them but to spring into jobs above their heads at a later stage, the real-life secretaries were lenient about our carelessness and indeed about everything, including the job of proofreading what we typed. "You passed the typing, hm?" Typing was the major part of the test we had taken to rule out nepotism in our placement.

That summer no matter what we actually did at our desks we were called interns, and heard lectures in one of the small, dark, deep-chaired auditoriums to be found in the building, like chapels, though there were actual chapels as well, filled in wartime, we heard, with praying employees. At any rate men spoke to us in a comfortable chamber, gray-blue, soundproofed because some of the movies shown there were about ordnance, or materiel. We all liked the word materiel, and liked to throw it into conversations. "But did you have any materiel on you?" The movies were presented as entertainment, as none of the interns that summer was an engineering student who might go into materiel. We were an unpromising group; most were English majors, displaying volumes of poetry or existential novels on our desks. The girls typed, the boys shadowed a deputy assistant for the summer. No history majors; only one in political science. The light went down and a blue glow stole out from a recess above the paneling. A silver cone crossed the screen to the music from *Exodus*.

During the showing of the films, we looked around and picked out people to have coffee with afterward. Romances began.

One stood out, flourished, for the first few weeks of the summer: Holly, a senior, tall and blond, and Alex, younger than she was, but from Yale. He was the one majoring in political science. They were the two glamorous ones. Holly, for Hollis, was graceful and Southern in a way that those of us who lived in the grass circle outside Washington were not. She had made her debut and gone to school in Paris. Her family was an old Carolina one, we heard, her father a general.

With every explosion on the screen Holly covered her eyes, and finally she looked between her fingers and said, "Doesn't matter who's doing it, I can't stand it." The boy from Yale looked over irritably but when he saw the blond hair hanging down he moved a seat and sat forward to talk to her, putting his body between her and the screen.

Holly's loose shifts, in shades of blue and lilac, were the style of that year. On most of us these were a neutral fashion, but on her they had a slipping, mussed air; they weren't ironed, or the armholes were big on her thin arms, or a button was missing just where the sharp shadow went down between the surprising breasts she had. "All I want to know is where somebody thin got those," one of the secretaries said, once they knew her.

Alex was tall too, with a shaven, silken, lean-cheeked face. Their eyes fell naturally on each other. Day after day, Holly brought a little more of her dreamy attention to bear on the blue eyes behind his glasses, the tanned fingers firm on his manila folder or his book, forefinger marking the place.

"Alex is going into politics," Holly told me. He had finished his freshman year at Yale, whose elevation above her college in Lynchburg was of no moment to her. He too was rich, we learned. His father managed a company making aircraft components.

Alex was always being called away from whatever he was doing and introduced to visitors by his supervisor, who was said to know more than anyone else in Washington about the missile gap. But when Holly walked by the door he would leave the friendly important men and rush to lean his arm on Holly's in one of the little stand-up coffee bars.

Soon they were walking out to the parking lot and she was folding her legs into his MG after work and telling me about the horse shows they went to on weekends so his family could get to know her.

I have never seen work done with the feverishness with which it was done in the Pentagon. People say bureaucracy, make-work, nothing gets done, etcetera. But vast projects are undertaken, brought to the verge of completion, redesigned completely, completed, cancelled. Thousands upon thousands work late into the night day after day, sweating and smoking, or they did then, coughing, drumming their fingers. Hundreds come in every few days while they are on vacation, just to keep up.

Mr. Orlenko was one of those workhorses. By the time we knocked on his door he would have been reading for hours, standing up, massaging his back, a bulky man in a white shirt and a tie with a silver clip, with dark hair going gray. He would lower himself onto the straight-backed chair he had brought from home, where he would write in longhand for hours more without stopping.

He would stand too close to us and order us, in his accent at once haughty and intimate, to type his tables of figures with their crossed sevens and curled nines. Few men typed at that time. Mr. Orlenko wrote with a fountain pen, making a lacework of corrections, holes rubbed and stuck through the paper where he used a typewriter eraser with a stiff brush. "Why not *pencil?*" we all groaned. With this pen he also doodled trees, all over his DOD blotter and in the margins of the legal pads he wrote on, and then scribbled them out.

He never took sick leave or even his full two weeks of vacation, despite the wife. There were children but they were thought to be grown. Nevertheless, the secretaries acted them out, saying, "*Da, Papa!*" and banging their heels together. His fingers were a deep saffron and the thumb, too, because he curved it under and petted the end of his Camel while he was thinking. Above his heavy, carved features flew thick black eyebrows.

From his brushed hair came a breath of nutmeg when he bent over your desk. He was very clean, and that—not all that common in those from his part of the world, the secretaries said—was because of the DP camp. He would shake out a white handkerchief and hold it as he worked. He kept a drawer of them, ironed, according to the secretaries. His wife ironed the shirts he wore, of which the garment bag on the door, they said, held extras for when he worked overnight. He never appeared tired, and kept his erect posture, arrogant and foreign. When a secretary had checked our lists and we took them in to him, his eyes meeting ours never lost their intense warning, though a moment before he would have been squinting into one of his folders with a kind of tenderness.

"You know, I'm intrigued by Mr. Orlenko," Holly said one day. "He seems like such an interesting man." We made fun of her accent, the way she said "intrigged," and "Mayan" for man, though indeed Mr. Orlenko was from another time. "So European," she said. "He *works* so hard. The N. is for Nazar, did you know that? Nazar. Nazar Orlenko."

Often when there is a gruff temperament in the office the gentler ones will find something touching in it, I did learn that. They will cosset a man who chews Maalox and slaps his blotter and bangs his telephone receiver. In the Pentagon we saw women attentive as mothers toward some bitter GS-9 who had to park in the farthest lot and walk in, and be spurned by the younger secretaries. But Mr. Orlenko did not have one of those office mothers, and in fact had nobody except his never-seen wife, for whom the accepted word was "pitiful." Nobody until Holly in her freedom—as Frost tells us the lovely shall be choosers—chose him.

In Frost's poem, the lovely woman is punished. When he wrote "The Lovely Shall Be Choosers," Frost was living in a world in which there was an audience presumed to believe, however mistakenly, that beauty conquered all. It may be the Kennedys didn't know the poem and really thought the lovely were choosers and that was that. We'll never know. Maybe they were not concerned with Frost's zeal to show them the bitter lot of beauty, or with anything except "The Gift Outright," in which there is the line about "many deeds of war" being the deed to the country.

The three of us, Holly and Alex and I, were traveling the outer ring of the Pentagon on our lunch hour, talking about Alex's future. He was going to run for office as a Democrat. He would start locally. The Secretary of Defense was coming toward us, surrounded by men with cameras on their shoulders and strings of spiral cord looped around them, and he was laughing, not exactly heartily but not with the craven note, either, of a man who would live to write a book about how bitterly mistaken he was in this period. He was not much further along than the interns, it turned out. He, too, had a lot to learn. "Hello, Alex," he said.

"Is that somebody?" said Holly.

"That was the Secretary of Defense," said Alex in despair.

"No, really?" Holly said. "Why don't we have one of those chocolate milkshakes instead of coffee." In the Center Court she sat down on a bench while Alex went to buy the famous double-chocolate milkshakes of the Pentagon concessionaire. Pressing my hand Holly said, "I have something I want to tell you. It'll surprise you, I bet. It's a little bit bad, now." I said, "Tell me." But Alex was already handing her milkshake over her shoulder from behind us. "Well, we'll talk later, hear? I *need* to. Alex, now you brought me—this can't be double chocolate, is it? Well! I remember it as so very delicious the last time."

A few days after she told me, I knocked on Mr. Orlenko's door. After a second he said harshly, "Come in." None of us sat down in that office, but Holly was sitting in the chair in which Mr. Orlenko seated his superiors, with their strange deference to him. She sat with legs crossed, in her lilac shift and the rope sandals she had started wearing to make her less tall, frowning, as if she had not been fervently talking to me in the bathroom half an hour before while she ran cold water on her wrists. Ordinarily Mr. Orlenko liked me; he explained my tasks to me with that exaggerated foreign intentness and then stood back satisfied to see me read what he had written. But he looked at me now as if I could be loathed as thoroughly as Khrushchev. I thought in surprise, almost in fear: Holly told him. She told him she told me. And I looked back at him as innocently as I could.

They both lit cigarettes as I recited my message and held out my document. "Put it with the rest!" he said with a jerk of his arm, hitting his t's hard and striking his knuckles with the cigarette on the side of the safe. He tore off his glasses and massaged the black eyebrows.

Then I saw them in the hall of war paintings. This was a still, wide gallery of a corridor, with tall doors bearing teak plaques. Hundreds of paintings. Cannon, trenches, foot soldiers of the Spanish-American War, the Battle of the Monitor and the Merrimack. Torn sketches taken from the pockets of the dead. Orlenko was stiff-armed and wore his sinister look, Holly was the one leaning and pleading. I saw her put her hand out and hook her long fingers with their oval nails in his belt, and then rudely, no longer pleading but with force, pull him against her.

That was what I saw. But a secretary who dared to open Orlenko's door when he didn't answer her knock saw more, and the story raced out, a spark along a fuse. The thing that lit it was this particular secretary's choice of the word "astride." Astride. Without that word the story might have died away. Somebody else repeated it. "She was right there, astride him in the chair." "Astride of him" were the actual words. Of course that was something you could not help picturing. Her long legs, her blond, hanging hair, his arrogant face thrown back, the chair.

No longer did Holly pause outside Alex's office and lead him off alone under the eyes of his supervisor. "Come *with* me," she would say to me. "Alex will chase after me if you don't." She no longer liked to be sent around the miles of corridor with documents, she liked to stay in our hallway, smoking dreamily in the ladies' room, drifting to Orlenko's door. She would knock a music of three knocks and then one, soft yet urgent, and lead him away. She concealed nothing; she liked to smile into everybody's eyes in a blinded way.

Orlenko began to take a lunch hour. His phone would ring, and at the nearby desks we could hear his chair scrape back, his terrible sighs, his scrabbling in the drawer for his Camels. Then he would come out, close his door, and go.

Alex would come up out of his chair and be at the door of his tiny office—he had been given an office—if he saw me walking with Holly. He would start right in signaling me to leave him alone with her, but Holly always said to me, "Come on, you promised." Holly walked ahead of him while he whipped his thigh with the manila folder. Then he began to hiss at her. "Why, Holly? Why?"

Late in the summer we were sitting in the Center Court, where the paved walks wound in and out of tended rosebushes. There were traveling clouds, an intense four o'clock sun in the hedges of arborvitae planted in half-circles around the stone benches. Someone tended them. Someone worked to keep aphids off the roses, as had been decreed by the landscape designers for this building, the Pentagon.

None of this was mystery, to me. "Leave something to learn later." That's what Frost said.

Holly was not sitting up straight. Her hair was tied back with a scarf as if to expose her two pimples and the darkened skin under her eyes. The scarf went halfway down her back, a relic of her stylishness. Alex couldn't take his eyes off it. Finally he took between his fingers the tiny rolled hem of silk he had been touching on the back of the bench.

"I don't know," Holly said, bending her head down so that the scarf puffed off in his hand, "Oh, God, I don't know. Nobody does!" and she jumped up, scattering the pigeons. "They don't know where he went!" With a sob, she covered her face. Because she was beautiful, everyone out on the sidewalk turned and looked at her.

I was sad for Alex, too, as he went after her with her scarf in his hand. Myself I see crossing the little garden, looking up at the inner walls of the building and seeing movement in the windows, a uniformed back, a flash of light off glasses, and half-thinking to myself that this love triangle—all at once it was one, now that it was over— was more important than what the people in those offices were doing behind the windows. It was this that the books we carried around were about. Even if they pretended to be about war.

That was what I thought at eighteen, in the Center Court of the Pentagon, ready for some passion to overtake me as it had Holly, steeped in my right to it. I am haunted now by the thought that some page in that sheaf of papers, that endless list we ridiculed as we typed it, figured in the death of a little boy like my own, the one I would have in ten years when the war that did not even have a name that summer was dragging toward its end. I can't remember. I can't remember a line I typed. There we all sat, typing. There we all stood, drinking our coffee and falling in love. What was I dreaming of as I typed so fast, the Selectric ball whirling the letters off my fingers? Did they land in someone's flesh?

At the center of that week was the safe: the failure of someone—Orlenko—to drop the rod down through the drawer handles and padlock it, his failure, one night, even to twirl the combination lock on the top drawer. Only by coincidence had the oversight been discovered and reported, by someone who stayed in the office even later than he.

"We are always at war," one of the National Security speakers told us. "Only sometimes we allow ourselves to forget that we are at war." Even so, the precautions were often forgotten; it happened to the summer interns all the time. In the morning you could hear the cry, "Oh no, here's my ribbon still in the machine."

All Mr. Orlenko had to do was make an appearance before a security board and be reprimanded. But instead he vanished. Within a week it was given out that his departure was a breakdown of a private sort. In other corridors the talk was of a college girl, a beauty, who had lured the head of a division away from his immigrant family that had lived on potatoes for three years in a camp on an unpronounceable border. And then she wouldn't have him, of course. Her family stepped in. The father an officer. That was what was said.

Strangely enough, though for days Holly was away from her desk all day being interrogated somewhere in the building, along with her father who had been called in from his base, in our corridor everyone shielded her. We pretended that it was all a matter of wild rumors having their origin in some other corridor. *People from—where he was from. They're paranoid. They'll bolt.* The secretaries even included Holly in the talk, bringing her coffee and aspirin, soothing and pampering her.

"I got a letter." She drew me into the auditorium and pulled the doors shut. She felt for the switch of the blue light, so that I could read it. There was Orlenko's crested, beautiful script. "He's gone, he's hiding. No address. Even if I could write him a letter I couldn't make him see it's *nothing*." She was biting her broken thumbnail. "Where can he go? He doesn't even have his family with him. He thinks he's running for his life, he doesn't know what *country* this is."

And what country is this? I could have said, but neither of us would have known.

"Terrible things happened to him in the war, you know. *Terrible* things." Her violet eyes went black. "But he never gave in. He drew pictures. His hero was a poet, a famous poet from there—oh, I'll get you the name—who drew pictures with a lump of coal when he was starving." That war was only twenty years in the past, but they were our years—we were eighteen and twenty-one—and we were both gazing into a history as uninvestigated as calculus. We knew the Allies and the Axis. We were majoring in literature.

"What else does he say?"

She looked away. "My 'beauty,' is what he says, made him careless." She held the envelope against her chest. I remember the crooked stamp and the elaborate capitals of her name: "Miss Hollis Baird." It had been mailed right there in Washington. "He's not here any more, though. I know it. He doesn't trust anybody. Everybody over there hurt him, Russians, Germans, everybody. And *this* place, oh, God, I hate this place. These *people* in here. They're the ones did it, up in Security, they're the ones *scared* him."

All the rest of the summer Alex comforted her, listened, took her coffee, walked her up and down the corridors, stood with her while she cried in the hot parking lot, until we all went back to school. "I just told poor Alex good-bye," she said on the last day. "She's going to marry him," the secretaries predicted. But she did not.

She sees him now and then, just as she writes sometimes to me. She is the mother of three grown sons who attended the same private school as his two. I have read that she is a Washington hostess, though she has nothing to say in her letters about that.

For some reason she got back in touch with me, years after this. For a while, she said, she went a little wild. "God, I went through the whole thing. In San Francisco I tripped, I marched, I hung around the Dead. I told my Daddy off." Looking back, she was glad of it all, except for what she had done that one summer, might have done, might have caused to happen—because we never knew what happened—to Nazar Orlenko. "Do you think there's a love of your life?" she wrote.

In the last picture I have, you can see she is heavier, though she stands behind the three tall sons. The arms are plump, the blond hair short. We have all changed, and any of us may change again, although Orlenko, strange sacrifice, will never come to her again in her beauty, nor a secret list extract itself from a torso, nor the Pentagon wheel back up into the sky.

kisses

One of the residents kissed Shannon. No one had done that for some time; her husband Garth did not kiss. A staff manual for the retirement village was already in print and it had a paragraph for moments like the one in the Kralls' living room: inappropriate situation arises, staff member reacts with calm, makes a report. But Shannon was her own supervisor, so there was no one to report it to. And she had returned the kiss, which began in sympathy but held for a beat. When Shannon stepped back Mr. Krall's eyes were still closed, lids dark as his wife's eye shadow. He did not look like an old man, he looked like a young man exhausted.

She had met him days ago but on this day he entered the room with his hand outstretched, so she turned off the vacuum cleaner and shook hands with him. "Not Mr. Krall, no. Ivan." And did she, with her high cheeks—he swiped his own cheekbone with his thumb, admiringly, she thought—come from central Europe? No? Where did her family originate? How many in the family? So small, no brothers, no sisters! No matter, what did she study in school? And no mathematics? And her parents? Ah, divorce, divorce. And her husband, the young man digging and planting, who was not here in the early weeks? A soldier. And was he from some other country, that he worked so hard?

And when she was on the porch next door—yesterday morning, was it not?—had she been crying? In the early morning, with the dog. Yet this was not, of course, for him to ask. And yet, her face. . . . For tears swell the lips.

The Kralls, Ivan and Duška, were the poster couple for a magazine piece about the village and its green ethos, though Shannon had to clean hard before anybody got in there to photograph their lifestyle. She had warned the founders, Mark and Dane. Mark said, "They've been here a month, how bad can it be?" About a house once the roof was on, Shannon saw, Mark knew nothing. He might be learning the ropes of construction but he was still a computer guy.

"'Green ethos,'" Garth said when he was first home and Mark was showing him around, telling him about the job. "Sounds like an MRE."

"Mark doesn't know what that is," Shannon said.

"I do happen to know what that is," Mark said. "Meals Ready to Eat."

In the old days Garth would have made friends with somebody like Mark. With anybody. He would have grinned and said, "Ever eat one?"

The counters, of a composite Mark said would outsell granite one day, were already hidden under dead plants, egg cartons, books held open with potatoes, cutting boards stacked wet, but the Kralls themselves looked good: a tall, lean, white-haired pair in turtlenecks, Duška with silver rings on her thumbs, Ivan with a voice as deep as Garth's smoker's voice and blue eyes wasted on an old man.

Duška was older than he and had something that affected her motor skills but not her mind. Her name had a little *v* over the s that made it a "sh." "You pronounced it wrong," Shannon told Mark and Dane. "Say *Dooshka*." At home she said to Garth, "I get to boss those guys around. Mark and Dane. They like it. Employee input. How you get to, like, consensus."

She was supposed to act out showing Duška the cupboards hung so low there was no need for reaching, but first she had to use the sink sprayer to run the dirt of plant roots off Duška's hands. "This child is an angel," Duška told the photographer. "Do you see her washing me? Take a picture! My dear, angels are often given this plain beauty that you have. You see? She does not hear. That is the mark of an angel."

The photographers kept wanting Shannon in the pictures. When the sun came out they stood her in front of the old truck with its painted sign, "Neat & Green." They wanted her plaid shirt and the soft broom from the Asian grocery store where she bought Garth's beer cheap. Her blond ponytail.

Duška laughed at her apology. "It is you, my child, who will sell the houses for them. Before our eyes, you prepare the home. To Ivan—ah, what a good thing you don't cook for him, he would be lost. I see you understand this. You understand men."

"I do," said Shannon without surprise. "Some of them."

House, barn, silos were gone. You crossed a bridge over a wide stream where the cows would have drunk, and arrived at the farm's original driveway, where a cow-sized boulder had been set, engraved with the name of the place, "Greenholm." The stream was waist deep in places, with currents tugging at the willow roots. Here the trees had all been left standing, their limbs brushing the water and already, to the photographers' satisfaction, littering it with yellow leaves. Sometimes Shannon took her sandwich and sat on the bank with the dog. The first week Garth was back from Afghanistan she had waded in with her shoes on and stood where it was deep and cold, to wash her eyes, but that had disturbed the dog, who splashed in and swam to her and back, and in and back again, and then ran in circles on the bank until she came out.

Eventually a pool and fitness center would go in, along with an assisted-living compound and a low cedar building devoted to continuing care, with wheelchair paths through the vegetable gardens, but for now the people moving in would be retirees roughly like the Kralls, still active and driving, the founders said.

Everybody working on the site met regularly with Mark and Dane—guys had to come down off the backhoes and sit with investors—to have their say about the village, or the first two paved circles of what would be a village in a year or two. Only three houses were occupied while the heavy construction was going on: the Kralls, a younger couple who had already driven away in their camper—the guy so frail Shannon didn't see how he would get the gas cap off—and now two old sisters, the Newells. But if one of them asked a question, or a visitor did, anybody working on the site was expected to know the brochure and answer.

Green Retirement, the website said. "A way to keep your footprint small when you're packing it in." That was Dane, at one of the early meetings. Mark said, "And for saying 'packing it in,' there will be a fine." They were two nice guys who had made a lot of money in software. More than a lot. They rode to work on the bike trail, and one or both of them would make a face when a backhoe fired up, even though Garth said it was all hybrid machinery they had out there, the new diesel electrics.

While they talked, sitting down, tipping back in their chairs, Shannon thought, the whole thing was going right past them on its own. Mark said, "We're offering our residents a way they can stay in the fight. They've been progressive people."

Dane raised his hand. "'Have been?'"

He and Mark would admit it was themselves they were thinking of, down the road. They had that quirk of rich people, agreeing ahead of time with whatever you might accuse them of. Shannon knew this from working in a good restaurant, where a woman would say, "I just take forever to make up my mind," and her husband would say with some pride, "I can attest to that."

When Garth first got home she showed him the brochure. "So these guys have no clue. They're like, 'Knees bad? Widowed? Here, have an ice cream sandwich!'" His squint made her add, "But they're OK guys. You'll like them, I bet."

A minute later he jumped up. "My jacket," he said, because he couldn't think of where anything was.

"On the hook," she said. "Pretty hot out, though."

"Ice cream. I'll go get some." He was back in fifteen minutes with beer. She didn't know whether he forgot things or never meant to do them.

Sod waited on pallets for Garth to unroll it in the main square for the only grass that would require mowing. Solar panels were up, on bungalows sited low so rooflines wouldn't mar the hills running up to woods they owned as well, said to cover hundreds of acres. Deer wandered out in the evenings to eat the grass, and tore out the surveyor's flags or chewed the salt from a cap left on the seat of a backhoe. They picked their way down into the excavations, where something would spook them back up the sides in sprays of dirt. "Deer will come to fresh dirt," Mark said.

Shannon said, "Ha ha, it says so on the deer website?"

The backhoes started so easily—Garth had shown her—that she said she wondered if a deer could hit something and start one, getting up on the track the way a little buck with antler nubs had done. Or activate the bucket, propped ready to start mouthing lump after lump like an animal that couldn't actually eat. She was always looking for a subject, now. She didn't really wonder, she knew about the dead man's switch so you couldn't jump off and run over yourself, and Garth didn't answer anyway, he slapped his cigarette pocket. "Left 'em in the truck." He went at a run-walk, straight downhill like the deer into and out of the pit instead of around it. When she got to the parking lot there was no one, but the air had the smell of his lighter fluid.

Going over her business plan with the bank, Shannon had lied. Or not an outright lie, but a certain picture of herself and Garth. The bank guy had a brass paperweight of that dollar-bill eagle with arrows in its claws, so she mentioned the war. "My husband would be at this meeting but he's still over there because you know, stop-loss." She could see the guy did not know. She told him how Garth had built a hand-cranked generator in shop, and rebuilt a vintage Sears bike—he would have laughed at the word "vintage"—instead of driving a car.

She didn't say nobody who knew Garth Moran in high school had ever heard him say the word "environment," and that the bike was to get around on because his dad wouldn't let him drive the car. To get a car, his brother had quit school and gone to work in a body shop. After hours he worked on a totaled van until he had the money for it, and then he got in and drove away. At first Garth thought it was just a trip. But although he would send Garth money, and call him every week from LA where their mother was, and listen to his despairing arguments for an hour at a time, he would not come back.

Shannon didn't say that right after they got married the boss in Lawn and Garden broke a promise to switch Garth to full time, and he walked off the job and enlisted. Walked into the army. Things went fast after that. Before he had his orders his father got him a T-shirt that said "Born to Fight Trained to Kill." At the pre-deployment picnic his father said, "Guess he's on his way."

"Sure is," Shannon said.

"Nothing to stop him," his father said. He looked like Garth but mean. She had the grill in front of her and she could have messed up his sleeve accidentally with the tongs but she stood there clicking them until he walked away.

Garth was coming, carrying a tray of bratwurst that he set down on the ground so he could get his arms around her while the smoke stung tears out of her eyes.

Garth looked good to the bank. The military, the jobs in high school. Knowing how to lay sod and bed stone looked good, she could tell, despite the fact that the man behind the desk spent the whole time studying her, up and down. When she finished talking about Garth he sat back and gave her a grin she recognized. "I'm hearing high-school sweethearts. Kids! But hey, you got married." She didn't answer because she knew they weren't supposed to ask about anything like that. He knew, too, because he wiped the grin off his face and said, "Sounds like a well-put-together plan."

"Some old guy," she told her friends. "Thought you got married so you could have sex." She still had all her high school friends and they got a laugh out of that.

· · ·

A boy born to kiss finds that out the way you might realize you can draw, or do math. His ways come naturally to him. He will not smile first. Sometimes he'll kiss you without putting his arms around you at all, just holding you at the mouth. You always know he's not just kissing, he's kissing you. His face will have a concentration like they get when they're playing Counter-Strike. She was explaining this to her friends, who were a few steps behind her at that time.

It was when the new shooter games were first in stores and she complained to her friends at sleepovers because Garth and his brother didn't own any games, so the two of them were always at some kid's house when she was looking for Garth. But this look she was describing was his, when they were alone. Think of the movies, where they're about to kiss and the man looks like he's ready to dive off a building. Her friends shivered. They all wanted Garth Moran or somebody like him. In the halls his teammates called him The Lover and shoved him against the lockers. He shoved back but not hard. He was easy on everybody and everybody was easy on him. "How did you get like this?" she said.

"My brother taught me stuff."

She was watching him take his shirt off. She said, "I don't see how he taught you this."

"So how did you get like you are?" he said. "Tough. But a little crybaby." She was as tall as he was and when she played soccer they weighed the same. "My little crybaby."

"You better hope your dad don't hear what you two are up to."

Shannon said, "Somebody would have to tell him and they would have to see him to tell him." Her mother was tired and had a funny little slowed-down shrug that Shannon hated when she was fifteen. People said their hair was the same color but it was not.

She had hold of the back of a kitchen chair and she knew how to fight it out with her mother, but this time she sat down. The cigarette smell rose from her mother as she sat across the table looking down into her bra, undoing the buttons of her UPS uniform. Shannon leaned forward. For the first time she had the thought of explaining something to her mother: how she loved and would always love Garth Moran. At first it was no more than his back in a white T-shirt, in class. His arms. His eyelashes, mentioned in the yearbook. The feeling changed. Into it came something that slowed her, filled her with a power of her own, like what got into her blood just sitting in the bleachers when he was on the football field, gradually stopped her talking about him to her friends. The knowledge that he gave everybody a chance came into it, that he was generous, that in love his concentration was fierce, yet he was always careful of her. That he was nothing like his dad, wanting to hurt somebody, anybody. He was good.

She looked for words for this love, an enclosure like a tent, with space for two lying down. But the words for the place, the love, did not come, and her mother got up and went to get out of her uniform.

"I have a name for you." Duška pronounced some long word in her language. "For the golden hair."

In the rubber band Shannon's hair was thicker than a wrist, streaked with tan and cream. Horse colors, Garth had said, winding it on his arm. Palomino.

"What are you thinking about?" she would say, in the days when she could ask him anything. "My palomino," he said. Once in the afternoon. He rolled over on his back to show himself to her. That's all we thought about, she recalled in wonder.

A box with five black puppies in it. Her soccer coach said anybody could have one who could get a parent's signed note that it would be neutered. Shannon ran to find Garth; she beckoned him out of practice and he got the last one. This was their junior year, when he had no job because of football. He tore off his gear, wrapped the puppy in his jacket, and nestled it in the bike rack. It was his for a week, but he couldn't pay for the vet or the canned food he planned to feed it and his dad didn't believe in neutering dogs anyway and made him give it back.

His dad did that kind of thing all the time, but he got a pass from Garth. When Garth was a married man about to deploy he was still trying to find some inside track with his dad, sharpening his mower for him or hauling his old couch away in a borrowed truck. The first thing Shannon did with her business loan was buy a truck, a rusted Ford F-250, full of chaff and spiders from sitting in a barn.

Her mother had warned her. "Look out for the dad."

"I know that," Shannon said. "Garth's the opposite of that."

"Where's the mom again?"

"LA. She has a whole nother family."

"She left those boys. . . ." Her mother sighed.

"Yeah and they were little, too. He wouldn't let her have them."

"Left them with *him*. She must have been something."

"I guess. But there must have been something good about her because look at Garth. He didn't get it from his dad."

"Left her boys," her mother said again.

"Hey, you kicked Dad out."

"I did. I know that. I'm sorry." That was the most her mother would say on the subject. To herself Shannon said, *I would never give up the way you did. Never.*

He would come home to a dog. Nothing was going to get in the way of it this time. At the shelter they talked her out of a puppy and into a full-grown dog, a tan Lab mix with short legs and a dark, expectant face. Her name was Zena, and on the way to work every day she sat motionless beside Shannon, watching the road like a driving instructor. With her tan worried eyebrows she was nothing like the glossy black pup, tumbling and squealing, that had been Garth's for a week. When Shannon ran a floor buffer this dog would sleep through the noise.

On the site she stayed just ahead of Shannon, often looking back at her, and did not have to be leashed. The first time Shannon took her out in the evening when the deer were out she stiffened but did not chase them. She seemed to operate under rules from somewhere.

Maybe she had started out to be a guide dog. Somebody had named her and trained her. Who would have taken such a dog to the pound?

"Knock knock. Mind if I join you?" Mark stepped over the batts of hemp insulation and sat down in the sawdust where Shannon was leaning on a stud eating her lunch. "That's the perfect dog." Zena panted as she looked steadily away from Shannon's ham sandwich. "Did you train her?"

"She came trained. She's super trained." A lot of the time Shannon thought Mark was coming on to her. Mark didn't seem to realize it himself; he had a girlfriend from his software days and Shannon had met her.

Mark got up on his knees in the sawdust and hugged the dog to his chest, which she let him do, twisting to give Shannon a flat-eared look.

Every evening the powertrains shut down at the same time and a quiet descended that was as full in the ears as noise. Garth had a wheelbarrow by the handle but there was nothing in it and he wasn't moving. At first she thought he was listening to something but he didn't have earphones any more.

"How's it going?" she said.

"Look at that."

"At what?" The sunlit green above the dug foundations ran up to the tree line where the woods climbed into foothills. Pink ribbons fluttered among the near trees, where Mark and Dane had found an old half-buried trail. Maybe the cows had made it. The plan was to get it in shape for easy walking, but without cutting any trees. "So . . . wooden houses. Kills me. Wood from someplace else." There was no way now to tell if Garth was seeing the funny side. In fact, it seemed safe to assume he never was. "Who are the fuckers, anyway?" he said. "Gotta have a place like this to die in?"

It did take money, she could see that. These were not the old you saw in the city with two coats on, pushing a Safeway cart down the street.

• • •

So far it's kind of virtual, she told her friends. Her mother drove out in the UPS truck to see inside a house. "This would be OK with me," her mother said, opening a refrigerator. "That new smell in everything."

"Except where the raccoons get in the garbage."

"They have garbage here?"

"Compost, I mean."

After that they took the dog up the hill and at the top her mother looked down on the rooftops and lit a cigarette. "Guess I better not leave a butt."

"Ha. Garth empties the truck ashtray in the parking lot."

"I didn't see him down there."

"He goes off at lunchtime."

"Look at all the little green fire plugs. That's cute. Is he doing OK?"

"Yeah. Yes and no."

Her mother smoked for a while and then she took a dog biscuit out of her pocket and Zena sat. "Good dog. Look how polite. And they don't ever bring you to see me."

"This is the only place she goes. He has her ride in the truck bed, and this is where we go."

"Ivan Krall." Duška would repeat the name as if Shannon should rec-ognize it. "He was my professor. A boy, just like your husband. In his classroom that year, he was the youngest. 'We see—' he would say. 'We see here—' But of course we did not see! Ah, but I saw that boy, with his chalk." Her made-up eyes sparkled and narrowed at once, over the boy who would be hers. And for life, a long life. Though without all that much of it ahead of them, or ahead of her, to be exact, as she had let Shannon know with what seemed like pride.

To Shannon, Ivan Krall did not seem like a professor of mathematics, a man with chalk. He would have looked good on a horse. But he had won a prize, an international prize, Duška said, in the field of manifolds.

"Wow," Shannon said. That would not be an engine. Garth would know. "My husband was good at math. I'll tell him. They had him tutor the football players."

"Yes, your husband when he is digging, he stops, he thinks, he forgets what he is doing. He is a thinking boy."

"Maybe he'll win a prize," Shannon said. She didn't like the sound of her voice. She sounded like his dad. "He works hard," she said.

Half the time in the two rooms she seemed in her own ears to be chattering loudly as if they had an upstairs and Garth was up there. When she told him about Ivan Krall's prize, he said, "No shit."

"But what's a manifold? Where are you going?"

"Gonna go get a phone. Phone died." He never used his phone and his driver's license had expired. She did the driving to work, but he would take the truck to the Asian grocery for beer. Since he got home he had gained ten pounds because of not working out. His collapsed cheeks had filled in and he couldn't get his wedding ring off.

"Why are you trying to get it off?" she said when he was twisting it. "Could you . . . could you just sit on the couch?" If they had a movie on he would be up and down, or go out and smoke on the sidewalk, or if he stayed put for a while it would be in the Goodwill armchair, lying with his eyes shut unless he heard the faint scratching she thought might be a mouse. That would get him up—a mouse.

"Here, really, I won't grab you or anything."

"No, don't grab me," he said without a smile.

Dozens of them in desert camo were streaming off the escalator. Who thought up those runny splotches that made people stop and look? Somebody had to design that exact thing, ugly and at the same time stupid. Halloween. But serious and real, in another place, something that hid you. Necessary. You had to remember that. There was Garth at last. Others were hurrying past him, waving, kneeling with arms out to kids. Some of the kids hung back.

Garth took a long time to get the duffel in behind the seat. He knew about the truck but he didn't say anything about it and he didn't want to drive. She had finished laughing and crying and reaching for him with one arm while she drove. When Zena ran up to him at the door he did not squat down to greet her. He said, "Is this ours?" She was sniffing his legs, wagging her tail. "Look, she knows your smell!" Shannon said. "She knows you live here! I swear she knows you've been away." The dog ran into the bedroom and came back to drop her worked-over knucklebone at his feet with a thud. Maybe she had been a man's dog. "And I mean, yeah, she's ours if you like her. I know you will. I bet you will."

"Sure," he said. Later, when the dog sat panting beside Shannon, he said, "Could you get it to lie down? Could you get that bone out of here?"

The custom refrigerator had a huge drawer. Duška rolled it all the way out on its quiet tracks. "We do not yet require the morgue." She pushed the ice lever and ice in the shape of orange sections clattered into the drawer. She knows I have the kind with two ice trays, Shannon thought. "This thing, this factory!" Duška went on. "It is as someone, someone, says, is it not? Factories in the private life. Isn't that right, Ivan?" Ivan didn't answer right away because he was looking at Shannon. Then he said, "The private life!" spreading his arms wide and smiling at them both.

"Oh, he is a bad man," said Duška.

"You, my dear," she said to Shannon when they were on their own, "I think you will not judge Ivan. About women, he is a like a little boy who will not come in when we call him."

Unpacking boxes for the Newell sisters, whose hands trembled and whose bright landscapes stood propped in every room, Shannon said, "Wow, you must have a hundred brushes. And both of you are artists? That's amazing." The shy sisters appeared to be twins, but she didn't ask in case one was younger and didn't look it. Mark came in and spread out street plans for them to look at.

When he reappeared she was sitting in the truck half asleep and had to start it to get the window open. Garth didn't like power windows;

you could go off the road into water. She had tried for wind-up but you couldn't find them even in a truck like this, parked in a barn with seeds sprouting in the liner. Mark said, "So Shannon, at the Newells' today. I was thinking. I wonder when social services are up and running if you might want to think about that. You'd be good. Oh, I don't mean quit your crew. Just, you'd let the others do that stuff." He didn't say "clean."

"Wanta know something?" She revved the truck a couple of times before she shut it off. "I like to clean. I like to *move*. You think I want to sit around all day typing up what somebody else oughta do with their life? Guess what, I have a business. I have two more people ready to clean when you have the things built. I have two more guys coming on—Garth has—for Grounds."

"OK, sorry, sorry." Mark backed away from the window.

"Maybe just put it in my contract and I'll talk to everybody and all like that."

"Is this about money?" Mark said, putting his hands up. "Want to go have a beer?"

"I'm waiting for Garth."

"He's down at the machine shed. So tell me, how are things?"

"Good."

"So I guess we've been a little worried about Garth."

"Who has?"

"Dane and I. Because it seems like he's having some trouble."

"You think so? Shit, I wish I would have noticed."

"You don't have to talk like that, Shannon."

"Gosh, did I say a bad word? Do you want me to fire him?"

Mark's face went red. "It's the war."

"Right, you were over there too? That's how you know? Why don't you fire *me*? Don't you know we're not supposed to yell at the boss?"

"Go ahead and yell."

"You go ahead. Go ahead and fire me. I don't care. I don't care what happens."

"Nothing's going to happen."

"Yeah, I guess that's the whole point of this place."

The Newells' niece Chelsea was in high school. She had short, teased hair with longer strands pulled free and waving around her head. "Who's the hot guy?" she asked Shannon the day she got there with her backpack and pillow. "His name's Garth," Shannon said. In an hour the girl was outside in shorts, pulling a board out of the scrap lumber. Her legs had dark bruises up and down them. She set up her aunt's easel near the bed of sand Garth was leveling for flagstones and she put the board up on the easel like a canvas. Shannon waited to see how long it would take Garth to leave. But once the girl was talking, twisting a brush handle in the belt loops of her shorts, he leaned on the rake and appeared to listen. Above the low shorts she had a roll of belly.

Mary Newell came into the kitchen and looked out with her at the two of them in the yard. "Oh dear," she said. "I'll explain to her. We forgot to say you're married. You and Garrett."

"Garth," Shannon said. "I am, anyway. I don't know about him."

Duška would have had an answer, several answers, but Mary Newell did not. She gave Shannon a look of frightened pity, wiped her dry hands on a dishtowel, and said, "Chelsea is our brother's daughter. We have her come every summer before school starts. I don't know. . . ."

"Can she really paint?"

"Oh, yes. Yes indeed, she's very good. She's still in high school but her teachers think if she can just . . . somehow . . ."

"Grow up," Shannon said.

"Yes, if she can emerge from the . . . troubles, if she can just . . . She's an artist."

Did that help you? A girl with bruises, Goth lipstick, troubles—troubles meant pregnant, Shannon was willing to bet: could being an artist help her? Did it help these two old women? Maybe not so old, if this was their brother's kid.

The girl had begun to put paint on her board, talking all the while to Garth, who did not seem to know she must be painting him. Could he be listening, as he looked off at the woods? Shannon wanted him to answer. She found herself wanting, in fact, to see him drop the rake and close his hand on the girl's heavy upper arm with its large blue tattoo of a bird. Maybe just to shut her up. Shannon could almost feel the skin herself. She almost willed him to take off his work glove and touch the bird. The girl had stopped painting and had the brush in her black Goth lips while she wiped her fingers on her shorts. Then she was showing him a bruise on her thigh. He bent to look at it.

Shannon was not going to open the door and go out. She was thinking it through and if she said anything it would be later, at home. She'd say, "Hot stuff, huh?" If he didn't answer, or even if he did, or if he turned his back on her she'd get up in front of him and maybe slap him, not to hurt him but just—and although he had never hit anybody he would hit her back, though not with the strength that must be in him still, or how could he work the way he did? She would yell and that would bring the neighbor out into the hall and Shannon would say a mouse ran out of the chair.

"There is your husband in the rain," said Duška. "He is in a hurry."

"Training for a marathon," Shannon said.

He went by fast, bent over, hands stuffed in the pockets of his overalls. Not the way anybody who *ran* would run. Shannon didn't know where he was going but she knew there was an army regulation that said you could not put your hands in your pockets.

"Don't have him deal with a lot of disorganized stuff," the chief warrant officer told her. His sergeant was the one she had gotten along with but his WO Mr. Coombs was back and had e-mailed that anybody could call him.

"Disorganized stuff. It's a building site," she said.

"Well, keep an eye. Is anybody bothering him?"

"Bothering him? No. Sir."

"You had a question?"

"About what happened. Like you say, I don't want to bother him . . . sir."

"It's a forward base. If they didn't get hurt they saw hurt."

"I know that." She said it in a friendly way so he would not put her with the antimilitary wives.

"In his case, that would be bones and fat where there was a kid, his buddy, a minute ago. Let's see. What else." They both knew a WO or anybody else with rank was not supposed to offer information in those terms, let alone over the phone. She could tell something was wrong with Coombs so she went ahead.

"OK if I ask you another question?"

"Fire away."

"It would be about you and your wife, sir." There was a silence except for his ice cubes clinking. "Please don't hang up on me."

"I don't have a wife."

"He said you were married."

"I was."

"I mean, I've been to the VA. I saw the guys. Maybe they don't have a leg. They're holding on to their wife, though."

"Everybody's different." She could hear him breathing. She remembered him, his way of grinning when she saw him in the PX. That was a couple of years back. She thought he was going to say he was different himself, but he didn't, he said he had to go, and then it sounded like he dropped his phone on the floor.

What if she yanked the duffel out of the closet and chopped into it with the hedge shears? Would he slap her back to normal, or get her in a chokehold like somebody from another unit had put on his wife?

She dragged the duffel out and sent it sliding on its cleats into the living room. Zena scrambled up growling.

"OK what's in there?"

"What?"

"That picture? Is that what you have in there?"

"What, now?"

"That day she painted you. Showed you her thighs."

"Jesus. A car hit her on her bike. She could be dead."

"She's not, though, is she. What's in there?" By this time Zena was pressed against her leg, growling.

"Stuff. My stuff. Elbow pads, gauze, knife. My canteen."

"Knife? Elbow pads?" Her voice was loud.

"To crawl with."

"Why do you need that? Why do you need that?"

"Stop it!" he yelled. Her own elbow came up before she saw he meant the dog. The dog was steadily growling, facing away from them in a kind of shame.

"Think I'm gonna hit you?" Garth said.

"No, I—"

But again, he was talking to the dog. "Gonna growl at me? Gonna bite me?" He squatted, took the dog by the head. "Think you might bite me?"

"She doesn't like that. It's OK, Zena."

"Wanta bite me?" The dog whimpered.

"Don't do that," she said. "I can't believe you're teasing a dog."

"Jesus, can't anybody just leave me the fuck alone?"

"Anybody? You mean me? I'm anybody?" For a moment she thought he was going to pick the dog up by the head, but instead he let go and stood up.

"Good dog," he whispered, as if it were a secret from Shannon like everything else.

"Because something's the matter, that's why. You need to get up here and see him—"

"Up where he's at?"

"—because he's out on the backhoe in the rain."

"He don't drive a backhoe."

"Well he's on one. I can't catch him. I can't stop him."

"Look, I'm due for my shift."

"Right. I'll just let him know that. You haven't seen him for two months."

"Take me twenty, thirty minutes and I got a job to do."

"Fine, Stanley. It's on you. What he does. You sent him to the god-damn war."

"What's he doing on a backhoe? Track or tire?"

"He's driving it, goddamn it, Stanley. Track."

"That's a trackhoe. Excavator. You got excavators out there. Any idea what one of them costs?"

The backhoe was running along the middle slope. It leaned at a steep angle and moved faster than you would expect.

"I couldn't find him, it was Zena that found him," she told Duška for the second or third time. "I ran, but it was so wet and I couldn't catch up."

Duška took her wet hand and put a tiny glass in it. They could just see the dog, chasing and barking. It was the first time Shannon had known her to bark. They could hear better than they could see through the pane, as the backhoe leaned in a wide circle and headed, increasing its tilt, uphill to the woods.

"Hear that? That's trees. He's running into them. And Duška, Ivan's out there." They could see him on the hill behind the backhoe. "I have to go back out."

"No, no, no. This is cold and you take it quickly. It's—" Duška pronounced one of her words, raising her little glass. Shannon's had a vertical crack leading to a rough edge that could cut you. That's what Garth would say. Many things could cut or drown you or reduce you to bone and fat.

The dog was running circles around Ivan, herding him. A rig like that could plow you under. That had happened to someone. A girl somewhere who thought she could stop men.

Duška leaned close to the window. "With our son," she said, "he always knew how to do."

"You have a son," Shannon said.

"We had," Duška said.

"Wait! Wait!" It was Chelsea, slapping the screen door. She ran into the kitchen pulling two phones from inside her wet shirt. "Don't call 911! I took their phones, see? I had to! If they call 911, if anybody does, he'll get shot. A vet, doing this stuff? They'll shoot him!"

"Thank you, child," Duška said.

"Keep these." Chelsea dumped the phones on the counter. "My aunts. Helping." She turned to Shannon. "I know he won't run over the dog." How did she know that? Did she know that you could turn a rig like that over, that you might want to, might long to, roll it into a pit? "Don't worry," the girl was telling her. "I'm going back in the house. They're afraid. Don't worry." She ducked into the rain.

Ivan stepped up to the backhoe and the noise stopped. A calm descended like an awning, with the drum of rain resuming on it. They could just see the dog, sitting now, while Ivan was slowly turning in the downpour and pointing, moving his arms in arcs as if to number the things that made Garth's effort—or any effort, from the way Ivan dropped his arms—in vain. Sky, mud, dog, machine; trees dark now and tightly ranged. After a time Ivan reached up into the cab with both arms. Was he going to pull Garth off the seat? But they were shaking hands, all four hands it seemed. Garth got down on his own. Then for a while the two of them walked around the backhoe inspecting it, the dog circling with them, and then they stayed out of sight behind it, at the tree line where some damage must have been done, and finally they emerged and set off down the hill.

After a while Ivan stomped on the porch mat and entered with his exhausted look, shedding rain. When he saw Duška he clapped himself on the chest in a way that struck Shannon as an old-man act, as if he might begin to sing, but instead he spoke to her in their language. Their son died, Shannon thought, holding the cold little glass. How terrible everything is. I want a baby. She would have sat down, but she was the youngest. "Where did he go?" she said.

"He is taking the dog to the truck," Ivan said. "The dog is wet. He will wait for you."

Maybe he would drive off the bridge into the water. No, he was in the passenger seat, and he had the dog in the cab with him. Her panting was the only sound until a high voice came out of Shannon. "Did you see her do that?"

"What?"

"Run after you? Keep right on after you up there? With no way to know, because how can she possibly, possibly know what you're going to do next? She came after you! She came, not your dad! Don't you like this dog? Don't you like her at all? Don't you like anything any more? Can't you at least like a dog?"

"Like?" he said, sitting back with his cap down.

The dog, still panting, looked from one to the other. Shannon couldn't get her own breath. "OK, so you don't even like a dog." She didn't reach over to stroke the dog because she saw that he had hold of her by the collar, both of them sliding on the wet vinyl.

"She got a spider off the dash," he said when they reached the freeway. "Ate it."

"Ugh. They're still in here."

"In Helmand . . ." He pulled off his wet cap, shook out his wrists, and took a fresh grip on the collar. The rain was loud on the hood and she got in the slow lane to hear him. "I drank a spider. Drank it down."

"No. No."

"It was in the canteen cup. Not one of those camel spiders. This was a little guy. But you could feel him going down."

"Oh my God."

"Yeah, I know, know what I mean?"

She turned to look at him. His face was white with a cap mark across the forehead.

"God. Oh, God, Garth." Her voice was hoarse. "What are we going to do?" It was her high school voice, the tear-hoarse voice that came out of her when the girls were all calling him, showing up at his house, even friends of hers, and she had accused him of things he did and things he would never do, and made him mad, and, worse, made him hopeless, because his brother was gone and who did he have other than her, and then with her words muffled against him she would soothe him in the dim hallway of her house in the afternoon with no one home, where because it was his nature he would take over and lean her up against the wall with care, the way he leaned the bike, and lean against her, moving his weight into the kiss the way he knew how.

you would be good

The burglar was stoned when he cut his way in. It was snowing hard enough that he had the stuff in his eyelashes. Somewhere inside, where even if he scared her for a minute he could maybe get through to her, was his ex-girlfriend. The place had one of those doorbells with pipes on the wall like an organ, and he could hear the dim clangs. He kept pushing the button through ten pairs of them, but she didn't come to the door. He went back to the car, got the stuck trunk open and found his glass cutter. Above the lock of one of the big double-hung bay windows of the living room he etched a curve. He knew she was in there, she had to be, she was housesitting. He pushed in the half-moon of glass, unlocked the window, shoved it up, and threw his leg over the sill. Before he got the other leg in he had the sensation that told him a house was empty. He would get that, a quick shim in the gut that said, OK get in, do your thing, get out.

Then his left arm was tight in the jaws of a dog. Jesus. The dog. The burglar had been a high school athlete and still had his arm muscles, and he got hold of the collar and twisted.

The dog bulged its eyes, pawed, choked, and sagged to the floor, a big black dog with a dark lolling tongue. He couldn't remember the breed but it was one of the biggest breeds, to go with the house. He knew the dog. That tongue.

She must have gone out for something. What time was it, anyway? Everything was quiet, as if it were early in the morning, but maybe it was the no-car quiet of snow. The dog lay flat out on its side. The window let in the smell of snow.

When left by itself the dog was supposed to be shut in the den, so it wouldn't dig its thick claws into various windowsills and slobber on the panes in its intense patrol for the family's return. They often forgot to shut it in and had to punish it when they returned. Erin always left it loose in the house and at those times, she said, it didn't claw the windowsills because she would be gone such a short time that its confidence would not desert it.

That's what she would do for a dog, reassure it, make its life easier. The rules didn't matter to her; she would let a dog up on the couch and into the bed. A small one like a pug she'd let up on a dining room chair, or hold on her lap while she ate. "Feel this," she'd say. "Here, feel the tension. He's so tense he's shaking. A dog shouldn't have to feel that way. They shouldn't leave this little guy. He can't get over it." A dog has ways to relieve tension, but if it is a good, trained dog, like the big one he had just choked to death, it is long past the callow relief of chewing furniture or leaving drops of urine where it alone will ever know they have dried in secret testimony to its anxiety and love. It must suffer unaided. She had taught him this.

He said, "Now he'll do this when they're here, get up on the table."

She said, "No, he won't, he knows them. It's them he loves, poor thing."

In the hall a scarf was dangling on the horn of a statue. These were the kind of people, world travelers, who would have in their front hall a wooden statue of a goat, bigger than the dog, a tall, thin goat with spiral horns, on a heavy base. Carved the way they do in Africa, so it spooked you more than a real one would have in a hallway.

She must have come early and gone back out for something because of the snow. She would have come in with her books and her ten days' worth of clothes, calling to the dog as it threw itself against the door of the den, and fed treats from her baggie into its big mouth, and let it stand up and plant its big paws on her chest, wagging and whining and squatting to keep the weight on its hind legs so as not to hurt her.

But instead of this, as he was to learn, she was lying on an ER gurney. Snow—expected as a mutant few inches at this time of year— had moved in over the city in a rolling bag of gray and the bag had opened. There was a pileup on the freeway and somewhere toward the middle of it two semis had crushed a couple of cars between them. A dozen drivers had arrived in this ER. She was the only one in a coma.

A year before this, she had been taking care of the house and dog while the owners were in Europe. In the huge oven of the eight-burner range she had roasted a chicken for him. They had eaten it on the terrace overlooking the lake, with their own white mountains in the distance, while the owners would be specks on skis on the same white above some pass in Bavaria. Then they would come down and visit cathedrals; some of the great ones were near the slopes.

On the terrace she had talked to him about the fact that he and she had both been raised Catholic. The effect on her was different, because of the big Irish family of girls she came from, with their understanding that any household not Catholic was abnormal, if forgivably so, while from the start there was no way he was going to get the good out of Catholic school, no way he was not going to hate it, being not only a boy but the kind of kid, unsupervised at home, who got in trouble every day.

They had used the owners' china and wineglasses, but spread a tablecloth she brought from her apartment for the occasion, because when she lifted a cloth from the linen pantry and shook out its heavy folds, it had occurred to her that if the wine left a stain she would have to send it to the cleaners. She couldn't afford that and certainly he couldn't. His money went for things she knew about by then and was set against, things that were going to part them.

He looked to one side as he passed the dog, and when he was out in the snow he dragged the window down with a thud. He didn't take anything. He wasn't going to anyway because that wasn't the point, the point was seeing her. He had to get out of there before she got back and found the dog. There was no buyer anyway for the kind of stuff in the house, all the silver crap, the dark carvings and creepy woven hangings, the carpets too big to move. These people took their cameras and laptops with them. What he really needed was cash. In this house there would be no cash. He got into his car and drove, doing twenty-five in the snow so he would look careful and not attract attention to an old car in that neighborhood. The snow was coming down hard.

In the late afternoon her sister Briah called him. For a second he thought her voice on his cell was Erin's. He interrupted. He could explain. Briah said, "I'm with Erin in the hospital." She was calling him, she said, because she thought he would want to know. For a time he didn't really hear. A bubble formed in his mind, with scenes floating and intersecting like drops of oil. The thought he was having was that Erin must not have had a boyfriend since himself, since he was the one Briah was calling. After all, Erin had not had somebody waiting at the time, she had simply gotten rid of him. She was right to. He was going downhill.

He had gone about as far as he could get, and now he was coming back up and he wanted her to know. He had known she was going to housesit; he kept up with a girl who knew her at school.

Briah was saying they didn't know if Erin would live or die. "I've got her key," she said between sobs. "I'm going over to feed the dog. I got in touch with those people. Their info's on her key. They're on a plane. I'm going before it gets so I can't make it on the hills."

"It's already that way," he said. "Got all-wheel drive? Or you won't make it now, down by the lake." He surprised himself by saying he would take her. He didn't have all-wheel drive and his tires were bald, but he was a good driver.

"You know what?" Briah said. "They're up there in the sky looking for somebody to housesit. They have a list and they're going down it. A list. Somebody to take Erin's place. Erin! Erin! They didn't even ask if I'd feed the dog. They said he could wait."

There was no doctor around and the ICU nurses wouldn't say, but when Briah went to the bathroom he asked them again and he could tell they believed Erin was in trouble. When Briah came back she had washed her face and had the key in her hand. The blue tag on it had Erin's looping g's and y's. He could hardly breathe. "This dog knows me," Briah said. "He'll let us in."

The dog is not dead. It's standing in the hall by the goat statue, with one big paw on the scarf it must have pulled off the horn. Again, it does not bark. At the sight of Briah, who goes in first, it begins to wag its tail slowly. To him it seems a little wobbly as it comes forward, sniffing first Briah and then him, his feet and legs, in a careful way. If it connects him to anything bad it doesn't show it. The big dogs aren't the bright ones, Erin has told him. Some of the little ones aren't either. Like people. But some are deeply wise. Those were her words.

He feels a jet of cold air pass his cheek, from the hole he cut in the window. Briah finds the dog food and fills the big dish, but the dog won't eat. It lies down heavily on a fine rug the people keep in the kitchen, a prayer rug, he knows from Erin. But when he sits down at the table it gets up and comes over and takes his forearm in its mouth. He sees that this is a form of greeting. The dog lets go and flops back on the prayer rug.

They let him out to pee in the snow and leave him loose in the house when they go back to the hospital. "He's a hospitable dog," says Briah, crying again. "He'll be nice to the list person."

She lets him sit with Erin by himself and he goes over everything again with her. How desperate he has been, how he has the prospect of a job thanks to his parole officer. He is off the drug and he thinks this time it's for good, his PO thinks so. All he had today was weed and not all that much of that. He still owes people money. He's volunteering at the encampment where he lived for a while after she kicked him out. Doing better than he was then. This hospital where she is lying, remember, is the place he once worked as an orderly, when they were both at the community college. When he met her. He is going to put in an application here today in case the other deal falls through.

He tells her how deep the snow is. How he wondered what she'd do when she saw him in the living room. The two of them in one room. How quiet everything was. No one was ever around in the daytime, in that neighborhood, except gardeners in the summer. How he talked to them back then and they were all illegals with more problems than he had.

How sorry he is—no way to say this, sorry needing a punishment, sorry beyond any look she could send his way to let him off, if she opened her sticky eyes. How he had been wasted, even on such a little, and forgotten the dog's name, forgotten the dog entirely, thought it was attacking him.

If she had been there, nothing like that would have happened. If she had gone out in the snow to start her car ten minutes sooner, or later, a minute sooner, three seconds later, this impossible crushing would not have happened.

He thought she was ignoring the doorbell. He had to talk to her. Would she have called 911? Knowing how he felt about her? No. No. She couldn't answer because she had a tube down her throat. He thought he could see her eyeballs flick under the lids.

When she died Briah stayed with him in the waiting room while the nurses were unhooking and arranging everything so that the two of them could go in and sit there for as long as they wished. Briah told him she would call him when her parents got there and they figured out the funeral. She was wiping her eyes on the hem of her shirt because the Kleenex box was empty, but he was breaking down, and she must have known about the problems he had when things got seriously bad, how he would go every time, no matter what he had promised, and find what would help him. She knew because she hugged him and told him not to despair. She got down by him on the floor where he was sitting and told him hospital floors were not clean and gave him a lot of advice. She had seen how he was in the kitchen with that dog. She said the thing that would help him now would be to get a dog. It was true she felt that way because she and her sisters were dog people, had grown up in a dog family, where it was believed that you should have two dogs because to leave one dog alone in the house for longer than it took for Mass to be over was a cruelty born of ignorance, and now their parents were on a plane and who knows how they had managed the matter of the one old dog they had at home. Briah had dogs of her own, but Erin, like a priest who had forgone marriage, had taken other people's dogs as her obligation. Once you had a dog you had to stand up, you had to get up every day and feed it and take it out, you had to meet its eyes, you had to be its leader, it did not know you merely owned it, had found it somewhere, it thought it had found you, its leader, the confidence it felt would shock you, make you worthy, you would stand up, you would be good.

He could see that. He could see a big dog out with him somewhere in the open like a beach. No one else was there. It ran ahead low to the sand in a straight line until it was out of sight. "They always come back," Erin said.

da capo

Before the musicians walked on, we sat there with the sad but alert expression worn by concertgoers. All around us were the French braids, the waved white hair, the freckled scalps, the university beards. Our organs were crowded by all the food we had eaten, but we kept a disciplined stillness. Paul shifted his shoulder away from mine.

We had been fighting in the restaurant. We had to fight quietly because the place was small and the owner, who waited on the tables while her partner cooked, scented our fight and kept coming in close to offer us the special she had just written on the blackboard, the wine label to study, the food itself in several stages, the peppermill, and in a last sally the pastry tray. Eventually four other tables were occupied but it was us she favored. We had to keep pausing for her in the midst of our eating and our fight, which should have become funny but did not, partly because of the woman's small tense face set forward at the jaw. She breathed audibly. She had some instinct like the one that makes our dog roll on dead seagulls at the beach. She even made us talk to her and got out of us where we were going after dinner.

When she approached the last time with our change she said, "Chamber music on a summer night! Wish I had tickets myself." She winked, as if chamber music were something between us that other people might object to. "You still have plenty of time to park," she said, following us to the door. At first I thought she said part. But she was not the Sybil, and she should have known how to be chilly with people who fight at dinner. She should have a remote, worldly air.

On the way over Paul did not drive recklessly, as he sometimes does when we fight, but with a kind of hunched carefulness, a meagerness in his steering, as if motion would hurt him. His face no longer looked swollen with anger, but tired. Fights like this, that leave you tired, are the worst kind.

I went back, in my mind, to the moment when our voices changed and that feeling came over me, of my head filling like a cup, to the ears, to the forehead, with daring and invention, and then brimming over with words. In the past there was joy in our fights, our blood rose against each other as chosen enemies, a pleasure could find its way into the shudders of insult and retraction. I was not tired the way he was, I could have gone on fighting.

His tiredness had to do with Sophie. A year ago Sophie had been determined to have him. Her determination had flagged, according to him, but she still hovered at the edge of things, did not pick up her bruised family and move away, kept up with her busy practice as a counselor.

Although Sophie has nothing more than an MA in psychology, and a job as a private counselor, she was the one brought in to give Paul's office a seminar on avoiding hierarchy in the workplace. After her presentation several of them took her down to the cafeteria for lunch, and she began to cry, because her cat had been put to sleep at the vet's that morning and she had not been there to say good-bye. Her crying, I am told, went beyond what might reasonably be passed over. Paul was the one who walked her to her car and questioned whether she should drive.

Think of that. Paul doesn't like women's tears, because of the many years of trying to stanch his mother's. Think of Sophie, always in tears, asking waiters for Kleenex, hunched over the ferry railing in the middle of the Sound, stumbling into elevators in her tear-fogged glasses, sobbing at the dentist's, lurching out of a movie in the middle.

Think of such a person trying to sort out the troubles someone is confiding to her.

I know about these things because Paul told me. He let them drop, so that I had to picture him at a movie in the afternoon. They did that. Both of them shirking jobs, watching for people they knew, wasting the only time they had. How could they do that? I was screaming at him. What movie did they see? Did they go to the grocery store? Did they put gas in the car? Did they pretend they were married?

Once I knew Sophie existed, he couldn't stop himself from speaking of her. He thought he was just letting out a few details to relieve the pressure. Crumbs I could follow to get him if he got too far. He came home once with a grubby shadow on his shirt where they had tried to rub off tears and mascara.

I know about this kind of abject love. About him, what he is like when you are going through it. He goes through it, too, he is not a bystander.

A lover of music, Sophie could be on her way to this concert. We were all here in this same hall once before. He and I had the children with us. Karen, the younger of our girls, said to me, "Why do you look like that?" They never knew that Sophie had us in her sights and was leading us, like a sniper. Of course they knew nothing of Sophie and her red hair and her terrible cramps and her MA, even when their father talked to them on the phone from the hotels where he was staying with her, because he had to make sure we could reach him in a family emergency.

And what would she think if she knew she was not even mentioned in the fight we were having only a year later, in the hurt we were taking and giving? One of my friends said, "Try not to fight with him, just for a while." She saw the need for caution. But we would have had to change, and if that change could be made, why not the one he was contemplating?

The children had thrown a match to our quarrel while we were getting dressed. They came in from riding their bikes, sighing and scowling because I won't let them stay out on bikes at the end of the day, in rush hour.

In a study, out of some number of children—in the thousands, I think—asked at random times what they were thinking about, none mentioned an adult. Sometimes you think of things you have it in your power to do, that would force your children to think about you, the power you have to break into the room of childhood, which they think is locked against you. Anyway, they were certainly not thinking about us, about our plan to go out, to face each other alone across a table and then sit in a darkened hall listening to music, and to reach underneath these things to lift out the buried excitement, distantly related to that of playing outside at dusk when we were their age, and try to keep it alive for an evening.

All three of them were getting ready to play Clue. Robbie had used up his time on video games for the day, and, having renewed his haggling for more time, had angered Paul and lost his game privileges for the weekend. His face dark, he was lying on the floor in the girls' room, drumming his thumbs, while they spread out the Clue board with its obsolete miniature weapons and detective notepads.

Not far into the game they began to disagree. "Goddammit," said Robbie, ten years old. I was standing in the doorway and Jenny and Karen looked up at me. Robbie bowed his head over the board.

I don't want to have brought forth a family in which a ten-year-old says goddammit, not as a challenge but with adult bitterness.

Robbie is not in adolescence, but he is drawing near; he has the size—big feet, big joints, and squaring jaw—and the melancholy that prefigure it. Because of his birthday he is with children a year younger than he is in school, and this summer he is perplexed at some of their interests. He tries to go back and retrieve his love for the action figures he put in a bag to give away. When you are that age, each year really is a closed system, a stage. Maybe throughout life each year is a stage that we are too distracted to recognize. "It's because she's forty-one." "Ah, forty-one." It might be that we would treat a year more respectfully if it were granted its own characteristics, even a name. There are not so many that we couldn't do that, greet each year at the birthday as it descends, original as a snowflake, with all the coming situations of mind and body sealed in it.

The year the alewives washed up on the Chicago beaches. Paul and I lived, new lovers, above a tavern in a neighborhood with shrines in the backyards, with the Virgin or St. Francis holding out their arms over little fountains. The people with yards and statues knew we were not married and, we felt, watched us. The smell of decomposing fish along the shore of Lake Michigan, the smell of the stockyards near our apartment—these not only did not repel us, though we indulged in rich complaint, they seemed to us to be the world in its real, as opposed to its fancied, glory. Our fights were the same thing, words dark, stinging and flavorful as the beer we drank.

What dispelled the glory of these fights, their predictable but mysterious descent, I do not know. By means of them, it was possible that year to descend into a dim red place of bodily pity and remorse, and desire to please, and pardon. A little room, a confessional.

The year I read half of Anna Karenina *on a plane, leaving the country for the first time, thinking about the dullness of Levin and Kitty as a couple. The question was why people married so relentlessly, when it was the nature of love to take place outside of marriage. Over the cramped hours in the air, the stodgy Karenin made his increasingly pathetic appearances. There was something I didn't know, even though it was there in the book for me to read and I read it and thought I knew it. The most important thing: the thing Anna lost, dwarfing lost virtue and pride and even the love of Vronsky. Her son—her beloved Seryozha!

I read it but didn't know.

The year of Mr. Mead, First Year Algebra in his hand as we all took a deep breath every time he turned, with his shoulder blades back, his layered muscles showing in the Banlon shirts his wife bought him, and wrote on the board. A full year of being unable to drag my attention from the way his wide back funneled smoothly down into his narrow beltless pants. When he turned from the waist, it struck me that his sides moved the way a slab of modeling clay does when you begin to twist it. I went over and over this similarity. I was hardly any distance from scissors and glue and clay. One minute in braids, stiff with pride, carrying up my clay man to put on the teacher's tray to be fired, the next tall, slumping, sore in the breasts, mysteriously weakened. Mr. Mead.

And that obsession was only a shadow of the first one. Lately I wonder if it all goes back to the way you begin, and after that you love in that way, or go sleepwalking after something that evokes the luxury, fatality, sorrow, whatever the strong taste was, of that first one.

The year of the bad boy. The year I was eleven I liked the bad boy all year. Because of that boy I am helpless in the hands of my son, who sometimes looks out with the same yellow-eyed look of a playing dog that would like to bite you, and barely restrains itself. A boy's look when he is finished with childhood and doesn't know it. That boy. Boy. A silly, jocular word for the mean, thin, graceful thing, the ghost-like thing.

He always had dark circles under his eyes, from having no bedtime, the teacher said. I waited for his high infuriated laugh after he stood in the corner while we read aloud, the sass he would mutter if she turned her back, the finger he would flick on the way back to his desk. Class, it wasn't funny, she said when he was in the principal's office. He was a serious troublemaker. He did things we could not be told about.

He knew something about the way I felt. When he passed close by my desk so he could rattle his knuckles on it I could smell the briny iron smell of the monkey bars on him, mingled with playground dust and a smell that was himself. I saw the unraveled hem of his T-shirt sleeve where his thin, hard arm emerged. Bruises all over it, lakes of bruise, disappearing onto hidden skin. Vague rumors about his father's meanness. We didn't have the word "abuse."

For a while I thought the others were pretending indifference to the dark eyebrows drawn together, the bitter, grinning look that so afflicted me. But I was the one pretending, turning my back at recess, making the face the girls made when a teacher dragged him off the playground. *She likes him.* The girls knew. But I could not stand up for a passion. I denied him.

It was a passion, although we called it liking. All the girls did. *She likes him.* Nothing I have felt since then has ever put it in the shade.

The children go back and start over and begin an elaborate plan to deprive Karen, the middle one, of the advantage she showed the last time. She chews her sandy hair casually. She takes part in the plan to handicap her, knowing she will win anyway. It is all established in the year each one of them is undergoing. Robbie will fare badly, thus he says goddammit.

I don't think in this actuarial way about the family for long. Soon the children have to go back to the beginning and start again because Robbie has used up his guesses early and he is crying. All three of them are oddly tenacious about Clue, as if they must expose a real misdeed. To the exacting oldest one's chagrin, her sister has put random objects on the board, a paper clip and a bottle cap, to replace the lost tiny pistol, the noose.

Then minutes later it happens again. They will not give in to Robbie's tears; he has made his mistakes and must play on without a chance to win. He cries loudly in his new way, with groans, the last—though he does not know it—that he may ever cry until somebody wrenches tears out of him when he is our age. Karen, the winning one, says something I can't hear. Her way is not to fight but to make observations about weaknesses in the others, which they think are secret. Robbie hauls up on his elbow and hits her between the shoulders with his fist, hard. She knows I'm there in the doorway so she does nothing. Robbie scrambles up, scattering the pieces, and begins slapping her on the head with the Clue board. The dog gets stiffly to his feet, points his nose down and barks. The board tears down the middle.

At this Paul begins to shout, "Stop it! Just stop it, god damn it!" All attention shifts off what is happening with the Clue game and onto his stamping approach. Robbie's eyes flash through his tears and the girls shift their hips righteously in their pink bicycle shorts. "Stop it,"

Paul says from the doorway, in a lower voice. He looks at his hands, and turns and goes noisily downstairs, throwing an angry look back at me as if I have allowed the children to make him want to hit them.

He would never hit them. Fatherhood he accepts as a vocation. Something happened when he was a boy that required this of him. He may not be a natural husband but fatherhood is a marked-off territory in his mind: there he will not be found wanting. He always preferred to stay home rather than hire a babysitter, and he doesn't have to pick one up now, because Jenny, the oldest, is almost fourteen. Downstairs the girls hug us loosely, waiting for us to be gone. I go back up to kiss my son. I have to kneel down because he's sprawled against the girls' dresser with his arms loose beside him. "Oh, well," he says, sniffing deeply and shakily. And he puts his head on my chest like a dog. Paul comes up, too. When I leave he squats down and talks to Robbie. I used to think Paul gave Robbie advice, but lately I have overheard snatches of their talks and I think it is more that he is begging Robbie not to be temperamental and violent and clumsy, as Paul was when he was a child, but to be happy.

Paul still calls home in the middle of the evening. But now that Jenny's old enough to babysit for other people, we think and say to each other, they're safe, the family won't let anything happen to itself.

Of course, we know a story to undo that faith, a story from Sophie's household. Sophie's toddler fell out of a doorway with no steps, in the house they were remodeling. All the while Sophie was crying with Paul at the movies and on ferries, her husband was lugging planks in and out and cutting drywall and breathing sawdust to turn the house into one in which she could lean back on the couch in front of the sunburst window, spread out her red hair, curl her thin toes and be happy. The little one fell several feet, onto cement, while in the care of her teenage sister. She was a ball of solid flesh and was bruised but not badly hurt anywhere, it appeared. Later in the day her sister could not wake her, and took her back to the emergency room, where she was found to have bleeding in her head.

The blood formed not one clot but two, it was said. It was a bad case, days of alarm, confusion, and guilt at the hospital. Sophie was not at the meeting in Denver that she had left home the day before to attend, but in a lodge on the other side of the Cascades with Paul, and could not be found. Fortunately Paul, daily envisioning just such a thing, had left a telephone number. But snow fell; an accident closed the pass, and he was unable to rush Sophie down out of the mountains to the hospital where her child lay, and thus, while the unconscious two-year-old was being wheeled in and out and having her scans and being operated on for the clots, many things had to be known, and said, and suffered over, on the telephone. And I saw how it was then, for Sophie's husband Stan and their teenage daughter, and for Sophie herself, and even for Paul, now that Stan knew, and I felt myself banned from the circle of suffering because I had known for months and my own knowing had not shamed anybody or set in motion any such spreading sorrow.

In the tiny restaurant with its ceiling fan going and its front door open to the cool air of the street, I observed, "You're confusing the kids. Lately either you give in to everything or you're yelling. What about quiet discipline?"

He said, "Quiet discipline. Like you." That was how it began, harmlessly enough. But something had been there all week, coming and going, flickering. Then we tried to get in everything over an hour's meal, but a silent agreement over the last few weeks not to bring Sophie into it blocked us.

It always used to come back to weeping red-haired Sophie twenty blocks away, in her house with its side cut away and draped in blue plastic, who never wanted to hurt anybody. Indeed after the baby's injury and long, stalled, only partial recovery, Sophie withdrew for months, more than half the year. Still, when spring came it was unusually warm, and under its loosening influence she was ready to sink back into desire and secrecy and tears. But Paul had had a chance to catch his breath and he was not quite ready, he was thinking it over.

It seemed possible to me that he was thinking he might have to stay the way he was, married. Bitter thoughts. When he was twelve, his own father left the family and married somebody else, and he was recalling that time of furious sorrow and hatred.

His father got married to a woman down the street whom they had all known. She was divorced, raising two sons whom Paul's father would later urge his own sons to think of as their brothers, during the brief visits he made. Those dwindled away in a year or two. The woman had pitch-black hair down to her shoulders and came out onto the sidewalk in her pink bunny-fur dressing gown carrying her garbage can. Fussing with the lid on the can, smoking. Paul always described her that way, on the sidewalk, inhaling. Long before they knew anything about their father's adventures, Paul and his real brothers had noted the hair, the pink fur. They had talked secretly about the woman.

As women did more frequently then, Paul's mother went on a downward slide. There were not many magazines telling wives in her position what their responsibilities were. She raved, she drank, she cornered the girl Paul took to the prom that year and wept in her arms.

Years later his father was passing through the town where Paul and I were in college, and he took Paul out to dinner. He boasted about the black-haired wife to his son. He said, "She's still a wild woman."

"Ugh," I said, when I heard that. Paul didn't tell me about it until after we were married.

Paul said, "I was through with it all by then."

"That's what you think," I said.

He thought for a minute. "If I had seen him a few years earlier and he had said that I would have killed him."

But maybe now he was finally thinking about how his father felt. I didn't know how long this period of thinking could go on. Thinking and waiting. Nine people waiting.

The concert was part of a festival, four chamber works by different groups. Two-thirds of the way through the first one, during the pause after the andante, Paul got up from his seat and crawled across me to get out. He was gone for the rest of the quartet and the two mazurkas. When the intermission began I threaded my way through the crowd in the lobby but I couldn't see him. Finally I went up to a pair of student ushers, a boy and a girl who were laughing and pushing each other, and said, "Did you see a man come out and leave, at the beginning of the concert?" The boy looked down at me, a woman with glasses and lines at her mouth. "Lots of people go out," he said in a voice meant for the girl. She stepped in front of him and said, "A man did sit out here for a while. I don't know, he might have left."

In an alcove by the cloakroom I found him in a telephone booth. This was in the time before cell phones. He was not on the phone, he was sitting in the booth with the door closed. He was leaning back as if he were asleep. For a horrible moment I thought he had gone into the telephone booth and died.

Though I had made no sound, it was too late for me to leave because he had seen me. He stood up as if he had been getting ready to come out just at that moment. He wrestled with the door, trying to push it outward instead of pulling it toward him. I remembered something I had forgotten, how when the children were babies I sometimes thought, at a certain stage of tiredness, of climbing into the crib with them. I saw myself, the wife standing outside the booth, as another person, the one who would have come into the room if I had been in the crib and said, "What are you doing?" Someone proprietary and without impulses, a balding Karenin, a jailer. "What are you doing?"

I wanted to say I saw nothing peculiar about his being in the phone booth and I was not there to bring him back. But he got the door open and came out, shaking out the knees of his pants, and without a word pressed through the crowd with me to the refreshment table. I could have said, "Are they all right?" pretending I thought he was calling the children. Or I could have said, "You called her, I know." But I didn't want to, because of the question of whether I had driven him to it. Not what if I had, but what if I hadn't? What if I did not figure into it at all?

We had come for the Schubert trio that was last, after the intermission. About the thin slivers of torte and the half cup of coffee that went with them for six dollars, we did not make our habitual jokes. Pale now, he went off to the men's room. When he came back he was standing behind me for a while before I knew it. Then the lights dimmed and everyone surged back.

A woman in a pleated caftan with shoulder pads pushed by me so hard I hit the doorframe. I looked back to see if Paul had noticed and I began to feel chilled and uncertain. He looked ill. Surely at dinner he had fought as fiercely as I, although I couldn't remember any of the things he had said.

We rustled, sat, settled, gazed at the stage. The musicians arrived onstage looking fresh and combed as if they had just laid aside aprons, washed their hands, and come out ready to serve us something they had prepared backstage. We grew still, the musicians smoothed their music, signaled back and forth tuning. Silence. Silence. The trio began.

It was to hear this trio, the B flat, that I had bought these tickets months before. In its andante an almost untroubled devotion would be told again and again.

When life is dark I listen to Schubert. I have taken books about him out of the library to learn why this should be so. Reading them the first time, and even rereading them, I have had such a strong feeling of woe, and of responsibility, as he stepped along his path, that it was as if I were reading about my son. For Schubert, there was no untroubled devotion. No wife, no proud children. He was himself the twelfth child of a teacher and a cook. Just five lived. So, seven deaths, for the teacher and the cook who had Schubert to bring up. He grew to only about five feet, not tall enough for the compulsory military service. He was known by the nickname Mushroom. Some of the piano music he wrote was too difficult for him to play. He drank too much wine, could not earn a living. No wife. No children. Even so, he was able to chart a despair and longing that seem to me to belong to marriage, although it may be I'm confusing marriage with life.

Schubert finished this piece in his last year, before dying at thirty-one of typhus, typhoid fever, or syphilis, depending on the biography you accept. Thirty-one. The year was 1828, *the year of mysterious pain, fevers, of businesslike attempts at sales. The year of death in youth.*

Here we were, hearing his lost idiom and understanding it, as though one hundred sixty years had not chewed through the world leaving nothing Schubert would recognize, except maybe the three on the stage, two men and a woman, with the violin and the cello and the huge piano with Bösendorfer emblazoned on its mirrorlike black side. The young man is bent over the keys guiding it. The air of an important but not—for him—difficult test hangs over him.

I fell in love with Paul in a class. I saw him bent over his spiral notebook, with dark circles under his eyes. He was carefully writing, shielding the page. I watched for a while and saw that he was not taking notes but writing a letter, which I felt sure was to a woman, a girl, as we said then. I started to think about how she would feel if she stopped getting the letters. When he looked up he looked straight into my eyes. He looked familiar. He had the flashing sad eyes of someone else. A boy. He looked like the boy from my grade school.

For a long time I used to say to myself, *no one can distract us from each other. Either of us.* It was impossible that anyone else could offer more than we were offering each other, in the days of the alewives coming in on the waves of Lake Michigan.

I did something.

I called Sophie. We arranged to meet at a restaurant. I knew whom to look for. I had seen her across the auditorium that night when Paul stiffened and I followed his eye. I knew she would get to the restaurant first because she was a therapist and would know that the seated person has the power. She was there, with a book, a novel. It was one of those novels that maintain the reputation of being for the serious reader while in fact everyone reads them. I wanted to say something crushing about it, for I had read it too, but I just said, "Are you liking it?" as I sat down.

"I do like it," she said, and she added, looking at me searchingly as though I might help her, "but it's taking me forever." Everyone complained proudly of the long climb of this awful book.

Was she pretty? No, but she had abundant red hair, and her eyes were large, and made up to highlight their blue-gray. Something about her did not look good. She had that skim-milk skin, blue under the eyes, that goes with the hair. She was not wearing her glasses. Things I had been afraid would come to me as I looked at her, physical things, did not. The need to be composed overrode any images.

"I don't know how to tell you how sorry I am," she said. Did this mean he had told her he was going to leave us? I didn't want to ask questions; that would make me the outsider. But I didn't want to let her ask questions; that would make me the patient.

"I know you are," I said.

"You must wonder what kind of person I am."

I knew this was a consideration of the utmost importance to her. "I have some idea. I assume this isn't your usual way."

"God. I would never have believed this could happen. Never. Never."

"But it did." We kept making these statements, one after another. Somebody was going to have to ask a question, or take a stand. The waitress came for our order and Sophie complimented her on her earrings. I could see she was going through life like this, making everything a little better for this person or that.

"So tell me what kind of person you are," I said.

"Oh, God. I'm . . . I'm . . ." She resisted the temptation to go on. Paul thought she was intelligent and maybe he was right. Her face grew intent. She had on black pants and a discreet blue-gray turtleneck, with a big necklace of hand-painted beads lying between her breasts. I could picture her without the makeup and the jewelry, at home like anybody, with her family.

"Tell me about your house," I said.

She swallowed, and then she laughed. "Oh, God. Why not. This is going to be a strange day. I knew you would be like this." This produced Paul, hovering as if she had passed her hand over a lamp, telling her all about me the way he told me about her. What would he say? *This is my wife's year of sadness, of strangeness. Of energy feeding out of ordinary life into her as it always has, but being turned into stasis, as if cries were being converted into print, or chords into notation, or dances into diagrams on the floor, and backward from there into just thought, thought, thought, so that she, my wife,* says Paul, slapping his forehead with the realization of what has happened to me, *does not do anything this year.*

And she is not like that, not passive, he would say, I hope he would say. Not a victim.

"My house," she said, leaning forward and waving her hand through the vapor of Paul's image. She was actually going to say something about the remodeling, I thought. Fortunately she said only, "It has come to a stop since Jenny got hurt." It's the worst irony that we gave our daughters the same name, but at least I know the thing didn't get its start until after she had Jenny.

Now her Jenny has what they call deficits. Jenny is not going to grow up to do anything like what either of her parents does for a living. She is not going to do much more than the basic things. Sophie is worried about who marries the kind of woman she will be. "*Mawwaige*," I said when Paul told me this. We always liked to say it the way Peter Cook does in *The Princess Bride*, at the wedding of the maiden to the vile prince. Paul grimaced. "She means who will take care of Jenny," he said hoarsely. He takes responsibility for the fall out the door, the ruined brain. "Let's face it, you may have to provide her with a dowry," I said. I could say anything. He knew how I felt about what happened to a child. He knew I would not draw the line at hurting him, though, and would in fact try as hard as I could to make his feelings of wretchedness more intense, until he would have to come closer in—because he always had to talk everything over, the worst, the most unassimilable things—closer, to be comforted. He let it go.

Talking of her child, Sophie had momentarily let go of whatever held the proud tension in her skin, her thoroughbred look. She mottled and sagged. Her nose reddened and her eyes clouded, and she took her white hands off the table.

"Let's be done with all this. I want to make a bet with you."

"What is it?" Sophie said, raising her chin with a determination not to be surprised.

"I want to tell you about us. I don't want you to interpret what I'm saying. I just want you to see the two people, the five people, you wandered in on. And then, I'm not asking for anything. But I'll make a bet with you that you'll get out of it. Because something that has been set going and gone for years, that is on its own course, something like *this*, something *made*—" Here I ran out of breath.

Sophie knew not to be friendly now or to supply me with words. She looked sick. We paused to look at all the men and women in groups having lunch meetings, with their personal lives set aside.

"Why are you asking me this now? I haven't seen him, we haven't seen each other, it's been—"

"But that's not your choice, is it? I'm asking you now because of a thought I had last week. I thought, I wish I could just shoot her, the way I could in a French movie. I did. That's when I decided to call you." I said this in a rush, though quietly. I had gone into a pawnshop because somebody told me that was where you should get the guitar for your child's first lessons, because they all wanted to be rock stars and yours might not be serious about the guitar for long. While the man was showing me a very expensive guitar a musician had pawned, I looked down and saw in the display case, nestled among the ring trays, a small pearl-handled revolver.

"Are you threatening me?" Sophie was cool, though her skin was muddy.

"I just wanted to meet with you." That sounded so professional, as if we could share ideas for a project.

"All right. All right. Have you been so happy," she said slowly, "that you think telling me about it is going to change my feelings?"

"I don't know about your feelings," I said. "What does happiness have to do with it?" Of course she knew how we have fought all these years. I moved and she jumped. What if I had the little gun?

"I do want to hear," she said. "I'll listen."

"And don't listen as if you're going to counsel me," I said. "I'm not your patient."

She drew herself up. "When you're finished, do I get to tell you my side? My story?" she said. "I realize I am in the role of the bimbo who appeared in Paul's life and deflected the—the chariot of your marriage." She went rosy at this turn of phrase, with the excitement of speaking more sharply than she usually did. She was used to other people being the ones who got excited. "And furthermore," she said, breathing unevenly, "people fall in love with the, the *spouses*"—she expelled this word like a pit—"of their *best friends*. So they know all there is to know, and furthermore they like or they even love their friend, and in some cases that doesn't make any difference at all to what has happened to them, what has happened is beyond their control." Her voice broke.

She's going to cry, I thought. *That's all right.* I kept still.

"You can't always control life," she said plaintively.

"No."

In the silence, she gasped. She gasped again and bent forward. "I'm having the most awful cramps," she said against her hands holding the table.

"I see you are." I felt a thrill of pleasure. Oh, I had heard about these cramps of hers. But she gave a groan.

"Oh God," she said. "I was afraid this would happen. All morning I was—" She pushed her chair back and got herself into a folded position, breasts against knees. She stayed like that and people looked over at us.

This is not really fair, I thought. It's a way of taking over. Though I did not doubt that she was in pain, because she had no embarrassment about the position she was sitting in. Now the people in the restaurant were going to some lengths not to watch us. The waitress with the earrings gave me a questioning look.

"Oh! Oh no!"

"What?"

"Oh no. I'm bleeding." She started to stand up and then crouched back onto her chair. "Oh no. Oh no. I can't stand up. I mean this—I'm hemorrhaging."

"Well, let's go to the ladies' room," I said, picking up her limp blue arm.

"I can't. Listen. This is not just my period. This is something else. This happened once before. There's blood thumping out of me. Oh God. I have to get to a hospital." The waitress heard the word "thumping" and ran to the phone. People began pushing back their chairs and heading toward us.

When the aid car arrived, a woman wheeled in the gurney with a casual speed. The sight of her settled everyone down. She gave the rest of us in the room a small gesture that said to get out of the way.

Sophie wept and grabbed the woman's hand on one side of the trolley and mine on the other. It was true, her chair had blood on it, though not a lot.

In the emergency room they gave her something that stopped the bleeding and made her silly. She lay holding my hand. She gave the doctor a weak wave of her other hand. "There's something so funny. This woman wanted to shoot me." Even in this condition she had her effect; the doctor stood there smiling down at her. "But you weren't going to, were you?" she said sweetly to me.

"No. I don't have a gun." The doctor gave me a stern look. "I would never buy a gun," I told him.

"I didn't think so," Sophie said. She craned her neck on the paper pillow and said to the doctor, "You look tired."

"But you never know," I said.

Sophie said, "I want to tell you something. Come here. I want to whisper." I bent down. "This is not a miscarriage," she said. "Don't think that. This is something else. I've had it happen before." I didn't answer. She pressed my hand.

I had never thought of that. I had never thought that could happen. That she and Paul could have a child. It had never, never before this, come into my mind.

I told Paul. I told him the same day, about everything, the pawnshop, the stupid book Sophie was reading, my plan to explain our life, the EMTs with the gurney and the shock pads. As I talked his face became slack and his eyes faraway. I told him how Sophie wanted to tell her side. How she had spoken of her children but not her husband. How a scene had come to me in the ambulance, in which Paul, summoned by her husband Stan for a talk, would not speak of me. The two of them would talk as if Paul had risen out of the sea and laid hold of Sophie. I told him how it all came to nothing with Sophie, nothing, because we had not even begun our talk when she did this. I said, why didn't I delay her rescue and just let her bleed to death? There was a moment when I might have pulled out the gun if I had had it. I didn't say what the moment was.

"I don't think so," Paul said.

"Women do. You think I liked her!"

Paul didn't smile. He would not let me joke with him. He would not let Sophie come into the realm of things that were ours. Ordinarily I could have said, "Turn around, talk, goddamn it. Don't stand there with your back to me thinking about when you can call her!" But the children came in from outside, not thinking about us.

Late in the first movement the cello broke a string. It was a particular seventeenth-century cello, according to the program. Crack! The sound echoed in the hall as if the bridge on the cello had snapped, but it was just a string. The three limped to a stop, all grinning, not as in Schubert's time, when surely humiliation and ruin hovered lower, in greater readiness to descend on one, than they do now. The most awful things happen now, but no one will call it ruin.

The gallant cellist, who had a thin humorous face and a little beard, left the stage to restring. The others got up and walked after him. Loud rumbling talk began in the hall. I had been in Schubert's world and I didn't want to come out. In the lapsed tension I had a desire to cry heartbrokenly. Paul had the armrest now and had propped his cheek on his fingers, hiding his face from me. "Are you crying?" I whispered very softly.

It would mean he knew, he had heard in the music, that he and Sophie had finished.

He dropped his hand and glared at me. He was not crying. That was not what he had heard in the music. "What?" he said haughtily.

I said aloud, "I meant about Sophie."

"I'm going to cry about Sophie at a concert?" he said, not so much angry as alert, now that her name had been mentioned.

It must be one of the strangest inklings afforded us in life to feel, momentarily, the coursing through the one we love of love for someone else. "It's the music," I said weakly. "It makes me want to cry about all of it, everything."

He said, "Everything. So you've been attacking me all night because of Sophie?"

"I haven't been attacking you," I said. "You always say that when we fight, so I'll think I'm a bitch and not fight."

"You are a bitch," he said. But he smiled. Our eyes met. He put his hand on the armrest as if he knew the sight of it, with its distended veins, would make me cover it with my own.

I didn't know whether he had talked to Sophie or not, and I didn't know how to find out. I didn't know what to do next. What would come next? I knew nothing, really. Nothing about how life could be conducted so that one did not have to go swimming with one arm like this, trying to hold onto someone in the current. It was not as if I were saving him. He wanted to swim away.

Many statements, rapid and theatrical, suggested themselves to me. They crowded up from the past, the kind of things I used to say when my beloved all through high school broke up with me to go out with girls who were new in school or girls his friends had broken up with. *Go see how you like her,* I would say. At the height of it there was half a year without him. *I thought I would die, at Christmas, when everyone was happy. I thought I was going to die, without you.*

The year I thought I would die, for love of that boy in high school, while somehow seeing at the same time a future in which he had utterly disappeared. In the vision—this was before I had decided against marriage—I was married to a man I can only describe as Paul.

Everyone in the concert hall seemed to be in a noisy, elated state. The cellist walked back onstage with his instrument held up and out like a puppy in disgrace. The applause that greeted him was a tremendous crowd sound, with whistles and cheers. Everything about this entrance was filled, for all of us in the auditorium, with inexplicable happiness.

The musicians settled themselves, lifted their arms, and went back to the beginning.

During the music my mind cleared somewhat, though the past had not receded and indeed it came closer, summoned by certain passages. I thought about how, when I went to the county high school, where students from all the little towns converged in the eighth grade, I looked for the boy I had loved in grade school. The bad boy. I longed to see him but he was not there. No one except the few who had gone to my grade school had ever heard of him, and it was hard to bring up his name and hear what they remembered of him.

For years I looked for him. If I denied him in school, I have kept faith with him since. Now that I have children I see that his condition was more serious than we thought. His stealing, setting fires. It may be that, just as our teachers said, he was headed for one of the jails that are the estate of such boys. Ruin. If he lived to be ruined. But something told me, when I was grown, that his father did not kill him, as I sometimes dreamed he had, and that he himself did not hurt anyone, that he was not in jail. That he went on and lived, found pleasures that no one refused him. Maybe his temper cooled, maybe he enlisted in the army—no, not Vietnam, no, he might have had a record that would have kept him out of the service. No, he lived. He straightened out, found his work. Or if he was the criminal they said he would be, a year came when he broke free, fought his way out of his earlier self, and in a face he saw one day, found me, the one who would love him forever.

the war poem

I n the last weeks of waiting for the opening shots of Desert Storm, Wally wrote a poem, the best he had ever written. It was 1991 and at that time the word "run-up" was new; no one was used to a waiting period before a scheduled war, like the overture to an opera. Carrying a "No War" sign to vigils beside the road for six months had left him giving angry drivers the finger and filled him with despair, but he was twenty-seven at the time, he had a girlfriend, a good job as a reporter, and a notebook of poems, and he put the despair into a poem.

Once he had some money saved he was going to leave the paper and write full time. He wasn't going to accept anything from his family. His girlfriend Janine, who was working at the paper as a temp while she learned Italian for her audition with the opera, said they could give it to her instead. She made the opera chorus, and during her performances Wally would take his press pass and stand backstage. It was a period when they both said they were overcommitted and overworked, they said they were poor, they said they were prisoners of the state. But looking back later Wally saw the time as full of a benign rushing—at twilight to antiwar meetings and opera rehearsals, at midnight to the half-darkened offices of the newspaper—and full of costumed dancing, the rumble of timpani, poems read aloud, exhilarating denunciations. Endless pitchers set down in wet rings, endless corkscrews sunk and pulled. Friends of his who could duel all night over who had dug deepest for background on Kuwait, friends of hers who could sing "Casta Diva" as easily as they sang along with Alice in Chains. They all agreed that Janine, in her villager's apron and puff sleeves, had a better mezzo than the guest soprano.

The poem Wally wrote in this period was about Elton, Oklahoma. The town of Elton was his own invention. He had checked directories at the paper and there was no such place. He worked on the poem in a trance of excitement: he had never been in Oklahoma, but as the town took shape in his mind he poured into it everything the planned war had aroused in him, every feeling for boys in towns around the country who were about to take part in a ground war, boys the age he had been a very few years before when he was sitting around a bong with his friends studying for the SAT, but boys who would deploy—word dropped into the news every night like salt—and then as intently and fairly as they might observe hunting season, go out to kill their counterparts, and who, being from a small town asleep in farmland, might know by name the stonecutter who would carve 1-9-9-1 into their headstones. In fact the thought of his own snug safety, in contrast to the risk these boys faced in carrying out their orders, shamed Wally, and out of that came the poem, a thing of some form, as he was proud to discover in the exhaustion of finishing it, but even more a thing of feeling.

He sent the poem to his friend Gustav, who had quit his job writing copy for the Auto Section and moved to the East Coast. Gustav had never really been a fit at the paper. He had come up to Auto after an editor got talking to him in the mailroom—though Gustav wasn't really a talker, more the kind of mild guy you bitched to in the cafeteria. He would rub his eyes, put down his carton of milk to listen. He was younger than the rest of them but he could not stay up late, and because of that he had rarely joined in the gatherings after work. If he drank two beers he fell asleep at the bar. In truth he was too gloomy for their company, too preoccupied with the care of his younger brothers while his mother was in and out of the hospital. Wally had met the brothers when he went over to watch a game with Gus. Over the afternoon he had noticed that if you talked during a game in that house no one answered. The wallpaper gave off the mother's smoke. Eventually the four of them picked up and moved back east so the mother could be near family, but once they were back in her old neighborhood in New Jersey, she died. His brothers finished high school and Gustav decided to stay where he was and get a teaching certificate. Even though he had written for a newspaper, the program required him to take a composition course, and there his instructor took a shine to something he wrote about cars. Through her offices Gustav got Wally's poem into the hands of an editor, and it was accepted at a literary magazine.

Wally subscribed to the journal immediately, and not sure the first issue that came would be the one with his poem in it, he ran his hands over the cover design of green and brown camouflage, seeing with a mild disappointment that the whole issue was devoted to the war. But there was his poem, lying in its own sunlight on the white page, fresh as a town in farmland—and there, just below the title "Elton, Oklahoma," lay the name Gus Horn.

Gustav called him the same day. The editor had made a mistake. The poem had arrived in an envelope with his, Gustav's, return address on it. Not really the editor: a student volunteer had made the mistake, but like Gustav, the editor was abject, and had given his word that it would be corrected prominently in the next issue. But there was no next issue; the magazine folded.

That such a mistake could have happened, and be saved forever in print! It was a punch in the gut. The second poem Wally had published in six years of trying was not to bring him a single reader. For several weeks before the demise of the magazine, he called Gustav every few days to find out what was being done to get the word out quickly about the mistake. Finally Gustav, in a voice of despair, told him that not only was nobody calling him back, but the magazine's phone was out of service and the fact was that nobody was in the building any more.

For Wally, the muddy camouflage colors of this event—for it was an event, no matter how Janine might characterize it when she tired of his depression—seeped into the next couple of years. A few more poems came to him, and then without any farewell he stopped expecting them. He grew more wary on the one hand and on the other freer in his habits, often drinking late with his coworkers and going home in a pugnacious mood. He lost Janine.

When he passed thirty he came out of this phase and into a time of expanding his goals. After a few more years at the paper covering union disputes with local industry he took his father's advice and applied to law school, got in, and did well in his courses. By the time he was in practice, his girlfriends were enough younger, enough used to war, that there was no point in bringing up a time when he had grabbed his head in both hands as a poem came to him almost whole. He couldn't even picture Gustav clearly, and there was no one except Janine—and that was a long shot—who remembered the matter. There was no way to show anyone the thing in print anyway, in part because although thousands had met their deaths in that war, almost every soldier who left the US to fight it had come back alive.

Some years later, he was going to New York to interview for a job. He was doing well in a respected practice in town; he had married and divorced, he had a new girlfriend with whom he was thinking of buying a house if he didn't care for the offer from New York. Planning his trip, he decided to track down Gustav Horn. Gus. The group of them at the paper had bestowed the name Gustav on Gus Horn in much the same way Wally had named his town Elton. Without any protest Gus had allowed the name to become his. If you called and asked for Gustav in the old days, you heard the mother say in her cracked voice, "Gus, I mean Gustav, it's for you." Wally couldn't remember if his given name had been August or just Gus.

It was easy to find Gustav, because he had not moved from where he had lived at the time Wally had been in touch with him every few days about the poem. He had the same phone number. He was glad to hear from Wally after years—was it twelve, thirteen?—and gave directions to his apartment in Jersey City. He was teaching the fifth grade.

The woman who answered Gustav's door shook Wally's hand with a strong grip. "This is Benilda," said Gustav, coming around her to give Wally a bear hug, as people had done in Seattle in the days when they were all working at the paper. Now it was the new century and there was less of that. Gustav had gone bald. "Benilda," said Wally, checking for a wedding ring. There it was. Benilda had long hair, dense and black, held back from her face with clips.

They took him into the living room where a dark-haired three- or four-year-old child, a boy, was sitting on the floor with a book. The child looked up at Wally for a moment with what resembled polite respect. Wally felt a power coming from Benilda directly at him as he looked at the child, a foreignness, some assumption that was going to trip him up if he wasn't careful. "And who have we here?" he said.

That was the right thing. "Gustavo," said Benilda. She had a pleasant alto voice but a way of looking at her guest steadily as if he were in the middle of some test of manhood.

"Age four," Gustav added with a grin of delight. Wally looked around at the furniture. Loud curtains and a big saddle-bagged couch of russet leather that took up half the living room. A madonna on the mantel, reflected in a mirror framed with tiles that looked as if they might have been painted by the little boy. Wally smiled. He began to relax.

The fight started when after a heavy dinner of rice and spicy meat and a lot of wine, turning Gus's pale wide face florid as it had when he was young, the new war came up, the Iraq war. Benilda had a grown son and he was over there in a city she named. Wally stayed in close enough touch with a couple of guys at the paper to know that the current protesters were justified in their chanting of the name of that particular place. In one siege, hospitals had been bombed. He knew two photographers who were over there. At the moment the bombs dropped, as in hospitals anywhere, people were on the operating table.

"Bennie, we got some more red in there?"

Benilda set another bottle on the table, and leaning back in his chair Wally began to bring in his rusty writing skills, hearing himself with some surprise. He could still make a person see it. The sick in their beds, trying to fall asleep. Babies in their isolettes. In the OR, open bellies.

"I am proud of my son," said Benilda. "*Mijo*, time for you to go to bed."

The little boy had eaten heartily without speaking during the meal, and did not ask for any dessert or protest his bedtime. He went to Gustav's chair to be kissed, and stopped at Wally's chair to say good night.

"Antonio would never take part in a thing like that. Antonio, her son," Gus said when they had left the table, and Wally heard in his voice an echo of Benilda's accent, a warning echo, if he had paused to interpret it.

Wally said, "Jesus Christ, Gus."

"Jesus Christ, what?"

"Are you following this war? Don't you remember? Don't you remember how this all got started?"

"I remember."

"Where exactly," said Wally. "Where exactly are you, these days? On the issues, I mean."

"What do you mean, issues?"

"I mean. I mean, are you on the side of the jackasses who are running these wars?"

"Why would you ask me that?"

"I look around me," said Wally, surveying the table from which Gustav had cleared the smeared plates and the many serving dishes.

"At what?"

"At this, this life you have. Jesus. What do you say to your students? What, fifth grade? Kids, get ready to fight in the Middle East. We'll have a war there for you, too. Be proud! Make your mothers proud!"

"No, I don't say that."

"Does Antonio come in and speak to your class?"

"Antonio is not in this country," said Gustav with a politeness that belied the red in his cheeks. He looked at his watch.

"Is it your bedtime?" Wally said.

"Not sure where this is going, buddy." Gustav was shaking his head in his old easygoing baffled way but with a keener look at Wally from under his thick eyebrows than he would have had in the old days.

Wally downed his wine. "Buddy, is it? Where's the bathroom at?" He had no idea why he added the "at." Anybody from the secretaries on up saying that at the firm, or using "lay" for "lie," had to buy coffee. To his embarrassment the tablecloth caught at his knee when he was getting off the chair and he pulled the cloth askew and staggered.

Gus pointed. From the table you could see down the hallway, where one of the three doors had to be the bathroom. He almost collided with Benilda coming out of the kid's room. She steadied him at the elbow. He got a little dizzy peeing and stayed in the bathroom for a few minutes, drying his hands and looking at the tub and the shower curtain with fish and bubbles. There was a kid's washcloth with a lion on it on the side of the tub. When he came back to the table he could see Benilda in the kitchen holding her hair up off her neck with one hand. She let go and the black hair fanned out over her back, almost to the waist. A photograph would have you read that as beauty, or at any rate as something more timeless or complete than it actually was. Wally knew that, he had worked with photographers. From the sink Benilda called to Gus, "Did you show Wally your book?"

"Your book," Wally said, still on his feet but not sure of his next move.

Benilda came in with a plate of brownies. "He will have a book. Next month. But this week the first ones have come."

"Reviewers' copies." A gloom was coming over Gustav.

"Reviewers, is it?" Wally said, holding on to the back of his chair while pouring wine for himself and Gus, who appeared to have worked around his old inability to drink. Benilda was not drinking the wine. Maybe Wally was putting away most of it. They were long past his two bottles but he was the pourer now. He lowered himself into the chair. "And so, the *book*. Tell me about the book. Do I get to see it?"

"Sure."

"What kind of book?"

"Novel," said Gus.

"And you . . . that would be you, you wrote it?"

Gus looked down at the tablecloth. It was hot in the apartment, and Benilda's big lids, silver with sweat from being in the kitchen, lifted to Gus a look so patient and intimate that Wally knew she knew the story of what had happened to his poem. He took hold of the table edge. "Just kidding."

Gus said, "Nope, you're serious."

"Aaah, man, no I'm not. I'm not serious. Hey, listen. My hat's off. My hand's out."

"Thanks. Thank you."

"What's the title?"

"*Strike*."

"It's about bowling?"

"It's about the general strike. Seattle. 1919. You know. More or less about that. Hard to say what it's about."

"It's about brothers," Benilda said.

"*Strike*," Wally said in a tone of wonder. Something stirred in him and he knew it would come out if he chose to allow that. "The general strike." He stood up from the table and crossed the room at a dignified pace. Benilda had opened the window to the fire escape where they had a big potted fern. He was pretty sure a plant on a fire escape was against the law. He pushed the window up and without making the decision to do so he climbed out. There was room for him out there with the plant but he stepped on its tray of gravel. Whatever he did next made the big clay pot turn over and dump out a lot of dirt on the good shoes he was wearing. "Jesus!" he yelled, kicking the dirt before finding he could sweep it through the grating with his foot. "Hey!" He waved a branch broken off the fern. "Got a view out here. I can see my car." Far below was his rental, small and white, not the model he had specified. "Come on out!"

"Hey, man, don't be out there." Gus reached and got him by the arm. Wally pulled the arm free and let it swing back, hitting Gus at the jawbone. At that he saw what was meant by "fire in the eyes."

Saw what a fifth grader might see if he made Gus Horn mad. "Look, buddy," Gus said with a teacher's quietness.

"Buddy!" Wally swung again, this time missing Gus with his loose fist and whacking the window frame. From that position, crouched and cradling his hand, he could see Benilda start for the window, but Gus moved her aside by the shoulders, saying in the same classroom voice, weary and stern, "*Por favor.*" Wally put his fists up and this time Gus came after him.

Next there was a little boy standing in the room in dinosaur pajamas, watching them get Wally up off the floor and stretch him on the couch. The boy said, "Are you OK, Daddy?"

"We're all OK," Gus said. He knelt down in front of his son. "Mr. Stover had a fall. Not out there, just here on the floor. That was the noise you heard. He's going to sleep here. But honey, you know what I told you, *mi cariño*? You never get out on that. You never get out there."

"*Nunca*," Benilda said, kneeling too, both of them speaking to the child with an intensity that suggested they were alone with him.

Wally was on the couch with his head back when Benilda came in with a pillow and blanket in her arms. He sat up; he wasn't sure how long he might have been sitting there. "Oh, no you don't," he said, without getting up. "No." He patted the arm of the couch with a sore hand. Gus. Gus had done to him whatever was hurting his shoulders. He had been on the floor and that would be because Gus had thrown him there. Of exactly what had been said or done immediately before or after that he could not be certain. He could see himself in the tiled mirror, waving his hand back and forth to say no, in a manner he would have made comical if he had been telling somebody the story. "No, no, you think I'm gonna just bed down on your new couch?"

Benilda made a gesture of serene dismissal of the couch they must have just bought with Gus's advance. If a novel about brothers in Seattle could have commanded an advance.

He put his head back and tried to picture Gus's little brothers. The times he saw them they had been doing homework or watching football. High school kids. One played football. He was bigger than Gus but ready to do what Gus asked of him—bring in the chips and salsa, give up the armchair, move his feet. The other . . . wasn't he a lot younger, maybe not smart? Three boys with a mother in the hospital. Where was the father? Gus was little more than a boy then himself. What did he even look like? What made the editor—sports editor, was it?—what made somebody go and pull Gus Horn out of the mailroom?

Now he had a blanket over him and a fat, hard pillow. The blanket had a cord dangling, not plugged in because the big couch occupied the middle of the room like a lap pool. Didn't these people know an electric blanket put you in an electrical field all night? He opened his eyes. "Hey," he said to Gus, who was in the room. "That kid. That kid you have is like the kid, remember, in that movie? Perfect kid, played piano, flew a plane?"

Gus said, "Yeah, he turned out to be a robot." He was in his pajamas.

"I mean, the kid's polite. You don't see a kid like that around." Why did he keep saying "kid," a word that grated when his colleagues said it? "My kids." In the courtroom you said "child." "The child is harmed." "Best interests of the child."

"Sure you do."

"I know guys—their kids are monsters. Right there in the house with them, right in the car. And they don't even notice."

"Who's that?"

"Nobody you know. Nobody from the paper. Those guys, wherever the hell they got to . . ."

"I hear from Kovalek. Hear from Janine."

"Are you kidding me, Janine? *DARYL.* That was the movie. Acronym."

"My brother loved that movie."

"Your brother—what was his name?"

"His name was Joe."

"Pardon me, I meant"—Wally got his head up off the pillow—"what *is* his name."

"He died."

"He died?" Wally tried to remember the brother. Not the football player. The young one. Something about him. Slow. "Jeez, that's—I dunno, man, sorry to hear that. When did that happen? How—?"

"His condition."

Little slouching guy who never had anything to say. Wally's memory would not supply a face, though he could see the room, the TV with a game on, hear the beat of the soundtrack behind the news that kept flashing on with the six clips at a time they put up in those days, the red and orange logos. And himself. There he was. In the house with its smell of smoke and hotdogs, he, Wally, a man as he thought, was standing, yelling over the TV to Gus about the coming war. His poem still to come.

lightning

When Mary Beth's uncle Cart got his draft notice he went north by bus and got off in Canada, where for two years he wrote Mary Beth every week. Some of the problems he went into in his letters were women, about whom she wrote back, "Don't tell me that stuff, just say why you got arrested." Still, he didn't really go crazy until he had been home a month—facing charges because the war was nowhere near over—and had the accident. He ran over a kid on a bicycle. It was not his fault; the boy was riding fast downhill on the shoulder, and for no reason that anyone could establish, veered left into the road. Cart heard the bike crunch and felt the tire heave up into the wheel well.

For everybody in the family except his mother, Mary Beth's grandmother, this was the end of the belief that while Cart might not seem cut out for a normal life, like most people he would eventually live one anyway. No one else from any family in the county had left for Canada. Coming back after two years, he had found his past waiting for him, a sheaf of papers recording truancies and scrapes, errors of judgment leading to misdemeanors and some minor felonies such as intimidation with a registered firearm, and charges of Interference with Marriage—the very things that had led the average person in town to think the army was just the right place for him.

But a change had come. He had lost the attitude that had cast him as the hero of these episodes, and although the ruling was that he was not at fault in the boy's death, he had a breakdown. He lay in his room staring, he didn't change his clothes or get in the car or chase women, and after weeks of this his sister, Mary Beth's mother, found a rope coiled under his bed. From the hospital he wrote letters to Mary Beth in crayon because they wouldn't give them pens or pencils. "They want to jolt me back a ways. Maybe back to the water tank." That was a memory between them. He had agreed, as an of-age patient, to a course of electroshock.

"We will think of it as beneficial lightning," Mary Beth's grandmother said. The notion came from a tattered little volume she had on her shelf, *Smith's First Book in Geography*, in which lightning served to cool and purify the air, as every piece of nature had a share in lending happiness to man. "Q. With what animals do rivers and most other waters abound? A. With fish for the benefit of man." Years ago her grandmother had read the book aloud to them, even though they had modern schoolbooks and the *Weekly Reader* and she was modern in her own reading and respected at the library for it, a farmer's wife.

"I hope those people up there can explain beneficial lightning to me," said Mary Beth's father, in the light tone he took with his mother-in-law. He had tried a case involving electroshock. But she was Cart's mother and as someone not well herself, she made a point of going along with the doctors, while her son-in-law made a point of not arguing with her past a certain point.

Everyone in the house, which now belonged to him and to her daughter, gave in to her as they always had. Until Cart came along years after her other four, the rules of her household had always stood, and she had not changed her ways for a late and wayward child. The rules were a mixture of strict and careless, but if one of her children committed an offense she was always practical, and did not look beyond the immediate occasion of it.

Once she was widowed and her daughter and son-in-law had come back home to stay, she turned over the reins of the farm to them and she let Cart fall more or less into their family. She continued to live there, fading from cancer in her sixties but making ready to die young in the same way she had readied herself to give birth old, and showing her lingering preference for Cart only by asking over the course of one feverish week when he would be coming home from the hospital, and rasping to her daughter and granddaughter, "Watch out for him, now."

When Cart got out of the hospital he was twenty-one. Mary Beth was nineteen, a junior in college. By then she was safe from him, from her old subjection to the eyes half-hidden by the slant of his high cheek-bones, her adoration. And his in return, as she learned, at a time when an attraction between an uncle and a niece, whatever their ages, would be thrown into a great locker of unnamed things.

But she had grown up, she had a boyfriend at home and another at school, and Cart was crazy.

Not long after he came home he took her brothers' bikes, which they hardly rode any more because they were in high school and both of them drove, and he wheeled both bikes, at night, to the cliff above the old gravel quarry secured with chain-link fence and padlocks, and dropped them into the pool of clay at the bottom.

"Cart, you'd done just as well to take them to the dump," Mary Beth's mother said when the man who had bought the quarry land called her. Cart allowed her, as his sister, some latitude with advice and even reproach.

How did the owner know the bikes belonged to their family? He wouldn't say. Probably Cart was seen. He was known in the area, though he hardly ever went out. Anybody on the road that late would have noticed a man wheeling two bicycles in the dark.

"No reason to ride a bike." That was Cart's answer in the flat voice he had adopted, perhaps to let them know he was now separate from them with their noisy family ways.

Mary Beth's mother treated him like the little brother he was, but without any patronizing; always with him she was logical and unalarmed, and that seemed to help. Cart was redheaded, and looking at him run his anxious hands through his dull uncombed hair she must have remembered, as Mary Beth did, the bright, coppery charm that had always spun off him when he was a boy. "Well, Cart, it was good of you to think of the boys," she said. It was odd how she did this, talking to him as a grown man who was at the same time a child. "Of keeping them safe. But anymore, they drive."

Mary Beth was sitting with her boyfriend Trey on the porch swing. When everybody went in he said, "What's that I heard about you and old Cart?"

"I don't know what you heard." She didn't know which of her brothers would have said it, or even known it.

"Heard you fooled around."

"Well, I'd have to say we did."

"Guess you were a hot little number." He knew this anyway.

"It wasn't that. He was my prince."

Trey was going to run his dad's beef operation one day and had no desire to go to college. He didn't read books and he let Mary Beth's remarks pass by him like the mosquitoes that didn't light on his tanned skin. He lived in a state of equilibrium. He was waiting for her, though.

"It was different for us," she said, to give herself, her child self, an air of mystery. "It was love."

"Sure it was." He pulled her against him without bothering to grin. "What do you say we take a ride?" he said, as if it were a new idea, and they drove out to a farm near his where the kudzu had taken down some of the buildings. Two machine sheds and a chicken run and a little house with a side porch were all being dragged to earth by big heart-shaped leaves blue-green and stirring, as if they had just come out at nightfall. The house was a tenant house, in a corner of a parcel that the tenant had stopped bothering with when the farmer's sons moved away and the farmer got old in his house and didn't come around in his truck any more to check on things. If you forget a tractor for long enough, kudzu can take it and grip it so that even if you poison the vines brown and leafless, you can see the machine inside bound like a fly you could never unwrap.

This little place bordered the quarry where Cart had taken the bicycles. He must have wheeled them a good half hour just to get there.

Her mother said Cart was not a bad boy but one who had always found himself in trouble. He took pleasure in trouble. Nothing corrupt or ugly: he never deliberately hurt man, woman, child, or animal. But he was a danger to himself and others. He ran a tractor too fast. He messed up two fingers with firecrackers. When he had a car of his own he souped it up, putting a V-8 in the rusted-out Falcon he rolled on the way to a dance. That time he got out unhurt. Fortunately the girl he was taking to the dance wasn't on the seat beside him, she was on the porch at her house waiting for him to get there. Chrissy Campbell. Her daddy never let her go out with him after that.

Mary Beth knew Chrissy Campbell, knew how she went on longing to sit in that little Falcon with Cart, and how in fact if he called her she would go out to meet him even after she became the banker's girlfriend.

Cart smoked and drank and drag-raced, and he broke into abandoned farmhouses and places where the owners were on vacation, and explored, and took things out the window with him. Stole. Nothing of much value. Year by year he refused to reform, or stay away from girls and women, or organize himself to apply to college. This was all before he went to Canada instead of to the war. Then he ran over the boy and went crazy, if indeed he had not been half crazy all along.

Mary Beth held Trey close and said when she came back from school next time, they would see. Already knew she was leaving him behind, with his sweet breath and his unruffled sigh and hard hay-making arms. When they sat up they saw Cart. He was crossing the top of the field. He had developed the arm-swinging, bounding walk that she recognized from the city where she was in school, where you saw it on schizophrenics and junkies.

At home he paid no attention to her, though he would look in when he passed the door of her room.

"Where's he off to?" Trey said, tucking in his shirt. It was hot and late.

"I don't know. He pretty much stays in the house. Mom and Dad don't think he leaves, other than the night with the bikes. They sure don't know he comes out here."

"Is he really nuts?" Trey was used to Cart at the dinner table, silent, eyes on his plate unless they suddenly grabbed onto you like a hand from under the bed. A scarred hand, two fingers mauled by the firecracker.

"He's damaged," Mary Beth said, sounding not like herself but like girls she knew at school. "He's better since he got back from the treatment but it didn't get him over the accident." That was better, being what her mother said.

"That'd be how long ago now?"

"A while. But somebody died."

"Can't get over you, neither."

"Don't be silly."

"He looks at you. At us. Uncle Cart. Pretty sad guy."

Trey and his father and brothers had a cabinet full of valuable rifles and shotguns. Every farm did. He was a crack shot at target practice and he went out in deer season, but Mary Beth happened to know he never shot anything. That was something even his own father never brought up. No one would have dared accuse Trey of not wanting to hunt.

Only years later would Mary Beth start to think about Trey in Vietnam. She would wonder what the worst thing was. Was it worse to kill deliberately when you didn't want to?

Or was it worse to kill someone deliberately when you were hot-headed and barely knew any better, as Chrissy Campbell would try to later, when she shot her lover's wife? Her lover was the banker and she, Chrissy, was head teller by then. She still flirted with Cart if he went into the bank, even though she knew he was crazy. He did go in because Mary Beth's mother kept a small account for him there, so he could get a haircut or a Coke in town until he had work. She trusted him not to get beer, with its strong effect on him.

Or was it the worst thing to kill somebody totally by accident, as Cart had done? Why had that particular one of the three ways of killing been the one to make someone go crazy, someone who had done things all his life of a reckless nature, unlike a girl who would love first Cart and then the banker and then both, or a boy like Trey who was ordinary and sensible and did what the army told him because he had respect, and lost his life?

She questioned her mother about whether a sister was the person to watch over Cart any more. Whether he might need to be where there were professionals to steady him.

Something unexpected happened. He met a woman. He didn't really meet her; she was the big sister of Chrissy Campbell, who was serving her time for shooting the banker's wife, who had almost died. That it was a crime of passion had shortened the sentence. The sister taught English at the high school and Cart had seen her around for years. He met her again when he visited Chrissy. Maureen Campbell. She took him out afterward and gave him a talking to, the kind his sister had been the only one allowed to sit him down for.

He told Mary Beth what Maureen Campbell had said. "Told me I'm acting like I'm crazy and I'm not crazy."

But you are, Mary Beth said in her heart. Aloud she said, "How come you went and saw Chrissy?"

"She asked me to."

"You do what some girl asks you."

He gave her the slanted look. "Some."

"Not me."

"What'd you ask me?"

She couldn't say, *you said you would always love me.*

"You know what?" Cart said. "She's not ashamed. Maureen. She acts like Chrissy just did what a lot of people would in the situation. She'll sit in intake with people the Campbells wouldn'a ever spoken to. Mostly it's men, visiting wives. It's a side of life you never would feature. The women in jail, the men the ones who behave."

"So you're the only non-husband."

*

He began to go out with Maureen. In a year they were planning a wedding. Mary Beth said, "You better watch yourself or Chrissy might shoot you when she comes out. Or shoot Maureen."

"Nope, right there in the jail she blessed Maureen."

"Were you there?"

"Course I was."

It hurt Mary Beth that he said this. The wedding hurt her. On the day of it and for days afterward, scenes from it kept landing hot and spitting on a kind of inner skin she didn't know she had. Maureen Campbell in her dress saying, "Now I'm your aunt." Thinking back on the wedding Mary Beth almost wished she was the crazy one so she could have made a scene the way the movies had people do when they gave a toast at the reception, usually but not always women, the way a woman never would in real life. She thought of what she would say. *There are things Cart doesn't remember. They shocked it out of him. To the groom.* She raises her glass. *You don't remember. That's how you are.*

A year later they were all talking about Trey. "You let him go to war," Cart said with his new judiciousness.

"What do you mean? I did not."

"You coulda stopped him."

"What are you talking about, Cartwright? Uncle Cartwright."

"You. You just allot a certain amount to one fellow and a certain amount to the next," he said, raising his beer. Maureen had changed all the rules; she turned a blind eye on beer.

"That's a cruel thing to say." There were other people on the porch or Mary Beth would have cried.

"Now, kids," said Mary Beth's mother.

It was the word "allot" that crystallized the second stage of her love. Where did he get that word? No school, little reading. Yet in him there was the word "allot." She was filled with shame. He had looked at her and said that word to himself, in judgment. If he was not crazy, if he could say "allot," why could they not have gone on and on forever as they had begun?

Cart was saved in Maureen's church and he managed the big Campbell farm that became Maureen's. Worst, for Mary Beth, he completed his domestication, the steps of alteration she will not call a metamorphosis, by having a family. There are two children, she knows, a girl and a boy, the boy with copper hair and a look in his eye. In the photographs they send her in Boston, he could be Cart.

It was said that at the sight of her Uncle Cart, the baby Mary Beth would run up to him and with a precocious sidelong glance drop her chewed-on cracker into his palm.

For years they played the play of children and they went beyond it. Cart was sent away to camp, something no one in that part of Virginia did with children at the time, when his mother discovered him with Mary Beth in the cattle trough. Mary Beth saw no reason to consider that this boy was her uncle. He was a boy, a particularly lithe and swift, funny and cruel boy.

They were sitting in their underpants in the round concrete tank, having combed out the drools of algae with their fingers. The cows had been shut in along the creek and had not used the tank in months, but several hills away Cart's father, Mary Beth's grandfather, shouting to his herd, alive as anybody and having no thought of dropping dead later in the summer, had opened a gate and tolled them through to the back of the farm. Following the lead cow over the ridge and down to the water tank came a hundred Herefords, including the bull, as bulging and sleek as the hippos in the zoo in Washington where Mary Beth's father had moved his family so that he could try his hand with a big law firm. The cows were fat with grazing in her grandfather's famous clover, the mixed Lespedeza and Big English Red of which he was so proud.

Mary Beth had been lying in the clover with Cart when they decided to get into the tank. As they lowered themselves into the water, a purple cloud had unrolled overhead, so heavy it looked as if could sink onto the woods.

"Watch out for that bug," Cart said. There was a big black beetle drinking at one of the puddles on the rim of the trough.

"I'm not scared of a bug," she said.

"I mean don't squash it."

She giggled.

"I mean it," Cart said. "Don't hurt it."

"You mean it," she said, reaching for him under the water.

When she comes to think of it, he never hurt her, whatever was said of him. She was only a little younger. He never hurt anything except the boy he ran over, and himself with his mistakes. With the herd surrounding them she didn't want to get out of the water. Cart had climbed in and out several times to show her there was no danger, but she was timid; the bull was near; four years away had turned her into a city child. It was the summer they were moving back to Virginia, where her father would settle down again in an office in the county courthouse and they would all, as her mother said, breathe a sigh of relief.

For Mary Beth and Cart it was the summer before the seventh grade. He had failed, as they all said then, the seventh grade. There was no such thing as "held back." He was tall for his age, and showing the family's heavy lids and high cheeks in a way that gave the family, though they were only Irish, a foreign, commanding look, traceable in portraits to Mary Beth's great-grandmother. This was her mother's, and Cart's, own grandmother, who had died during her first childbirth while her husband was fighting World War I. "My mother grew up an orphan," Mary Beth's mother always said, causing Mary Beth and her brothers a shudder—though they never saw the tragic person, the orphan, when they got out of the car and ran into the arms of their grandmother.

Mary Beth's mother, too, had the eyes, and they were part of her authority. Mary Beth did not have them. They made Cart look older than he was. He did not look like a child at all and in fact was not one, as Mary Beth knew by this time. The feeling she had about him in this summer of coming back was the strongest she had yet had for another person. It was new to her that there could be a person who had no say over you but ruled you anyway, even made you go in fear of him, and yet sometimes gave up everything and let you rule him.

Over the hill her grandmother came striding. "Here comes Mama," he said. They remembered they had been out all day. They saw her before they heard her faint voice. When she scanned the field and spied them at the bottom she pointed at the sky, which was a purple-toned gray across its whole expanse, pressing down on the one strip of bright afternoon light still left, like a stripe around a bowl, close above the fence buried in honeysuckle, and the woods behind, with thick arms of poison oak around the trees. They had had a run-in, both of them, with poison oak in the woods that summer.

"Better git out," Cart said. "Right quick."

"Why?"

"'Cause it's going to rain. Going to lighten." He said "goan-latten." Living in Washington DC her family had lost some of the talk.

"Lightning?" she said, pleased with the progress she was making at having him see the absurdity of the way he talked.

"What I said." There is a pleasant "say-id" used for "said" in that county. She knows now it is pleasant; then it was laughable, because she had gone away and been seduced into another way of talking.

"She's coming down to make us go in, I just know it. Why can't we sit here while it rains. Come on."

"Come on, y'self, and git out. These ole cows don't care." He was out, sleek and wet, and the cows lowered their heads and crowded backward getting away from him.

By then his mother was near enough for them to see her face, and Mary Beth became aware that she had stripped down to get into the tank and would have to stand there in her underpants as her grandmother approached, unless Cart snatched up their shorts and T-shirts, there on the grass being nuzzled by the wet sandpapery lip-nose of a cow. The cows' sides were bulging with the calves Cart told her they were going to have in the fall. Her grandfather liked to bring his calves through a winter young, so they would be tough. The bull stood farthest away, not curious like the cows but watching sideways.

"Cahhht-*wright*," called the voice of her grandmother. "Y'all come *right now* before it lets loose. Pick up *this minute*."

Mary Beth still sat in the water and Cart stood, while the clouds got darker. They had nothing to say and neither of them knew why they were angry and sad, unless it was that the cows had been too timid to come in and drink while they sat there—the same ones that took feed from the hand of the man who didn't care about the angry tears his son Cart could shed when their yearling calves were pushed into the squeeze chute and up the ramp to the stock sale. They had waited, they had pretended not to be thirsty, they had stood swinging their heads back at flies while two humans sat in their water tank.

The lightning came on, lighting the ridge, and then a long growl of thunder. Cart helped Mary Beth climb out, and yes, his mother was right, they were more than children. She was not looking at her granddaughter, she was looking at this son of hers. Unspeaking, she looked all the while they climbed the hill, though he did not glance at her, but only at Mary Beth who kept turning until she couldn't see the tank any more in the field where all three could read the downward course of their love.

aiken

Bridget's parents had taken somebody from the soup kitchen home with them and installed him in their house as a tenant. A sure sign that the days of their independence were coming to a close.

Her brother Kieran, who saw them more often, called to tell her. "So now they've got this guy, what do they know about him, a guy who mooches off eighty-year-olds?" He paused. "Bridget? Are you listening?"

"Oh, sorry, I was looking at the rain. There's a river in the street." At the window in her nightgown, Bridget rubbed her eyes. She had gone back to bed after Nat left early for a weekend of hiking, even though the radio said rain was sweeping fifty miles inland all up and down the coast. Now it was skidding along the street in wide V-shaped ripples that made her building, from the window, seem to be riding steadily forward.

Kieran sighed. "I mean, of course, are you free to come up here?"

If she opened the window and hurled the flat staticky little phone out, away it would skim on its back—unless it snagged in the whirlpool over the storm drain—calling shrilly, while she shut the window and got back under the covers and reentered the dream Kieran had interrupted. She had been wading through a campground, under pine trees, pulling her feet up out of tree sap as she went. She was looking for somebody. One of those exhausting dreams in which a reason for the grief is not made clear.

"Eighty-year-olds!" her brother said again as if Bridget had denied their parents' age, or perhaps caused it.

No, Kieran said, he would not describe the tenant. Bridget would see for herself. The guy was going away for a few days, and while Bridget was driving up from Portland—she did think she could leave? Nat wouldn't mind? Or was he off "on assignment?" (this was Kieran's phrase for Nat's self-assigned efforts to write things that would sell)— Kieran would leave his family for the day and take their parents out so that Bridget could have a look at the house while they were out. They had to make a trip to the dentist anyway. The new one. It had been like pulling teeth to find a dentist who worked weekends—and then the only one who did was a woman—so that Kieran could go along to keep track of the two of them. Make sure they didn't stagger out full of nitrous and get behind the wheel. That was how they were now.

Aiken, the man's name was. Something Aiken, the kind of man people called by his last name. In a very short time Aiken had taken over, hauled things down to the cellar, made the house his own. Not her room? Not her Santana poster, framed by her father with strips of molding, not her frilled lamp and the rug she had hooked in Camp Fire Girls? No, Kieran's room, not hers. Hers had not been touched.

"You read about guys like this, drifters."

Drifters. *Murder.* That was the unspoken word.

She had driven half the day from Portland. In Tacoma the blowing rain had thinned to a drizzle, and by the time she reached the north end of Seattle everything stood out in that clear afternoon light that came in the wake of rain, with vapor streaming up off roofs and tree trunks.

It was warm for February. Under the dripping trees her mother's bulbs already showed green tips. Bridget was tired and sweaty from gripping the wheel but she did not go in right away. Key in hand she walked a wide path around the empty house, like a prowler.

In the back, beneath the pines and firs that had dwarfed the house long before the big places came in on either side of it, she came across a patch of the biggest toadstools she had ever seen. She knelt down. The one she touched had unexpectedly firm suede flesh. A dozen or so of the orangey-fawn things were standing up in the dappled shade, eerily straight as if holding still, one or two with pine needles dangling from their heads. She was glad she hadn't stepped on them. It would have been like mowing down a proud group from a spaceship, with no idea yet of creatures bigger than themselves.

When she raised her head she was looking into an eye. An animal eye. Catching herself with one hand in the wet pine needles she saw the wire hutch, and the long form of a rabbit pressed against the wire not looking at her, or not seeming to, though the eye must have taken her in. The eye was half-closed, the ears lay flat on the scruffy, gray-brown coat.

"Hello." She spoke to it because a human silent and crouched might threaten an animal in a cage. It didn't move. So. This Aiken had a pet, a sickly-looking rabbit. What was the disease you caught from rabbits? Or maybe it was starving. No, a feeder and a water bottle were clamped to the wire, and darkened lettuce lay in a corner. On the ground beneath the wire floor was a loose pyramid of round black droppings.

She stood up, dizzy from squatting by the toadstools in a kind of half-witted suspense, and surveyed the yard. Her parents' house sat some way down from the tall firs in a clearing at the edge of a little lake. When the north end of the city was deep countryside this had been someone's weekend cottage. Her parents had moved into it when the store began to lose business, when Bridget was still in grade school. It had a front porch big enough for two people to stand on and a drainpipe that still ended in a rain barrel, from the days before the house had plumbing. A metal cup had hung there, out of which she and Kieran had scooped sharp-tasting rainwater to drink, but that was gone. Now on both sides rose the big places built of cedar shake and glass, with steep angles to their roofs.

What would a man in his thirties be doing here, in walking distance of no shopping or activity, boarding with old people like her parents? Yet Aiken was not a client of the soup kitchen where they had met him, but a volunteer. Bridget remembered all about that—the thin boundary between the clients and the volunteers, some of them. On Sundays her parents still drove into the city to the old parish, to work on the hot meal served after Mass. Bridget, too, had volunteered there during high school, looking for excuses to get out of it.

Her parents' car was neatly parked in the carport. No truck. Aiken drove a panel truck for a carpet store, parking it up under the fir trees, her brother said, so that he could get in the back and smoke dope. He climbed in and out at all hours, and came into the house with a smile on his face even when Kieran was there to smell the smoke on him. And he was getting into trouble of some kind. On one of Kieran's visits he had a closed, seeping black eye.

Murder.

According to their parents, Kieran said, Aiken was beaten up from time to time because he drove a truck and didn't belong to the Team-sters. It did not surprise her that her parents had come up with this explanation. In his store her father had been removed from the notion of unions, except for the occasional drivers making deliveries in the big rigs, and although through the church her parents had sided with Cesar Chavez, they had not given up selling grapes, or eating them, or drinking the wine that spread a bloom on the fine-grained soft cheeks they both had, Irish cheeks.

But she could not really blame her parents, sealed as they had always been, even before they were old, in an irreversible blameless ignorance. Her high school friends thought their own younger, more suspicious, angrier mothers and fathers knew nothing, but Bridget could have told them those parents knew a thousand things that could never intrude upon her own.

She might have blamed her parents, if they had ever thought them-selves in the right, if they had ever found fault. If they had not been *orphans.* But her father had his lifelong diffidence, and her mother, put out to relatives in the blessed country running a Catholic for president in 1928—her mother did not presume then or later to judge the affairs of the country where she had presented herself at thirteen in her moth-eaten cape to be fed and clothed.

"So there they are, without a clue, in the house with this scam artist."

Kieran was two years younger but he had always been the responsible one, the one in charge. He had married a good Catholic girl with some money—it appeared she had some, enough to have "Kim and Kieran" embroidered on a cloth napkin for each guest at their wedding in the old church, which Kieran now called "a working-class parish," where the smell of stew from the soup kitchen filtered through the heating ducts to mingle with the freesias as Kim was kneeling in the folds of her wedding dress. To marry Kieran! So love was something that could lead you to marry—Kieran. And could change you: as the husband of Kim, Kieran had learned not to argue with his sister.

The rabbit was the same color as the leaves blown around the grove the fall before and lying in scales on the tree roots. It did not move when Bridget bent to look at it, inhaling the smell of the hutch. I won't jump to any conclusions, she said to herself. I'll get a sense of what's going on. She could start with the rabbit, which must belong to Aiken; her parents wouldn't have pets. Her father steered clear of dogs because of having been bitten when he was a mite delivering milk, and cats scratched up the garden and squatted in it.

Bridget let herself into the house and stood for a minute. You were smack in the tiny living room when you stepped inside the door. There were her mother's magazines on the coffee table with the TV remote, her father's cardigan on the back of the recliner, there on the mantelpiece the Infant of Prague and the two little varnished saints, Ciaran and Brigid, underfoot the green carpet, bald in patches, that Kieran threatened to rip out with his own hands, and on the wall two seascapes in frames lined with shells, bought by Bridget herself with her allowance on some school vacation, and breathlessly given.

There seemed to be no smell, certainly not the remembered smell that stood for this house, of moths baked in the porch light fixture, of lake mud drying on tennis shoes, of wet sheets and tablecloths strung across the cellar on rainy days. All the life so repetitive and dim, the life in which Saint Brigid, who had taken out her eye, their mother always said, and put it back again only when she won some favor for the poor, and Saint Ciaran, who had left home as a little tyke to be a monk, looked down on them from the mantel with painted blue eyes and silly chipped smiles they made fun of in their rooms. All that they had escaped, and dipped up now and then, before the tin cup disappeared, in leaf-clogged, dark water they downed on visits as a medicine, a weakened strain of that life.

She went down the narrow hall and opened the door to Kieran's room. It was dark, with the shade pulled down and plastered against the sweating window so that it had stained at the edges. The room was hot; the baseboard heater hummed. Here was a smell she couldn't identify. She didn't want to take it down into her lungs. The bookcase had been pulled away from the wall so that a gun—she jumped—so that a gun—it must be a shotgun, in the instant of seeing she noted the two barrels, smooth tubes lying side by side like organ pipes—a *gun* could be propped in the narrow space and held upright by the doorframe.

Don't think of that.

Of someone coming in and living close, close by, part of the household, and then, and then . . .

She was filled with wrath at her parents, for bringing about a dark, wet day in which, instead of going away to work on things with Nat, a lovers' weekend—but Nat had not invited her. He wanted to get away from her. Why would she not apologize for herself, the contentious self she felt ready to discard at any moment, and laugh her forgiveness when he admitted his own faults: his endless pleasure-seeking at the edge of safety, his wish to tease God, in whom he did not believe, past that edge? Why not hike beside him, and sleep beside him while rain beat on the tent fly? But instead she must drive the interstate in blinding rain, in the roar of tire spray, to arrive in this dark smelly room, her own little brother's room, and make this discovery.

The spines of Kieran's ordeal-and-triumph books slumped under piles of *Popular Mechanics* and *Car and Driver*—so many that dozens of the magazines had dropped onto the floor, and on the wall where their mother had tacked Kieran's drawings of robots hung a tapestry depicting slim does drinking from a mountain stream while a muscular stag stood guard.

The smell in the room reminded Bridget of the onions her father had kept in a bin in the store, when one or two had a soft patch and they had to start bringing them home fast, and peeling off layers so they wouldn't be wasted. She bent to see what was crunching under her shoes. Nutshells. They were all over the carpet.

The bed was made. Sticking out from under the pillow was the fringe of a blanket. She raised the pillow to look at it. It was a baby blanket, pink faded to gray. She shivered, slid her hand under the bedspread. No, the bed was not actually made, just covered up.

Instead of opening the door of her own room across the hall, she went into her parents' room and stood in front of their dresser. There it was, as it had always been. The milk glass Pietà. Nothing of her father's out to be seen. Her mother's tortoiseshell mirror, brought from Ireland wrapped in the rags they used and laundered in those days, lay in the middle of a litter of sales slips, pill bottles, Vicks inhalers, and pink stocking tabs. Bridget had one of the tabs in her fingers before she even noticed, smoothing the rubber button with her thumb as she gazed. You slid them into the slots on girdle legs. One girdle succeeding another, through changing sizes, for an unimaginable number of years. Her heart contracted. Why did she not beg her mother, before it was too late, "Tell me. Tell me what happened."

She picked up a cloth-covered lump, a beanbag of some kind, with a satin bow on it and a tag on a plastic thread. "Healing Heart," read the tag. "Place me on your chest when you are lying down, my gentle weight will help to heal your sorrow." She read the run-on sentence again, and looked at herself in the mirror with the lump in her hand, heavier than it looked, her hair frizzy and damp from the watery air outside. She thought the gingham-covered blob with the bow had made her smile but her face was tired and sullen.

She jumped at the sound of a key in the front door, and the next minute heard her brother's voice. "Bridget? Bridget? She's in here somewhere, that's her car." She dropped the heart on the dresser and quickly shut the door behind her.

Kieran was already in the kitchen rummaging in grocery bags.

"Hello there!" Bridget cried. "Mom, Dad! What's this? I thought you were going out to dinner!" She hugged them, trying to avoid looking straight at her mother's puffy face. She helped her work her arms out of her coat sleeves. "Why Bridget!" her mother said hoarsely, as if surprised by an encounter on the street. "Dear," she added, patting Bridget's cheek. Her father kissed her and said, "How long did it take you? Did you stay on the freeway all the way up?" He always followed the details of her route with frowning concentration, for use on the trip they were planning to make to Portland, "though we daren't do the speeds." She knew they shrank from coming to her apartment, where they would see Nat's things. And this year, instead of coming at Christmas, she had left them to Kieran. "Five hours, because of the rain. I thought you'd go out to eat with Kier. I wasn't sure what time I'd make it."

"We were *going* to go out to dinner, Bridget, after we saw the dentist and shopped," Kieran called from the kitchen. "But we decided to come back on the chance that you'd be here, and have spaghetti. Bridget? Lenten spaghetti of course. You haven't eaten, have you, Bridget?"

Kieran sounded manic, repeating her name that way. He had always been excitable, irritable, in need of some appeasement supplied by their mother and now by his wife Kim. He came to the door of the kitchen, a balding man with raised eyebrows. Was this the boy all bones and curls, two years younger than she but a little pike in the water, their father bragged, who had taught his big sister to swim? In one long afternoon, flinging drops of sunlight off his head? Bridget could remember his endless game of Monopoly on the coffee table, and her furious pitying love for him when they took away his prize for the soapbox derby because he had oiled the wheels of his car. "Bridget?"

"Well, I stopped for coffee . . ."

"Let's just whip it together, then, Mom. Mom? Then if Aiken does get back there'll be some for him, too. Now that we know he might. I'm sure I've bought enough. Bridget! You haven't met Aiken!"

"No. No, I haven't been up since he got here, but I've heard about him from Mom and Dad." That was not true.

"You'll meet him," her father said with a bob of his head and a sly humble look, as if they were discussing the new priest, while her mother looked around vaguely. Kieran came out, kissed Bridget—"No, you stay there and relax with Dad"—and steered their mother into the kitchen with him.

"She's slowed down a bit," her father said.

"Is she all right, Dad? She looks . . . her face looks stiff."

"She's fine, she's fine. She's been to the dentist. No problem of the sort for me, I just take 'em out and put 'em in her hand—we've a girl now for a dentist. And how are you, me girl?"

"I'm fine." *And how's your friend?* she thought.

"How's your friend?"

"He's well. He sends his best. He wants to come up next time if he can get away for a couple of days." They both mulled that over for a moment. Here there was no question of her sharing a room with Nat, and now the couch would be the only place for him. If he would ever come. If he would put down his crampons and his kayak and all the rest of it and just come with her, once, to see her family, instead of saying, "You don't exactly make it sound like a treat."

She heard her father's thoughts. *Just marry him! Just marry, me girl! Have your baby or it will be too late. Don't ye know that, ye modern girl? Don't ye know time? Your own mother knew it, and past forty she was when she had you, and then went on for her boy.*

And if he won't, the devil take him.

They had finished their plates of spaghetti and as a second course eaten Kieran's salad made of four kinds of lettuce with no tomatoes or cucumbers, or anything really except greens. Bridget knew this was how salads often were now but her parents didn't. "Did you find all you needed for the salad, Kieran dear?" her mother kept saying. "I can't think I put everything out for you. Weren't there some carrits?" Bridget had always, except in high school, liked to hear her mother say "carrits."

Kieran said, "This is the salad, dear, in its entirety."

They were eating at the kitchen table as they always had, but they had lit candles and drunk the burgundy Kieran had poured, and they were flushed from it, as they all got, in the family. They all drank too much. Nat said so. "Even Mr. Clean," he said, meaning Kieran. *We do it because* . . . Bridget could get no further. Rain was drumming steadily on the shingles. Out the sink window she could see the lake water heaving in lighted patches, so the lily pads crowded up to the edge, sagged back, and jostled up again. She liked the familiar shiver it gave her to look out from inside the kitchen. Momentarily she liked even the cone of yellow light from the pull-down copper fixture. Her mother seemed more herself, bustling to the refrigerator to get milk for their coffee. "Oh, but we've no dessert!" she cried, her hands falling into a gesture from the Pietà on the dresser, and Kieran rolled up his eyes as their father said, "And we'd be wanting more?"

There were thuds on the porch steps and the doorknob rattled. Bridget jumped up from the table and Kieran hissed, "I knew it!"

"Hoo! It's *raining* out there!"

Her parents turned in their chairs. Bridget stared at the smiling, dripping man, who looked like an actor coming onstage in makeup: black, wet eyelashes you could see across the room, deep lines drawn on the cheeks. As he shed water on the linoleum she almost laughed. He seemed to know his looks were excessive and silly, the handsomeness of a comic book figure, and to have partially covered them up in long hair that didn't look clean and a day or two's growth of beard. He turned away from them as if he might undress in the doorway, not just pull off his windbreaker.

"I'm a mess," he said. "I better shower before I even set down." He had a drawl that was not really Southern. Western, maybe. Cowboy. Fake, it might be. Movie cowboy.

He crossed to her father's side in two steps and shook his hand. "How's it going, Thomas?" "Right as rain," her father said, whereupon the man executed a gradual turn like a bullfighter, saying as he drew his heels together in front of her mother, "Mary Frances!" and then with another half turn, "Hot dog! This must be Bridget."

"Why—! *You* know Bridget!" her mother said with genuine reproach.

"Well, it feels as if we've met—" Bridget began, to spare her mother confusion, and gripped the chair back in case the man should try to shake hands with her.

"I had heard you were out of town," she said. Kieran had risen from the table and thrown a dishtowel over his shoulder.

"Fell through on me. Don't let me get in your way. You're eating! Here, set down, Mary Frances. Eat up! You—! If you don't look like a rose, with your rosy cheeks. What's up, Kieran?" He pronounced the name as if it were Karen. He hung his windbreaker on the calendar nail to drip. "Mary Frances! All right if I shower? Enough hot water?"

"Oh, whenever you need, Aiken, and you know that."

"Daddy," Bridget said, nudged by Kieran into the living room when the man had disappeared into the back of the house, "who *is* he?"

"Who, Aiken? A chap from the church. The dinner, ye know." Every week, in canvas aprons, spattered glasses sliding down their noses, her parents chopped vegetables and stood on tiptoe to stir the tall pots on the church's ancient range. Dozens their age did it, retired people with old Reagan bumper stickers, whose concern was not the dirty lineup outside the social hall but the chunks of ground beef to be thawed, the potatoes and carrots to be chopped and boiled, the pots to be washed.

Bridget waited with an expression of encouragement, until her father added, "Works down there with your mother and me. Needed a place."

"Well, do you like having him here?"

"Sure. I'd say we do."

"Is it your idea, or Mom's?"

"Well, both. Both, I'd say. What, ye don't care for the man? Barely got a glimpse of him."

"Of course. I don't know one way or the other. He seems fine."

"Kieran thinks well of him."

"Oh?" There was sloshing and clattering from the kitchen as Kieran washed the dishes. Her mother's voice wavering on alone. No word from Kieran, who must be straining to hear them. "And he fits in, with you and Mom? Your life?"

"Sure he does. We don't have so very much going on. We can make room."

"I guess you can. Well, does he help out?"

"He pays his room and board!"

"I mean, is he a help to you?" She had strayed close to the subject of their being old. Her father did not like any reference to his actual *self* to be made, and shied from it. He hid himself in "your-mother-and-I," a friendly entity that went about in the world leaving him free to work out his unspoken views.

"He does this and that. And your mother does this and that for him. And if it's to inspect the lease you've come, we haven't one."

"Oh, Dad."

"Now then, girlie, let's hear about those students of yours and their nonsense." Her father liked to have her quote to him the ungrammatical and godless writings of her composition students. He liked her to bring their papers with her and grade them in the living room; he approved of the red "Help!" she scrawled in the margin when a student wrote, "the triple murder of three people," or "she lay the baby," or "Organized religion, throughout history." She knew he liked to see her this way, as daring and up-to-date, but at the same time rather soberly guiding and shepherding the young as she had been shepherded herself by the nuns, keeping the young from some pit with stakes at the bottom, of illiteracy and indifference and license. Because even though she shared an apartment with a man, she knew her father still considered her absolutely, indefinably, unchangeably pure and immaculate.

"Well?" He was rubbing his stone-colored hands lightly and incessantly now, so that she had to stop her own hands from grabbing them to keep them still.

"I do have a couple of zingers for you to look at but they're in the car. I left my suitcase out there."

*

"Did you look in my room?" Kieran was whispering, buttoning his raincoat at the door, his eyes bulging. "Did you see under the bed, the rabbit shit?"

"Kier, go home. Just go home to Kim. I'll take care of everything."

When she came back into the living room she said, getting tiredness and finality into her voice, "I'll show you in the morning, Daddy. My students' papers," she said to Aiken, shaved now and with his longish hair comb-tracked, the little black teeth of it slowly dripping into the collar of the white shirt he had put on for some reason. For an hour or so he had been settling deeper and deeper into the couch beside her mother.

The man fancied himself a storyteller. Until Kieran abruptly got up, Aiken had been telling stories, stories of characters who double-crossed him, of rodeos, purchases of unreachable swampland, mysteriously hindered border crossings that kept him from ever getting into one of the swank air-conditioned combines that ran all night on the Canadian plains during the mustard harvest. Going on and on, abandoning himself to loud, juvenile laughter with his head back, showing newly shaven neck and jawbone, and then soberly straightening up to say, "Whew! It takes all kinds!"

At the mention of her students' papers he sat forward, as if the subject had a special interest for him. Quickly she looked away lest he launch into tales of his own schooling. Lies, all of it.

"And what have the rascals come up with now?" Her father turned to Aiken. "Bridget brings me this and that for my amusement." He prided himself on his reading; he liked it when Bridget didn't know who had written a best seller, he liked to make a certain face when she uttered faculty-meeting words, "diversity," "norm." He liked to correct her if she ever said "you know" or "I mean." She had noticed all evening that he did not correct Aiken's speech, or look her way as the "ain'ts" and "he don'ts" rolled off the man's tongue, punctuated with knee-slapping and her mother's marveling "I never!" and "Don't tell me!" while all three of them went on oblivious of Kieran's baleful look and Bridget's coldness.

"The ones I have with me aren't as funny as some," she said. "It's getting late in the year for the real howlers. Or I hope it is. I hope I've taught them something."

"Now there've been one or two," her father said, winking at her and finally getting around to loosening the tie he had put on to go to the dentist. Her mother had poured a bag of his peanuts into a good glass bowl, for Bridget's sake, and he began to crack them. "The one that tickled me was the *personage*"—he turned his mouth up impishly—"without a face."

"Oh, that was when they had to invent. They stretch so hard," she said, turning to her mother but speaking to Aiken when she saw her mother had begun to doze, "for the most unlikely thing. It's partly to shock me."

"And doomed to failure it is," her father said.

"Like *Darkman*," Aiken said decidedly, lounging back and sticking out his legs. "That got me. Guy with a messed-up face."

"No, no. No, this one didn't lose a face, he never had it."

"What's so funny about that?" Aiken said.

"It wasn't supposed to be funny. They were supposed to write about a lack. First write about a character who possesses something, anything, and then about one who lacks something. It was just an assignment," she said as the man continued to look at her. "The point was—" She came to a stop. It was no use.

"The lad was a little off, she's tryin' to say," her father declared peaceably.

"I have to get my suitcase."

"I'll get it!" Aiken said, jumping up.

"No!" she said, and all but ran to the door. Outside it was damp and mild. She shook her arms and shoulders. For the time being the rain had stopped, but the trees were dripping musically onto the car roof, and pine needles sent up clicking bubbles where she stepped. She saw the patch of toadstools wet and gleaming, and behind them the rabbit hutch. With some relief she saw that it had a pitched roof with an overhang to keep the rabbit dry. It was dark outside the ring of dim, brownish porch light, though the houses to left and right, through the trees, had white radiant spotlights illuminating their docks.

When she came back in, her parents were on their way to bed. They kissed her in the hallway. Her father said, "In the morning we'll be fit to be seen, with our wits about us." The expedition with Kieran, it turned out, had involved not only groceries and the dentist but driving miles in search of a muscle ointment they had seen on television, which could not be found. Bridget could imagine Kieran's sighs, his edgy driving, coupled with his insistence on trying the next place, and the next.

She sat down. Aiken picked up a magazine with a long breath, the way she had always done herself once her parents went off to bed.

"Why do you have that gun? Do you hunt?" With her hopeless, specialized talent for giving an out.

"No, ma'am!" he said, dropping the magazine. "I'm keeping it for somebody."

"Who?" she said.

"My buddy." He gave her a guarded smile. "At the church."

"Somebody at the *church* has a *gun*, and doesn't have room for it. So—" He looked at her. She was not sure he was faking the slow reactions. "So you have to store it," she prompted.

"Right."

"That's odd, Aiken." Using his name, like a teacher.

"I mean he can't keep it, where he's at."

"Where is that?"

"He's in the shelter."

She sat back. "Well. Well, thank God for that, at least. They don't let them have shotguns in the shelter."

"They sure as hell don't!" He laughed, throwing back his head.

"Why would he need a shotgun?"

"I never asked him." He cracked his knuckles, though he held onto his grin as if she were an entertainment. "I bet you don't ask your girlfriends why they need stuff they have."

"I would ask my girlfriends, as you call them, if one of them tried to get me to keep a gun."

"They probably have someplace to keep it. But I'll ask him, I'll say, 'How come you got that thing, anyway, dude?'" He palmed the smile off his cheeks. "Did you feel how it turned warm out there? Pretty near a spring night."

"I did," she said, in the voice she used when one of her students tried to make fun of something serious in class. Aiken seemed younger than her nineteen- and twenty-year-olds but she knew from Kieran that he was in his mid-thirties at least, maybe more, maybe her own age. "It's yours, isn't it," she said.

"What? The shotgun? I told you."

"I know but I think you're afraid I'll say you can't live here with a gun in your room."

He put his elbows on his knees and sank his jaw into his hands while he looked up at her, grinning. "Uh, are you the landlady?"

"Let's say I'm the daughter of the landlady and I try to take care of her. And the landlord."

"Well, I can't say that shotgun's mine because if I did, I would've stole it. And if you don't want it in here go ahead and say so. I mean that. If you think it would upset Mary Frances."

"Don't mind me, I've just come back to take my pill," said her mother's voice from the door. She peeked in.

"Good night, sleep tight now," Bridget said, blowing her a kiss. When her mother had finished in the bathroom and felt her way back along the hall, Bridget said, "I do want to say something. Not just about what you keep in your room—and it could use a little work, couldn't it? The rug, the nutshells? I mean about *them*. My parents. Just come outside for a minute, would you?"

She waited under the porch light, and when he shut the door behind him she led the way across the wet grass to the soft boards of the dock. Behind her he said genially, "I've been telling them they oughta put a light right there where the step is. See those lights, those spots they have at the other docks? Those are on account of prowlers."

I bet they're because you moved in, she thought, but she said, "All these boats. On this little lake. It's hardly big enough for boats any more."

"Oh, I see, it's smaller than it was?" He used her father's tone, her father's rhythm. Her face went hot. He, with his gun and his baby blanket! His fights, his black eye, his stupidity. Mimicking her father.

The water hit the dock's legs with a *clock, clock,* and the air had only an invisible slow spray revolving in it.

Bridget turned abruptly up the dark yard to the hutch, where the rabbit crouched in the same position. But the self-feeder was empty, and it had eaten the lettuce as well. For some reason this made her feel like crying. "This poor animal—it's sick, isn't it?" she said loudly over her shoulder, but he was right behind her. "What use is it to you out here? It's not much of a pet. And doesn't it get cold?"

"Well, right now she's warm as toast. But if it's nippy we have her come in." The smell in his room. "And she's not mine, she's theirs, your parents'."

"Wait a minute. My parents never had a pet in their lives."

"Aw, come on. Your mother loves animals. She gave her kid an animal name. Your mother loves this girl." He brought the animal out, hanging the length of a sweater sleeve, with its back legs tucked up in its matted belly fur, and draped it over his arm.

"My mother loves a rabbit? My mother? That's ludicrous. She spent years here fighting the squirrels and the deer—"

"That was your father." Aiken had the rabbit balanced on his forearm and was giving it a heavy stroking.

"Seriously, my parents don't care for animals."

"They had a cat hanging around when I got here."

"They hate cats. My father does."

"I bet he doesn't. People who hate cats hate women."

She laughed in exasperation. "What if they're women, who hate cats? And what animal name?" Had she ever had a nickname, other than "girlie" or "dearie?"

"Their daughter. Robin."

"Look, Aiken. I'm their daughter."

"Uh-uh. The other one."

"They have no other daughter. They have me and Kieran."

"The one that died."

"What are you *talking* about?"

"I mean the one they lost. Robin."

"They never lost a child."

"Damn, I'm not doing so good here."

"This is ridiculous."

"Well . . ." He watched her with speculative pity. "You got me."

"This is unbelievable."

"Hey, I don't know. Maybe they never told their other kids. Maybe they didn't want 'em to know."

"Them? *I'm* them! I'm serious, Aiken. You're not hearing what I'm saying. No such thing ever happened!"

She tripped on the slick roots. He put a hand out but she shook it off. Did he want her to believe her parents had told him a family secret? But it wasn't true.

"My parents married late in life," she said sharply, holding onto the tree. "My mother was forty-two when I was born! Kieran was born two years later."

"Whoa, I didn't mean nothing. All's I was saying—"

"There was no other child!" She unclenched her fists. "So let's drop it."

Or he was lying to her, for some reason, pretending her parents had told him such a thing?

Or was it possible? Was it possible her mother had indeed told him there had been another daughter? Her mother, not her father. Her father could never make anything up.

What was the matter with her? Already she was imagining that her mother had *made something up* to tell this man. "*So*," she said harshly. "What happened to the *cat*?"

"Cat?"

"The *cat* you said was here." She felt certain there had been no cat.

"Folks up the way took it in. Kids wanted it."

"Probably to torture it," she said bitterly.

"Now why would you say that?" he said, with interest.

"Oh, forget it. Forget it."

"I might. Or I might remember it. Look at that there." The lilies were sloshing against the bank. "Big old bullfrog." He was smiling as if nothing had happened, as if he had not made Bridget argue angrily with him until she tripped over a root, about a nonexistent child.

"You have a lot of things you're very sure about," she said, her voice shaking. She felt herself digging in, getting ready to wrangle pointlessly the way she did with her brother, and certain students, and Nat.

A half-moon had come out and thrown a glaze onto the lily pads. The water had slowed its tossing. "Well, I'll tell you a story about this here lake," he said easily, but with a note in his voice that let her know he was up to something, the way her students often were, wanting to exhibit some cleverness. "A kid got out there in a boat and pushed his friend's sister in. In this exact lake. Kid had trouble with his dad, had trouble in school, got out there one day and whoosh, there she went."

To her distaste Bridget was imagining it.

"When?" she said in the practical voice she used to make students account for what they turned in.

"Long time ago."

"And what happened? Did she drown?"

"Yes ma'am."

So he had come back here. That was why he was here. "And that was you."

He laughed loudly enough to wake her parents. "Whoo. Like to have you for a teacher."

"Why is that?"

"You're a funny gal."

"Not so funny. Was it you?"

"No, it was not me. It was a feller I met. It ain't always me. Everyplace I go they want to say, 'You did time, it musta been you. You musta done it, you're the *type*.'"

"You did time." Of course he had been in prison.

"I did. But I didn't put no *peanuts* in the bedroom, your dad did."

"My dad?"

"He'll be in there talking to me, and you know him and his nuts."

Bridget felt a sag inside her. She could see it exactly, her father knocking on Aiken's door, sitting down in the chair by Kieran's little desk with his bag of peanuts. Trusting. Not even looking at the shotgun, for fear of being rude.

"I'll be honest with you, Aiken. I'm suspicious of you. You don't seem to have a good reason to be living here. It might be you want something from my parents and I don't know what that would be. Or how you might plan to get it. Maybe you're planning to drown somebody."

He made a turn into her path so that she bumped into him. The eyes were right in front of her. He was close enough that when he ran his hand through his hair she could smell the shampoo. She stood still. She couldn't tell if she was afraid or not. Finally he said, "Some people wouldn't get away with what you just said. I'll let it go because you don't mean it. So I'll let it go."

"My parents don't have any money." She went on reasonably, like a person with no fear, herself, of being drowned. "Can't you see, from this house, how they live? They have this house, and that car, and an income that can't be any bigger than yours. Just one little check that comes every month. But you probably know that."

"I don't want their goddamn *check*."

"OK, I'll take your word for it. Why do you live here? What do you want from them?"

"I like 'em." He had narrowed his eyes so that the exaggerated lashes met.

"You—like them."

"Yeah."

"Do you like my brother?"

"He's all right."

"Do you like him?"

"No."

She began to laugh soundlessly. "Oh, God. If you had said you liked him . . ." But at the same time she was thinking of how she might explain Kieran to him, show Kieran in a different light. She could describe the afternoon Kieran had taught her to swim, or the way the scoutmaster had taken back his soapbox derby prize, lifting the silver-painted trophy out of his hands.

"Your brother gives them a hard time. He's always after them. Can't do nothing about it but I don't like it."

"What's in your van?"

"Weed. Yeah. Guess you caught me."

"So I hear you spend time in there."

He sighed, looking around the dark grove. The air was moving in the firs with a soft ticking. Then he grinned, shaking his head as if he had run out of ways to stall her, and carefully transferred the rabbit to his shoulder, where it laid its ears back and performed a soft scramble for footing. "Come here."

"What?"

"Come take a look."

"What do you mean?"

"I like to lie down in there and look out through the trees. I like the view." He cupped his fingers and wagged them toward himself once, twice, as if he were guiding somebody backing a car. "Come on and take a look."

"Oh, no way. No, thanks. No." She folded her arms.

His hand closed over her wrist. He got hold of her elbow with the other hand and pulled her by the folded arm, until she felt the rabbit press her shoulder with a forepaw to keep its balance. "Let go."

With his other hand he unlatched the door of the hutch. He eased the rabbit down his arm and in, and started, holding Bridget by the wrist, toward the van. "Wait a minute here, Aiken," she said. "Hey." If she had to slap him she would. What would a man like this do, if you slapped his face?

But he let go of her arm, or he didn't so much let go of it as hand it back to her. He put it against her chest, upright between her breasts, and reached for her other hand and crossed it over so that she was holding the arm like a bottle. Shaking his head, he wrenched the handle and opened both doors into the back of the van.

For some reason, instead of walking away Bridget said, "All right, I will. I'll sit. I'll look at the view, only there's no view." She hoisted herself up and sat with her legs dangling, while he grasped his lower back with his hands and bent to one side. "Back trouble?" she said. "You can sit."

"Yeah? I can sit?"

"It's your van."

"It's my van. I maybe stole it, though."

"Thou shalt not steal," she said.

"Thou shall not covet thy neighbor's house," he said over his shoulder, walking away. "Thou shall not covet thy neighbor's wife, nor his manservant, nor his maidservant, nor his ox, nor his ass."

"Where are you going? And it's 'shalt.' *'Shalt* not.' I bet you're not even a Catholic."

"What makes you say that?" He came back.

"Catholics don't quote. I bet you're some kind of evangelical."

"Not me."

"Lots of the people who work in the soup kitchen aren't Catholic."

"Not me."

"Say the Hail Mary."

"Come again?"

"Say it."

"I'm gonna say it for your entertainment?"

"Say the Act of Contrition."

"You say it."

"Hey. I bet you don't have anything you're ashamed of."

"If I do it's none of your business. Yeah, I'm ashamed. I'm ashamed of a lot of things. Yeah, though, see, but if I am it's my business."

She swung her legs childishly. She couldn't help it. "Say it."

He stepped closer, frowning. "You got a problem."

"OK," she said. He had grabbed the doorframe so that she had to lean back. "OK."

"Don't do that," he warned her.

"What?"

"Don't make no sign of the cross."

"I'm not, I'm just getting—out of your way. See?" She drew her legs up into the van and laughed. "Are you a werewolf?"

"No. No, ma'am, and you're not a priest. But I'm pretty sure you think you could be."

"I do, as a matter of fact, think that I should be allowed to be if I wanted to be, which I don't."

"Right," he said. "We won't see that day. See anything in there? Hey, you don't need a warrant. I'll show you around."

"I was just looking. Did you see *Silence of the Lambs*?"

"Nope," he said. "I don't go to that kind of show."

"'*Show*,'" she said. "Where did you grow up?"

"No matter where I say, you're gonna say something," he said, shaking the van as he sat down. But he pushed himself back and got all the way in, onto on a roll of carpet. He stretched out his legs. "Aren't you? You're gonna say something. New York City, that's where I grew up."

"Really?"

"Where did you think?"

"Nevada? Florida?"

"That some kind of insult? I was born in Indiana."

"Gary, Indiana?"

"Terre Haute. So figure out the rest."

"Guys from Indiana, aren't they supposed to be basketball players?"

"The tall ones."

"Do you think of yourself as short?"

"Do you think of yourself as bitchy? Where's that boyfriend you're supposed to have?"

"I don't know."

"Up some mountain with a lot of fancy gear, that's what I hear."

"That's what he does."

"What do you want him to do?" He said it quietly.

Oh, no you don't, she thought.

But he had her by the arms again, he was using them to bring her into the van with him. He held her weight against his chest and then went down on one arm, stretching out on the carpeted floor in an easy motion that had nothing she could argue with in it, though it brought her down beside him. Lying down could just as easily have been her idea. She let her head hang back but her body came forward.

*

"How come it stays warm in here?"

"It's warm outside." He didn't say the obvious, that they had raised the temperature in the dark van. The doors were still open, with the limbed pines standing on either side. She could see the brown glow of the porch light.

She rolled over, propped her bare ankles on something and crossed them. On his knees he pulled a blanket down from the logs of carpet and spread it over her. What on earth was she doing here, under an army blanket in the back of a van? She said sleepily, "You got my mother that thing, didn't you, that heart."

"Somebody gave it to me. I gave it to her."

"Somebody. A girl."

"Yeah, a girl. You're one of them know-it-alls."

"A girl thought you needed it."

"Guess she did."

"Knowing about your life. The story of your life. The *stories*. You're quite a storyteller. You had my folks pretty amused tonight."

"I get into trouble in bars. I get going. I like a story."

"I've heard you get into trouble."

"You heard that."

"Heard you get into fights."

"Well, yes I do," he said. "Or I use to. Half the time I liked the guy thrown the punch."

"I see," she said, in a classroom voice. Maybe she always had this voice.

"People get acrost me."

"You didn't mean it when you said you like my parents, did you?"

"What now?" he sighed at the ceiling.

"I know what you meant. You meant you love them."

"I guess you could say that."

"And you think I don't. Love them."

"You better hope I don't think that, if I make a pass at you."

"This was a pass?"

"I'm not going after some girl that don't give a damn."

"Are you going after me?"

"I got you."

"Oh, you think so?" She put her finger on the crease in his cheek to feel the smile.

"Definitely." With one of those slow shifts of his that she already recognized he got himself lying with his head on her thighs. He was outside the blanket and she could make out the white of his legs in the dark, and the dark sockets of his eyes. He turned over, sighed, and moved both hands up her legs until he had her hips in his hands the way you would hold somebody's, a child's, shoulders, if you had to gently lecture her. He rubbed his jawbone heavily against the blanket. "You're a beautiful girl," his muffled voice said wearily, as if it were a lesson he had had to teach too many times.

"Funny, you said."

"Don't fight about it," he said. He was holding onto her. Both of them slowly adrift. It might be she was drifting and he was towing, though without effort.

"So . . . my mother told you a lie. And you gave her a Healing Heart to comfort her."

"I reckon I wouldn't use '*lie*,'" he said after a while, "if it was my mother."

"Where is she? *Your* mother?" The baby blanket under his pillow.

"Couldn't tell you. I left home when I was eight."

"Eight."

"Eight."

"Why? Why would you have to leave Terre Haute, Indiana?"

"You don't wanta know."

"No, I'd like to know. I would. I'd like to hear you describe it," she said humbly.

He shrugged himself under the blanket with her.

Describe it. An assignment. But one he declined with silence.

Describe a time you were praised. This was for her night-school students, the Vietnamese and Samoans. *Describe a view from a window in paradise.* The Muslims liked that. *Envision the world with a key improvement.*

And her students would write, striving—against their work-study schedules, their mono, their hangovers—striving to please her, it had to be that, by means of an imaginary world with a key improvement: three sexes, or plants generating the power, or no composition courses.

In the world I envision there would be only this one power, no other. Love, it was, though she frightened herself with the word.

When she woke there was no sound, not even the dripping on metal to which she had gone to sleep. She sat up in the dark and tried to see her watch. She would have to be quiet getting back into the house. But not yet. She put her fingers to the back of her head, where the hair was matted. No one could see her, her prettiness at this hour gone puffy. It was arrived at, anyway, not to be found in the middle of the night.

It was not that that made her catch her breath as if she had been sobbing. It was not betraying Nat. When had Nat ever wanted her exacting loyalty? It was not that a few hours ago she had been gasping under this stranger as if she were being murdered, and taking pleasure in being murdered. It was an absence. A sound of roaring, or rushing, not close to her but half-heard and ever-present, the sound of her life, had stopped, rolled back from bare beach, herself.

Her ears were stopped up as if she were yawning, and the leg doubled under her had gone to sleep, while Aiken lay at ease, on his back, breathing peacefully. The black eyelashes fanned out along his cheekbones. That's what it was, she thought, looking at the hollows of his face. That's what happened to me. That's pretty simple. That's a first. I just gave in to it. Is that what it was?

She had only to wait. She knew the life would run back in. Her voice would begin in a minute, in her own mind, she could not escape it. But she could sit here until then.

What if it started in and she stayed anyway, watching him?

"We snuck in and watched you," her father would say when she was little. "Your cur-rls were spread out and you were sleeping the sleep of a clear conscience." "And the baby, too. Little angels, you were," her mother would say, as if the shock of this family formed out of nowhere, out of nothing but two orphans, could never weary her. As if two ordinary children were beauties, and if they were, as if beauty were goodness. She could see why her parents had forgotten her and her cruel brother and imagined themselves the mother and father of a girl who had died and Aiken.

americans love dogs

On Brianne's first day as their au pair, the French couple tested the dog. They were going to observe its reaction to her presence near the baby, *l'enfant, le bébé,* whom the dog, said the father, lived to protect. Their dog was a sober animal, he said, not playful like those Brianne would be used to in the US. "*Asseyez-vous,*" he instructed Brianne. He opened a door and the dog, an untrimmed standard poodle, gray and tall, stood calmly sniffing for a moment before it entered the room and crossed the rug. A male, Brianne saw. The dog came to her and laid its muzzle on her knee. "Poof!" said the little girl, Nathalie. She was not yet four but she already knew English and was said to like the idea of having her own language and of speaking it at all times with Brianne. The father Luc gave a clap. "*Les Americains aiment les chiens!*"

On that afternoon Brianne barely took in his glowing eye and early silver at the hairline. Everything she said was directed at the mother, Clemence, who nevertheless let her husband do most of the talking.

Clemence was tired and losing weight but had not yet had all of her tests. With his small taut briefcase Luc arrived home every day on a gust of fresh air. He told Brianne her name came from a cheese. Or from the masculine Brian, which came from *brecan*, meaning "break."

At any rate, a mimicry of French, one of the silly names so American. Brianne fell in love in the first week, recognizing this kind of talk for the warmth it concealed, like a béarnaise with pepper flakes. "Spicy!" he said with relish. "For me, it is better to have not very much cayenne," Clemence mentioned in private. In addition to speaking English to the children Brianne was to do some of the cooking as well as clean a little. At home her friends had said, "They're French and they want you to cook?"

At home Brianne had been a nanny, until she exiled herself from American loves. For four years now she had been putting off college and getting into difficulties, most of them arising at the edges of her workday, with the fathers. Her mother had given up and just wanted her to be married.

Clemence came home in the middle of the afternoon from her appointment with the specialist. She sat down on the ottoman in front of the red armchair—the furniture was colorful and small—where Brianne watched TV while the children were having their nap. The French were serious about the nap. Every day Brianne had two hours of freedom while the two children slept, one in his crib and the other in her little French-sized bed. On this day Brianne was watching TV with her Mauriac novel open on her lap. She was not reading and had formed no plan for improving her French or reapplying to college. The dog was at her feet.

"*Ma chère*, will you bring *un petit Dubonnet*," said Clemence. When Brianne came back with the little glass of ruby liquid Clemence said, "*Mais toi-même aussi.*" Brianne didn't like Dubonnet but she poured herself a glass, drank it in the kitchen, and poured another. Clemence was still on the ottoman, with her head in her hands. Among the curls her fingers still had the tiny glass in their grip. "I know that he makes some advances to you and I think you love him," she said, sitting up straight again. "But do you love my children?"

Always say you love the children. But Brianne was sincere in this, whatever her effect on men—and it was not her fault that they had a similar effect on her, though only certain ones, very nearly a type, to be exact, and to give herself credit, for her the type was not the matter of looks and fresh youth that it was for them, but some sense of a person at once a father well established in life and a pent-up little boy. The truth was she liked the boy side better, preferring children to adults. She would have at least two of her own. But she would take care never to slight the beautiful pair sleeping down the hall, who were half hers already, as was the dog, who stirred against her feet and opened his intelligent eyes when he scented the tears of his owner. He did not get up and go to the ottoman, where Clemence had wiped the tears, swallowed her Dubonnet, and fluffed her curls. Luc was at the door. With his head still high the dog shut his eyes as if asleep, as Brianne cried, too, and absently picked up and laid down his silken ears.

sleepover

ngie sat up. "Come in," she called, but no one came and there was no second knock. She got out of bed stiff from hard sleep and opened the door. A woman stood there in a purple bathrobe very like her own, long and quilted, with a satin collar. It was Cham. Cham, the housekeeper. Angie put her hand on the commotion in her chest. No need for it. She was in her daughter's house, in the guestroom. One of the guestrooms. Cham was here.

"Somebody here," said Cham. "Boy."

"Who is it?" Angie responded foolishly, reaching for her own robe. Hers was red, given her by Bill Diehl just before he got married, as a consolation. A size too big, owing to her loss of weight. Cham helped her with the inside-out sleeves, not even glancing at the arrow of scar where it sank cleanly down the neck of Angie's nightgown when she reached back for the armholes.

"Boy," Cham said again. "In there, with girls. One girl turn off al-ahm." *One girl.* Not *Erika, your granddaughter.* Cham's face gleamed with oil and she had a purse in her hands. Would she keep a gun? In a special purse, for the nights she was alone with a child in this out-sized house?

Would thirteen-year-olds at a slumber party let in someone they didn't know? A sleepover. "Don't say slumber party," her daughter Pat had warned her. "Or pajama party."

"We're in this together, Cham," Angie said. Cham's feet were bare and a strong smell of nutmeg wafted to Angie, perhaps the oil Cham had on her face. I don't see why she can't be friendly, Angie thought, following her down the long hall like a child, but they had reached the great dim room and Cham was already turning without a word to leave her there.

The moon was high and the skylights spread four pools of gray light on the floor. At the far end of the room where candles were burning on the glass table, the girls huddled in a cloud of pillows and sleeping bags. Sniffing for marijuana Angie got only nail polish remover and candle wax. The heavy couches with their rolled backs seemed more ponderous in the semidark, under the vaulted ceiling. A hushed laugh drifted in the room.

"Your grandma!" someone hissed.

Next to her granddaughter in the circle sat a blond boy.

Angie's heart attack had been written up in a medical journal. She was proof that women might have a reaction all their own to having their arteries blown open with balloons, or cut up and spliced. They might repay the most delicate and constructive of procedures with clots, wild rhythms, ugly infections, fevers. "Now, Patty, would you not give me that look," she said to her daughter on the first day of her visit. "Just remember, when you came down to see me I was using a toilet chair. I've come a long way. And what about you, if you get any thinner you can live in that wall of yours."

Pat's wall was a block long, built high enough that no one on the curving boulevard to the lake could see a house behind it, even the roofline, let alone the lake below. Apparently no law said a city ought to be able to see its own lake. The wall was a foot thick and had its own miniature roof of slate tiles. Pat said nothing, but went on looking at her, and it was true that in the vast, smoky mirror over the fireplace, a wraith could be seen standing with Pat, nodding and pointing, instead of a solid woman with round arms and a good neck for sixty-seven.

Sometimes, Angie did not say to Pat, it seemed the blood pumped off during her bypass and fed oxygen for all those hours had run back into her carrying seeds of despair. But at least she had not lost her wits to the pump, as people her age frequently did. They woke up confused and stayed confused. Pumpheads, the doctors called them. Once it was clear it hadn't happened to her, her friend Terri had told her about pumpheads. Terri was an ICU nurse.

Angie was not a pumphead. Still, she had not really picked herself up and gone on. She was waiting to decide. Decide what? Pat would say. Pat had her own copy, from the Internet, of the article about Angie's case. Nothing would convince her that Angie understood it. Coronary artery bypass, or microchips, or the human genome: Why should somebody like Angie try to catch up? Angie's territory was the past. But the past that clung to her was mixed up, for her daughter, with movies that had come out long afterward, and dressed things up. The Summer of Love, and Woodstock—it didn't matter to Pat that Angie had not been at Woodstock and had in fact been a pregnant woman in her thirties at that time, with a husband too sick some days to get out of bed.

Pat didn't remember her father Rudy. Angie could supply her with dates: How she and Rudy had started in before there was any such thing as a hippie, crisscrossing the country in a van and signing people up to buy record albums that might or might not come out. How long she had been married and how tired she was, by the time Woodstock came around, how hungry to go back to Oregon and live alone with her husband and, at last, their baby. Pat.

"OK, so a beatnik," Pat would say. And she didn't mean the real past, anyway, she meant the past-in-the-present. She meant Angie's shawls and posters, her friends who got arrested on picket lines. Her boyfriends, who might be younger, in their fifties, and wear those thin ponytails—or like Bill Diehl, fluffy blow-dries—and see no harm in accepting loans from a person like Angie who always had work.

*

Early in the course of the birthday party, Angie had angled the big suede armchair to give her a good view of the girls. Just when she thought one face was perfect, another would come up from the tray of colored bottles—they were painting each other's toenails—and this one would be dreamier, longer-lashed, more perfect. Then fine red hair would fall across that face and another would look up, skin taut, full lips parted. That was her granddaughter Erika, getting up with the phone to her ear. Then a composed, high-cheeked face with shining bangs: that was Tamiko, who had come to the door in the company of her uniformed driver. Then another, fringed in unruly curls, a child's face, black-browed, heart-shaped.

I'm old! Angie thought, without any real opposition. I don't envy beauty any more!

The girls had on T-shirts in parakeet colors that bared the studs in their navels. "Our birthstones! Stick-ons!" they crowed, pulling them off to show Angie. "Except Erika's." Erika had a thin gold ring threaded through a real hole. They all wore ankle bracelets and multiple rings. With that high agonized laughter of theirs they kept falling on their sides on the rolled-up sleeping bags.

"Don't let them fool you, these girls are tough. They all do sports," Pat had told her. "Basketball, track. Wait till you see Erika run the four hundred meter. And the relay! See those legs?"

Angie thought of saying, "Long, all right. Eric's genes in action," because of the important tone Pat gave the word "relay," when it was just another form of tag, something you did at recess.

Or she might say to Pat, "Is she as smart as you were?" Angie saw Erika roughly once a year, she didn't have much to go on. Erika didn't seem to have the brains Pat had had in school.

"Erika's the leader," Pat went on patiently. "You'll see it. They all follow her like ants."

"Maybe because she's tall," Angie said. "The tallest ant." It must be that they considered Erika the prettiest, she decided. And their standard must be just this blondness and slenderness and height, and the air Erika had, patient but dissatisfied. Like a woman in a store trying on shoes, nothing unfriendly about her but nothing obliging either.

Angie watched the muscles slide in Erika's telephone arm as she moved away from the others, talking seriously. When the call ended she spiraled in one motion down onto her back, laughing and slinging the bag of cotton balls in the air so they rained down on the others. "Wait, wait—it's on my foot! Hey, Jessie just did my third coat!" The girl with the innocent, triangle face drew her black eyebrows together in a mock scowl. Then she, too, lay back with her arm over her eyes, gracefully waving the foot with the cotton ball stuck to the toes. She was a pretty little thing, more a little girl, perhaps, than the others. Watching her, watching all of them with their long waists, their pearly collarbones, was like being sung to, Angie thought. One of those songs in Gaelic or some old tongue. Rudy's material, sung at county fairs when he was first starting out. Ballads. Before the war heated up and all those lords and maids and cherry trees and narrow beds were put away, and the guitar took up a harsh line.

She could see him, in the full-sleeved shirt she had embroidered with birds and ivy, and in tiny script on the collar—it was when sewing machines first did that—his name, Rudy Rudeen.

Now the five girls were on their backs with their hair spread out on the rug, waving their legs, all talking at once. Erika was on the phone again. They had on that three-chord harmonizing stuff they listened to now. Boy bands. When the time came, Angie's job was to light fourteen candles on the cake and carry it in. She didn't see any presents. These girls might be beyond presents.

The armchair in the computer alcove was so big there was room for a small child on either side of her. And this was no alcove, really, it was an area as big as her own apartment, enclosed by plants and low bookshelves, with two computers and a copier and two fax machines on a counter of grainy stone. It was part of the same room where the girls were, but Angie was some distance away from them. The whole center of the house was laid out in an open design, with divisions suggested by slate inlays in the shining maple floor. You could lose your balance out there, as if you had wandered into a bullring.

Tropical plants in stone tubs marked the inlays at either end. Most of the lake-facing front of the house was glass, and four skylights poured light on the tall, muscular plants and the area rugs and scattered islands of furniture.

This was a famously dark, rainy city, but in her daughter's house you would think you were out on the lake in some kind of a glass atrium. Maybe on a cruise ship, where you could unwrap yourself behind a palm and quickly slip out of sight in a warm pool. Angie had been on a cruise, to Mexico. Her daughter had sent her on it, along with Bill Diehl. "Why not take your pal Bill." That was what Pat called him the whole time he shared Angie's place. "The car salesman," she called him after he moved out and got married, although Bill didn't sell cars, he sold boats, a harder job, more uncertain.

Bill was sixty-some, a few years younger than Angie, but Angie's friend Terri, the one he married, had just hit her forties. Angie was the godmother of their baby girl. "Well, you remember Terri," Angie had said when she called Pat, after she sent Bill off in the U-Haul with his couch and his cat, "how pretty she is." She was half hoping Pat would offer up some female curse and half relieved that she did not. "And beauty is everything," Angie went on. She liked a conversation that would go from there, even an argument. She would have welcomed "Beauty is nothing!" or "Are you kidding? We're talking about sex!" so that she could reaffirm her hospital vow to keep clear of the negative and appreciate everything. "I'm not making excuses for Bill. It was one of those things."

"Right," said Pat. In the past she would have said to Angie, "What's with these men? Why is this the story of your life?" But by the time the godchild came along, Pat was no longer making painful or intimate remarks to her. "I don't know about my daughter these days," Angie said to Terri and Bill. Terri had placed the baby in Angie's arms and she brought its wide-eyed face close to hers. "What do you think? Think maybe aliens took my girl and sent a copy?" But what happened with Pat is a secret, she thought. A secret from me because I was the mother.

The metal stairs at either end of the huge room were like the companionways on a ship. Guests, if there were any guests, climbed up them to the second-floor wings, where they could settle into one of the balcony rooms, or the suite with its own kitchen, where Angie would have been staying on this visit except for the fact that her daughter had taken one look at her and said, "Wait, I'm going to put you in the little courtyard room down here. Rika, ask Cham to make up that bed."

Erika's bedroom was up the metal stairs. Angie had an idea it was something to see, but she had not yet had a look at it. She had tried to, going up hanging onto both rails. At the top a metal walkway ran the length of the great room, a sort of open-work bridge. When she got close to the top she turned and sat down to rest. She waved to Pat, who said, "Come down. Now. And hold on."

Pat said the previous owner, a man whose company had done business with hers, had hardly finished remodeling the house in this semi-industrial style when he retired and moved to Hawaii. He had left a full wine cellar behind. "Well, sure I will, I'll have a glass of wine," Angie said.

"Oh," said Pat. "Sure. I never think of it."

"Red wine is good for me. And you said he was going to live here all by himself?"

"Not for long," Pat said wryly.

Angie had heard the stories about shirttail relatives who turned up in Seattle when the software fortunes were first being made. Right from the beginning Bill Diehl kept her up on those things. "Pat's going to break the bank up there. She's smart, she's in the right place at the right time," he said. Bill had no money of his own but he could always sniff it when somebody else had it or was going to get it. "Some people get kinged," he said, "just like in checkers." He was a man of no resentment, and that was what Angie had loved, she had loved his gleeful accounts of sudden, undeserved windfalls, occasions of wild luck. In fact when he and Terri realized they wanted to be married to each other, he told Angie this could almost be one of those, the first of his life.

Angie could not stand in the way of such a thing. "So what are you waiting for? She's the one for you," she said. "I know about that. I had that. There's only one."

Of course she did not believe this. If one, why not more than one. Fortunately Bill would not think of it in that way. His way had always been to skip over twenty-five years of Angie's history and treat her as a widow. Early on she had made the discovery of his serious gift for comfort, his knowing at what point to pour the wine down the sink and wipe a woman's tears with a clean handkerchief. He had bowed his head to the story of Rudy more than once. So let him see himself as an episode late in the day, for Angie, someone with whom she had joined forces for a couple of years, and shared one vacation, and a cat that gave birth in the closet. Though for his sake she had been at some pains to keep up the idea that their arrangement was a romance.

"We bonded over a stray cat," she would tell people. Bill was the cat-lover, but they spent weeks united in the search for homes for the kittens. In the end the cat went with Bill, even though she had won Angie over in her solemn hunt for each of her given-away young.

"Why did the guy put these railings all over the place?" These were of a luminous metal and had a decorative, all-purpose look. Angie had taken hold of one herself a time or two. They were in all the downstairs bathrooms and ran along the first-floor walls.

"He had a fall. Rock-climbing. I'm going to take the rails out but I haven't had time to hire anybody."

"What happened to him?"

"A chunk of the rock face fell on him. Crushed his legs."

"No. That's awful. Does he still have them? His legs?"

"He does. Lots of rehab. Listen, he's out of the wheelchair, he walks. Don't worry about him, he's a tough guy." Was Pat's voice bitter? Had the man been her lover? "He tried to take me over. My company."

"So you ended up with his house?"

Pat smiled. "I bought his house." In her head Angie heard what the old Pat would have said to her. "It amazes me the way you're always ready to sympathize with some guy. It could be anybody. Somebody's always hurting these poor men. The guy fell. He went to rehab. He moved. End of story."

• • •

Pat did not give Angie a tour; she didn't boast of anything in the house, or the garden with its tall fountain, blown out wide some days like a sheet on the line. While Pat was at work Angie gave herself a tour. She sat on the rim of the fountain by herself. *I'm not kidding, I wouldn't trade with you.*

Oh, because I'm not a good-time girl like my mom?

You're not the only one, Patty, who's had more than one life.

They didn't say these things any more. Why was Pat lost to her?

When Pat came home the first day Angie said the high ceilings made the place echo, but Pat had her yell to prove it, and there was no echo, only her shout.

Pat had not indulged herself, beyond Erika's school and this house. She didn't travel except to meetings and she didn't buy cars or wear good clothes. She didn't join a health club. In Oregon Angie lived among people who were barely making it, who swore by health clubs. But Pat ran. Her legs showed knots of muscle and her hips were narrow from the miles she ran, as if she were training for Erika's relay.

After she ran and showered, Pat came out and flopped down with her feet up on the coffee table. This was the best time of day to approach her, sitting around the huge table, a metal ring on tube legs holding up a four-inch-thick slab of clouded, pocked glass. You had to be careful where you put a drink down on it because the glass had hills and valleys. "I bet this thing cost you," Angie said the first day, not sure about swinging her own feet out and raising them to the level where they could be propped. Anyway the table might be for Pat's feet.

"Do you like it?" Pat said. She never took offense or acted like she didn't care for Angie's meaning, as she once had; she never argued any more. She was above argument.

"Yeah, I sorta do. It's weird but it appeals to me."

"Weird," her daughter said with a dreamy expression.

Angie knew this expression. "I know, honeybaby," she said. "I know it's art."

"Well, a sculptor did it." Angie wondered if the sculptor was some-one Pat knew. Other than the wheelchair man, Pat hadn't mentioned anyone she knew. If the phone rang it was for Erika; Pat didn't even look up. I know about that, Angie might have said. I was blank that way after your father died. But as far as she knew, nobody had died.

"By the way, you don't have to do the wash," Pat said. "Cham will do the wash."

"I just put a few things in. I like having something to do."

"Right, well, maybe you'd do something for me. Rika's birthday. Four-teen." As if Angie didn't know, didn't have presents in her suitcase. She wasn't sure about them, though. She knew to stay a little ahead of the game, but she could see that Erika had suddenly taken a step. Mention of her previous interests would bring a vague, regretful smile.

"I'll be here for her actual birthday but then Friday I have to go to Palo Alto, and the party's that night. If I change it, half the girls can't come. You have to get these things on the calendar. I can hire a party coordinator but Erika won't like that."

"A party coordinator? Are you kidding? You asked me, I'm doing it."

Cham would be in the house, of course. The girls couldn't put anything over on Cham, a woman who had run into a burning grade school. You could see scars on Cham's neck and jaw and only guess about the rest of her, always covered up. She had hidden in a sow's pen, swum through sewage, to get out of Cambodia. Angie knew that. Somewhere back in the dark of that period was a family, children Cham had had, the ones who had been in the grade school. A com-plicated story of who had gotten out of the country. None of the chil-dren. Cham was alone here, suspicious of everyone but Pat. Cousins were here in the city but there was a problem with them; they thought Cham had cursed some relative. She had been with Pat for years now, arriving with a double name that Pat had shortened.

Cham would be right there, in her bare feet and khaki pants, keeping an eye on everything. But it would be better if Angie met the girls at the door. And you had to be careful with sleepovers. Some-times boys this age came around. How they got there Pat didn't know, since none of them drove yet; they were kids. They would come in twos and threes, with cameras or flashlights or masks, after the parents were asleep, and not do anything, just occupy themselves in stealth and heckling and making the girls hysterical enough, as these skinny prepubescent boys could somehow do, to burst out with confessions to their own parents the next day.

Sometimes drugs turned up, of course. Nothing big so far, knock on wood. And some of the parents had a high enough profile that they had to worry about their children for security reasons. Guard them. One of the party guests was in that category, with her own bodyguard. Or custody disputes, same thing.

"Some of them know boys from I don't know, a previous school, or camp, or even church. Or community service. They have to do community service, through the school."

"Well, good for them," said Angie. She knew Pat expected it of her. "What do I do if they show up?" She pictured a string of boys sneaking up the bank from the lake, past the fountain, with knives in their teeth.

"Send them home. Say you'll call their parents. But you won't have to, they can't even get in the gate. Oh, now you're going to worry. Hey, even if they cook something up, they're pretty much a joke to these particular girls. At this age the boys are way behind the girls. This group has a lot to keep them busy. The boys they see in school—they're so-and-so's son but these girls know they're twerps. Erika does. She's like me," Pat added, and it was true. But not in the way Pat meant it, not the way Pat had been at her age, full of tears and threats and some display in her walk, Angie thought, some sad teasing, some heat coming off her that might have been called slutty before they all, Angie and her friends, knew slut was a patriarchal term.

Angie remembered sitting around on the floor with the women she had lived with when Pat was little—women considerably younger than she was, leaning on radiators as they nursed their babies. Every once in a while they dropped a new term into the middle of their sleepy talk, like cloves into the stew. Their subject might be the commodification of breasts. But they would slip back, they would sigh over Angie's little daughter's rounded beauty, her awareness of her limbs and body as she bathed and danced and fastened her barrettes, her languorous, sweet manner with their boyfriends. But smart, too. Very smart. Competitive. Up in the high percentiles when she got to school, skipping second grade. So there was some connection, after all, between that little girl and the Pat of today.

And no father. A father who was gone, dead.

Pat had no memory of Rudy. So she said. None. She had seen the pictures, heard the tapes. When she got to be seven or eight she didn't want to go with Angie to the cemetery where Rudy was buried, but once, later, she let her boyfriend Eric take her. The Grave of the Unknown Rock Star, she called it. No, she wasn't especially curious beyond that.

Pat didn't have Angie's problems with pregnancy; she could have had ten babies. But she had only Erika. Rika, now; Erika had renamed herself, just as Pat had. "Pat" was not Pat's real name, of course. Her name was Parvati. Angie was not going to apologize for that. She and Rudy were back in Oregon; it was 1969 and they had moved into a double-wide just before the home birth—trailer-birth, Pat called it—with Mount Hood visible above the pines. Parvati. Daughter of the mountain.

In your thirties, in those days, you thought time was running out. Angie had been pregnant four times. "I'm staying put this time. I'm going to have this one if I have to stay in bed the whole time. You do whatever you want. Go on. Go with them!"

This was after she had scattered the carload of girls who followed the band. She got up from the bed and routed them out of the motel parking lot where they were beating tambourines on their hips. Pregnant, Angie was a terror. *Get out of here! Leave us alone!*

There were always pretty girls around, in droopy long dresses, with cracked heels and no makeup. But they weren't the ones she had to worry about. She had to think for a minute, remembering. Those two who had traveled with them, and had some right to be there, those were the ones—Mariah? Mara. "Mara meaning bitter," the girl would introduce herself, twisting her ripe lips. She sang with the band and had crying fits on the road requiring Rudy's presence in the room she shared with her friend with the made-up name. Sky. Mara and Sky. Names Angie had imagined were written on her skin, dug into her palms. And she had forgotten! Or almost forgotten. She was old.

But she hardly ever felt old. On the contrary, she had been old then. They were old, she and Rudy, for what they were doing, the company Rudy liked to keep. They were on the far edge. All around them were kids. Rudy was tired of the band and they were tired of him; during his guitar solos they liked to wander around the stage talking and drinking. He wasn't all that well because he was careless with his insulin. When he went to the free clinic for his cough the nurse told him to quit smoking but she said it was the diabetes that was going to get him if he wasn't careful.

Rudy was trying to quit smoking. He did quit. He got a job. The baby was born and then the changes came of their own accord for several years, and then the diabetes went out of control again and this time his kidneys failed and then his heart, and he died.

"I wish he could see this house," Angie said. They were having breakfast on the terrace, on the second day.

"Who?" Pat said patiently.

"Your father."

"Why is that?"

"Oh . . ." Angie took off her glasses to wipe off the fine spray from the fountain. Why? Why this wish to get the attention of the dead, force them to marvel at some exceptional thing? As if the sight of the living themselves, fighting and sleeping with each other and crawling through sewage, would not be enough to shake the husks of the poor emptied-out dead. "It would . . . mean something to him." But what, exactly? She felt a flash of conspiracy, the arrival of an undermining opinion, cool as the spray on her cheek: Rudy would laugh at this house. "Well, he didn't have money in his pocket till near the end. You know"—she turned to Erika—"when my dad hired him, he was out on his own. Hitched all the way from West Virginia to the Oregon coast. The reason he came at all was to play music at the carnival—we had a timber carnival in town. He was thin as the neck of his guitar.

That kind of diabetics aren't fat. He had to give himself shots, and my mother was a goner when she saw that, that and the smoking. She was going to put a stop to that, and feed him up. But he was a grown-up sixteen." The quality of Erika's listening changed. "He went right to work in the yard. The lumberyard. You could be a man at that age, back then, if you had to."

"Don't tell her that," Pat said.

"We ran off together a year later. I was a bit older."

"She's heard all that."

Erika said, "I have not and I don't remember."

Angie pried the picture of Rudy out of her wallet. She looked into the green eyes until the restlessness showed itself, as if the eyes would look away from hers if they could, and then she handed the picture to Erika. "We had to come back, though, we didn't have a penny. I knew my parents would take us right back, poor things, they wanted grand-children. But they never lived to see any, did they."

"No, they didn't," Pat agreed, looking at her watch.

"I'm not going to have kids," Erika said.

"Is that right?" Angie said. "So Rudy put in ten years in the yard with my dad. He was good at it. Then the strangest thing—folk music came in, overnight, and we packed up. We thought it was now or never, it was his chance. Oh, we roved around the country. It was before anybody ever heard of hippies. I just followed along. That's the way things were then."

"Not any more," Pat said. "Nowadays girls don't tag along after some guy they married, do they, Erika? Rika."

"Whatever," Erika said.

"Come here," said Angie. "I want to kiss the birthday girl." She was never sure Erika would come, but she did, she leaned across the table holding out her smooth cheek smelling of apricots.

"It's a whole different ballgame," Pat said.

Pat's boyfriend Eric played basketball. In their senior year the whole state knew Eric. He had the longest leg bones Angie had ever seen, and the biggest joints; he had a long neck with a prominent Adam's apple, and the fact that he was not, at first glance, a handsome boy didn't bother the rows of girls at the tournaments, chanting and holding up cutout letters of his name.

Angie loved Eric. She would be the last to find fault with a boy who noticed whatever you had left that was feminine. But she knew that politeness of his, that warm look of attention, she knew a ladies' man. Don't cling, she warned Pat silently.

Pat had lipstick on and her curly hair fell down over her shoulders. Women were getting permanents for just that soft look. But Pat was not exactly soft, even then. She and Eric were going down the porch steps, lugging the metal sides of a bed frame. Eric had to prop it so it stuck out the back window of the car, too big for the trunk where Pat had crammed most of the books from Angie's house. "You don't read, Mom." She hugged Angie to her. "Say me good-bye," she crooned, as she had as a toddler when Angie left for work.

"But I'll see you in a month," said Angie in sudden fright. She already had the time off, to be there when the baby was born. Pat was eight months pregnant but she was going to college. The state university had offered her money. Only one of them could go, to start with. "He'll support me and then I'll support him," Pat said, and that was what they did, after a fashion.

Eric shut the trunk and came back up the steps. "I'll take care of her," he said, putting his arm around Angie.

But Eric wouldn't be like Rudy—Angie was willing to bet on that— always making that wide circle back to home, because down deep Eric wasn't forsaken, and making up for it, the way Rudy had been. He didn't have Rudy's sadness, his need. He wasn't going to stay in a sporting goods store in Eugene for long, losing his chance to play basketball while he put Pat through college.

Angie was wrong; Eric did stay. He stayed faithfully, taking care of Pat. But the thing that happened to Pat was underway, by then. Pat didn't cling at all, she did the opposite. She wouldn't set a date to marry Eric, and then she wouldn't marry him. She floated away, lighter all the time, quicker, smarter. In no time she was someone whose job paid a sum she wouldn't tell either one of them. Then she was someone who talked on the phone with her feet on the table and said, "All we need is the space and three hundred thousand dollars."

Eric turned out not to want anything for himself, except Erika. When Pat took her away to Seattle Eric surprised everybody by not going to school on the money she offered him. He took off for Alaska.

From the first, he stayed in touch with Angie. He wrote that he had a job on a fishing boat. Every winter he appeared, tall and wind-burned, in her doorway. He had girlfriends but he didn't marry them. He didn't change. Angie decided he was one of those men pledged, with no loss of manhood, to his high school self. "I'm ready for this sunshine," he would say, hugging her. "Saw my little girl on the way down. She's about ready to do a summer up with me." He had been saying this about Erika for years.

Erika jumped to her feet. It was the fastest Angie had seen her move. The others were still in their jeans but Erika had put on a white cotton nightgown with ribbons trailing from the neck.

"Hello," Angie said lightly, crossing the room. She didn't exactly swoop in, she was slow at this time of night. "And who have we here?" Smoothly, the boy got to his feet, while Erika cried "Grandma!" in a stagey voice. "This is Jonah."

"Jonah," said Angie, holding out her hand. The boy shook with his left hand because he had a cast on his right arm. He smiled, a smile devoid of excitement or fear. A small boy, thin, shorter than Erika, with hair peroxided white-blond and dark eyes puffy on the upper lids. Small, flattish nose, deeply curved mouth, surprisingly adult. He looked familiar to Angie. She said, "Have I met you?" At that some of the girls choked with laughter.

"I don't think so."

"Well, Jonah, I'm afraid you'll have to go. I didn't see your name on the guest list." She didn't like the sound of that after she said it.

"OK," the boy said. Standing up alone in the ring of girls he went on smiling steadily. His face was like a chunk of carved and sanded pine. The swollen eyes made her think of Bill Diehl. That was it. Bill's came from alcohol.

The boy didn't say he was sorry or make a move to leave, he looked at Erika, who was playing with the ribbons at her neck. He was waiting for her to say she had turned the alarm off and let him in. Angie knew that. But Erika was not going to say it. "Bye, Jonah," Erika said, waving her fingers. She made a little kiss in the air.

When the boy moved, Angie followed in her trailing robe. "Where do you live?" she demanded.

"He lives—" Behind her somebody covered the speaker's mouth.

"Near here," he said, facing her at the door with a mild defiance and ringing the hanging pipe chimes of the doorbell with his knuckles. His eyes in their full lids suddenly flashed at her, like a dog's when you try to take something away from it.

"Can you get home?" Angie said. "It's after one."

"Sure."

"Do you need a ride?" she persisted. "Should I call anybody?"

"No!" the girls cried. "You'll get him in trouble!"

Cham was back. Close behind them, she gave a hiss, a dog-shooing noise, whereupon the boy slipped through the door and was absolutely gone.

With a dark look over her shoulder at the girls, Cham punched the keys of the alarm. She had the purse with her again. "What's in your bag?" Angie said. She couldn't help it. "Luck," said Cham. Angie pictured dried roots, a nutmeg, something sewn into a cloth. Cham opened the purse, let Angie look, and quickly snapped it shut. There was a rock inside.

"Stop it, Rika!" The girls were play-slapping each other.

Angie said, "Well, I think that's that, Cham. I think we can get back to bed." To the girls she said, "Don't think this is any surprise to me. I had a daughter, you know."

At this they crowded around her, touched her arms, flirted with her, eager to have their say. "He would have been in big trouble if you called his house." "He would get it. His father—" "Not his father, dummy." "His foster father—whatever, he's crazy." "His foster mom's pretty bad, too."

"Well, did you consider that when you invited him?"

"Invited him!" They all mimed shock.

"You invited him, Erika," Angie said. "You called him. I saw you on the phone."

"He just came," Erika said, quickly sullen.

"You might think about him out there at this hour, trying to get a bus, if there is such a thing in this neighborhood." They nodded solemnly, all but Erika. "How old is he?" Angie had a sudden feeling the boy might be in his twenties.

"Fif-teen," one of them said, drawing it out. The dreamy-faced redhead, Jessica. "Fifteen? I think? Right, Rika?" They all smiled and swayed. So they were all in love with Erika's boyfriend.

"He is not," said Tamiko. "He's older."

"He's sixteen." Erika folded her arms and recited in a patient singsong, "He's not from here, he's from Alaska, the caseworker took him away from his father, they always do that, they don't understand his people, he missed school so he's a grade behind."

"Only a grade," Angie said.

"He's smart," Erika said with the pride of possession.

"You can see that," Angie said. Erika's fingers with their light blue polished nails lay on the skin of her folded arms without pressing. I bet you don't usually get caught, Angie thought. I bet you get away with a lot. "So now, go to sleep, girls. Get down in those bags. Otherwise I'll have to stick you in bedrooms and you'll never find each other. Anybody need a pillow?"

Crawling on their knees over the sleeping bags they grabbed their pillows and began to thump each other with them. "Hey, quit it, I give up!" Then quickly with their ringed fingers they smoothed the pillows and held them up for Angie's inspection, subdued now, a devout little group. Tamiko hugged her two pillows and laid her head on them. They all copied her. That was the one Pat had referred to, the one with a bodyguard. Tamiko. Her driver had taken off his hat and handed Tamiko's two pillows to Angie with a bow.

. . .

When Angie woke again it was just her three o'clock habit. Wide awake this time and knowing where she was, she found the bathroom without turning on the light and sat getting her breath. Along the rail under her hand were nicks and scratches where the poor fellow must have backed and tipped his wheelchair getting on and off the toilet. "Don't worry about him, he's tough." So Pat had said. The girls, too: "These girls are tough." And Angie: "You'll do fine, you're tough." And it was true, Angie had done fine. All the same, if everyone was tough, then no one was heartless. When she came out she stopped at the window and parted the half-open vertical blinds with a finger, to look at the fountain. She could see its plume drop straight now with no wind. The moon still cast full light. She saw the blond boy, leaning forward—was he crying?—with his forehead buried in the tangled clematis on the wall that half-enclosed the courtyard.

There was someone else. Someone he was leaning on, against the vines. Arms unwound from his back. The girl pushed him away from her, just enough to get a gulp of air, and then she stretched herself out against the wall and drew him back. She was smaller than he was, hidden by his body. It was not Erika.

Angie could feel, along the front of her own body, the straining and pressing of the two small frames. The boy had made an effort to get the cast out from between them and had it propped against the wall over the girl's head so that they could lie together upright in the vines. Finally he stepped away, shook himself like a dog, and faced forward, leaning back heavily on the wall and fitting his shoulder to hers.

It was the little girl Meghan, with the flower face and black curls.

Now the boy threw his head back and Angie could just hear his voice, a faraway moan. The girl answered, slowly but with an up-note, a question. Gradually, without looking at him, she made some quiet argument to him and twined her arm in his, taking his hand. With their backs against the wall, holding hands, they turned their heads slowly to face each other. It was as if the kissing had been forced on them, and now for a minute they were free of it. They could have been on a stage, holding hands, about to open their mouths and begin a duet. Something unaccompanied, lyrical, medieval, with pain as its subject, pain and secrecy. Secrecy enclosed them.

So maybe it was not Tamiko, but this one, who required a bodyguard. If that was so, they would have to plan around it. They would have to figure it in, they would know all about how to pretend, how to see that suspicion fell on someone else. On Erika.

The boy let her drag him against her chest and back to her mouth. She had him around the ribcage as if she might lift him off his feet. His knee was between her legs. Of course. Of course. That was how it went. Angie could feel her own pulse, keeping the same old heavy beat of curiosity and objectless longing.

Then she saw Erika. She was standing on the balcony of her own room, above the wing that was Cham's, looking down into the little courtyard. Angie saw her white face, her hair hanging forward, and followed her gaze down to the embrace against the wall. No, there was no argument, no way to refute what was going on. When she looked back, Erika was gone.

Angie turned from the window. Was she out of sight in the dark of the room? She wanted to get back into bed, into Pat's soft sheets. But she would have to take charge, the boy Jonah would have to leave. At least the girls should all be in the house, wherever the boy was. She didn't like the thought of Erika up on the balcony. In the tantrum years, the years of the forming will, she had taken care of Erika—never a child to be shielded, pitied. And what could Angie say now, if she went now and found her? *Don't let it hurt you?* For a long time she stood by the bed. Finally she pulled the red robe back on, tied it, and softly opened the door. Cham was standing a few feet away. "Same thing again," Cham said. "Girls get up."

"Are you familiar with this scenario?" Angie whispered. "Is this what happens? What's the story?"

Cham said doggedly, "Girls get up. Erika and one girl."

"I mean, are we supposed to take action?"

"This boy is not for birthday. Not for girls."

"Well then, I'll see what I can do." She swept past Cham down the hall, and counted the girls in sleeping bags. Erika was one of the four.

At that moment the house exploded in blaring sound. Angie tripped and almost fell. Her hands found the rail, but that drove the buzz up her arms. As it poured in on her, the girls clambered up screaming. Cham was running flatfooted to the door. She peered through the hole and stepped back, making a violent crisscross motion with her hands at Angie to show—what? "Stop it! Turn it off!" Angie shouted.

"Girl," Cham said, raising her voice angrily. "She try to open. So—" She pointed at the top of the door. A metal plate had dropped two inches to block it.

"So let her in!"

The girls had their pillows over their heads, all except Erika, who yelled, "Turn it off! Turn it off or the cops will come!"

"Oh, no, the cops!" The girls' heads came up. "Jonah! Rika, Jonah's not here, is he?"

"Cham!" Angie shook her by the arm. "Turn the alarm off this minute and open the door. We don't need the police here. It's Meghan!"

"A man," said Cham. "A man is here."

Angie pulled Cham away from the peephole and looked. First she saw the weeping girl, then a badge, held like a playing card between two fingers. Behind it a short heavyset man stood grinning, moving the badge aside to show himself, then bringing it into view again. "For God's sake Cham, it's her—employee! OK! It's all right," she yelled through the thick door. Cham was finally punching in the code.

When the alarm stopped, the house seemed to sag like a parachute. Angie shot the bolt back and the man turned the knob, stepped back, passed Meghan neatly in before him and stuck out his hand. "Kirby Wells. With her dad's firm." He had thick brown hair combed steeply back from a creased forehead. He gave a short man's bow, leaning into the handshake as if from a height, flicked the badge into his right hand, and offered it to Angie. "If you don't mind—gotta catch up with somebody."

"I do mind," Angie said, taking care to stand still and give way to no fluttering, elderly gesture. "Who?"

"Little guy out there. Party crasher."

Angie smoothed the robe and raised her chin, gathering herself, like Katharine Hepburn. "Oh, dear, you don't mean Jonah? He is an invited guest."

"Excuse me, ma'am, but this young lady has a few restrictions on her."

"Ah. But this young man wouldn't be one of them," Angie said.

"Wrong. Watchit there." Angie had backed onto her hem. "Sorry, ma'am, but that's not the case. This kid is a menace." Meghan looked straight ahead, her swollen mouth clamped shut, paying no attention to the three girls rocked back on their heels among the pillows, or to Erika, who had crawled down into her sleeping bag and hidden herself. "So like I said, I'm sorry," the man said, "but the kid's going back."

"Back where?"

"Juvie. Sorry about that. "

Angie thought he actually was sorry, sorry that she, his opponent, was silly and old. He wasn't all that young himself, the hair might be dyed. Above his muscled neck he had a low-slung face, engaged in some inner calculation, at once gloomy and self-satisfied. Gauging his own supply of whatever it was that kept men going at his age. "Why, I'm surprised to hear you say that," she said. She was getting into her role, not so much Katharine Hepburn now as any old woman invested—self-invested—with a secret authority that could turn dire. "His family are friends of my daughter's."

The man positively spluttered. "No! No, ma'am!" He rubbed his big short-fingered hands together, then jammed them into his pants pockets. "Nossir. These girls are shitting you. Excuse me. This kid's a problem from way back. I can guarantee you your daughter does not know this family." Wells turned his lower lip out in a cartoon face of disgust.

"I know them myself," Angie said in the dowager voice. "There's no telling who another person is acquainted with." Though looking at Kirby Wells she was in the process of guessing a whole life for him. "Now, I don't know where you're stationed tonight, but I bet it would be all right for you to go off duty now. Please tell Meghan's father we had no idea he felt this way. I certainly never got any such information from her mother."

"Mother don't have a thing to say about it," Wells said. "He's got a court order."

"Now, Mr. Wells. I promise you I'll watch Meghan. I'll be right here where I've been all evening. Well, actually it's morning, isn't it. How about a cup of coffee? Cham? And do you have a partner out there?" Cham gave her a baleful look and did not move.

The man's hands in his pockets were balled into fists. He took them out and shook them. "I'm a one-man operation," he said. "Tell you what I need, and that's a restroom."

Angie sighed. "That way and down the hall. All the way down, on the left." It was over. She felt mildly winded, as if she had been gripping the ropes of a swing.

But it was not entirely over. The door chimes rang out, echoed, rang again. Angie put her eye to the hole again. Two policemen stood there, with the boy Jonah between them. They had hold of him by the elbows, loosely enough that he was unwrapping a stick of gum.

Angie opened the door. Her high spirits drained away as the two men nodded soberly to her, creaking in the straps of their holsters and radios. But the taller one said in a friendly way, "I think we maybe have us a cat burglar. Is this what set off your alarm? Says he knows you."

"'This,'" Angie said, "is a friend of ours. Jonah, what are you doing outside at this time of night? And who called the police?"

"Your alarm went off, ma'am. We respond to that. The company gets the call and a few minutes later"—he showed his watch—"we get the call." He was speaking to her a little more slowly and loudly than necessary. He was young but bald, and the other one had a buzz cut that showed his scalp. Both of them had the attractive neat police mustache.

Angie took a breath. "I'm sorry, Officer," she began. "I'm Angela Rudeen. This is Jonah, and Meghan, and over there are my granddaughter Erika and her friends Brianne, Tamiko, and Jessica"—she spread the names out with their mild distracting power—"having a slumber party. It's Erika's birthday. If they've been in and out I'm to blame. I can't tell you how sorry I am about the alarm. But it is a birthday party. Fourteen," she added.

The tall one said, "These false alarms—they'll get you a big fine. If this is your first one you're in for a shock."

"Oh, it is," Angie said.

The shorter one said, "We get them all the time. The dog sets it off, the maid sets it off." He glanced at Cham's bare feet. "They call us, we come out. Pretty soon, no police response for anybody. I'm just letting you know, ma'am."

By this time they had let go of the boy's arms and he had begun to smile and crack his gum. Don't do that, Angie thought, don't smile. They're ready to go. They'll leave if you stay still.

Of course he was smiling for the benefit of Meghan, who was haughtily pushing the stuck curls off her face. She had been shooting looks at him from under her black brows, one after another like rivets, and he was replying with a message of his invulnerability. Her smile in return was radiant, if radiance could be secretive and not wholly benign. She put her shoulders back and her breasts up and Angie saw that for all her slightness she was not a little girl at all.

Far away the bathroom door opened. Kirby Wells was coming. "Well, here comes Mr. Wells!" Angie cried as he came striding on his short legs. "Mr. Wells ran over when he heard the alarm."

"Well, looka here," said Wells. His face was deep red, as if he had had trouble in the bathroom. "Hey, you got him."

"Please," Angie said. "I was just explaining the situation to Mr. Wells," she added.

"The situation is, here we have the man himself, Mr. Smartboy," Wells said.

"And Mr. Motherfucker," the boy said with his smile.

"That's enough!" Angie said. But she sagged at the knees and the tall policeman's hand shot out for her elbow. "And Mr. Wells—! But let's sit down, why don't we," she said. The door was flanked by granite benches, where no one ever sat. Angie was the only one who did so now, and as the boy took a gliding step in the direction of the open door Wells grabbed his good arm so fast it spun him in his tracks. What struck Angie in that second was how ferocious a small thing like that could be, not at all like people throwing each other around on TV. It was as if a sharp gas had been released into the room. They all breathed it. Both policemen stepped forward.

"That's assault," the boy said, shielding his narrow chest with the cast in a way that would have brought tears to Angie's eyes if he had not, the next minute, grinned around at all of them. OK, my friend, she thought, you can take care of yourself. This was a boy who was aware of his effect. He must get by on it, the pang stirred up in others by that combination of looks—for of course the girls had chosen him for what only now struck Angie as his beauty—and the suggestion of a misery, some error he was set on compounding.

"What's so funny?" Wells demanded. "You. What's so funny?"

"Oh, dear," Angie said. "Mr. Wells is trying to help, I'm sure, but really, at this point I'd be happier if he'd just—maybe he'll listen to you."

The tall policeman looked at her and at Wells in turn. His eyes swept the room. "Having fun, girls?" he called. "Whose birthday?"

"Hers," they all said, pointing to Erika in her sleeping bag.

"Looks like she's sleeping through it," he said. The radio on his belt gave off static and then a voice, numbers, an address. "And we've got your guest here, Mrs.—?"

"Rudeen," Angie said. "Yes, you do."

"Uh-huh. We apprehend a guest from time to time."

The younger policeman got up close to the boy and spoke to him. "Buddy, you might be a guest, you might be whatever, but you need to clean up your mouth."

"Rudeen?" said Kirby Wells. "Any relation to Rudy Rudeen?"

"My husband," said Angie.

"Uh-huh. Well, things seem to be under control here," the tall one put in easily. "Don't you think so, Frank? I think we can all just get back to business. And you're a neighbor, Mr. Wells?"

"I'm security personnel for Mr. Nicholas Pappas," Wells said, rocking back and flapping his trousers from the pockets. "I keep an eye on the safety situation of his daughter. Yeah, I'd say things are under control."

This satisfied the tall one. "Do you want to file a complaint?" he asked Wells.

"Wait a minute," Angie said. "Mr. Wells is in my house. My alarm went off. Wouldn't I be the one to file a complaint?"

"All we'd need is, we'd need to run a few checks, maybe get your boss on the phone. And if not," the policeman went on comfortably, to Wells, "you may as well call it a night." His radio blurted again.

"No complaint," Wells said. "I'm outa here. Whoa. Rudy Rudeen."

"Uh-huh. And ma'am, you might want to shut down your borders. The gate. Gate's wide open. You can go ahead and shut it when we leave. Give it two minutes." He stepped aside so that Wells could precede him through the door.

"Well, yes, I will. Thanks again, all of you." Angie stayed sitting down, to conserve her energy. "Thank you, Mr. Wells. Good night. Seriously, don't worry."

The moon had swung to the rear of the house, and from the bench she could see long, pale washboard clouds. Cham shut the heavy door. "All right, now," Angie said after a minute. "Girls, get back in bed. Meghan, go to bed. Wait, Jonah. I don't know what I'm going to do with you."

"OK, see this?" Meghan had come to life. "See his arm? Wanna know who broke it? Ray. His quote-unquote father. And look." With a rough sweep, almost a blow, she pushed the boy's nylon soccer shirt up. Across his chest ran what looked like a purple tattoo, but proved to be a band of raw skin with scabs clustered along it. "That's rope burn." At that the boy sat down beside Angie, shaking his head modestly as if Meghan were listing his accomplishments.

So Angie had been wrong again, wrong in thinking such a boy could take care of himself. And once she had been so unfoolable. She leaned back against the slate wall. Pumphead. "You'll have to stay until morning," she said to Jonah, keeping her eyes closed, "and then I don't know."

"Just take this off!" said Meghan, plucking at the neck of the boy's shirt. "It's pulling the scabs. See? Oh! See? They tie him up, they break his arm, and now he'll get killed."

A loud, strangled sob burst from Erika's sleeping bag.

"Oh, yeah, Rika! Yeah, hear that? How do you like that? You got him over here. You turned the alarm back on. You got him into this." Meghan's lips had gone white and she bared her small sparkling teeth as if she might sink them into Erika.

"That may be, Meghan," Angie said, "but she was a little bit duped, if I'm not mistaken. And I can guarantee you he won't be killed. He'll stay right here until we're sure." Sure of what? What could they manage for this boy? And Pat was getting back at noon. But she, Angie, was the mother. She was not afraid of Pat. "And now, and I mean this, you're all going back to bed."

As Cham stood ready to push the buttons on the panel there was a knock on the door. "Hold it!" Angie got herself off the bench before Cham could take any action. "Great, now we have the police force again." But when she opened the door, it was Wells.

"I'm back," he said, walking straight in. "I'm thinking, wait a minute, you don't wanna leave the fox in with the chickens." At the same time he held his hands up to indicate some possible compromise. But Jonah had already ducked into a dive against the man's belly. "God—damn!" Wells hollered, catching at the bench but going down, sitting hard on his haunch and ankle with one leg out. Angie heard the bent knee crack. From the floor he grabbed Jonah's pants leg and yanked until the boy fell on top of him. They began to roll absurdly to and fro on the flagstones, rocking one of the stone tubs with their feet so the tree in it gracefully dropped a leaf. The boy's body arched as he strained to get his knees under Wells and throw him off. He didn't have to; Wells toppled heavily of his own accord. What kind of bodyguard was he?

This all took place rather slowly, giving Angie time to think how stupid, ugly, and yet coordinated it all was. As Wells rolled on top of Jonah and pinned him she had time to see the man's sweaty scalp, the white in his part where the brown had grown out. She saw the back of his hand, a dry old thing crawling with fat veins, as he got a grip on the floor. He had on a wedding ring. His head swung low between his shoulders.

Suddenly Meghan was in the middle of it. "Dammit, Kirby! I told you!" She had him by the hair, wrenching his head up. "I told you! I told you, stay outa my life!" The cords in her neck were standing out like tree roots and it seemed to Angie, who let out a yell, that this was a girl who might not stop before she broke a man's neck. "Christ!" Wells had a hand up, flapping at the girl or protecting his head, and she had bitten the hand. It was then that Cham charged, in her purple robe, driving Meghan off with an elbow, not to spare Wells at all but to slug him with the purse. She hit him in the spare tire toward the back, where the kidneys were. "Cham, for God's sake!" Angie snatched the purse out of her hands. The boy rolled free and Wells let himself down onto the floor with a groan.

Meghan got Jonah by the cast. "Get outa here!" she hissed, dragging him. "Don't go home! He's nuts, he'll go to your house, he'll get Ray up, get outa here!"

"Oh, no he won't." Wells hung from the bench by one arm. "I quit." The voice came out of his belly. He brought his watch in front of his face. "I'm nuts? You're a bunch of maniacs. As of now—3:55 AM—I quit."

Wells knew the music of Rudy Rudeen. "The man had a voice," he said. He knew because of course he played the guitar. At least half the men Angie ever ran into played the guitar, Bill Diehl being the exception.

In the eighties Wells had played with two bands nobody ever heard of. The good one, he said with the picky, musician's air familiar to Angie, was modeled on the E Street Band. He considered that he had been pretty good himself, but too old by the time he got good enough. And not in the big leagues, like Rudy. Not with those stubby fingers, she thought. She did not correct him and say, "Actually it was the minor leagues."

"I'll tell you, it was drugs messed me up for a while there. In the service you could get anything you wanted. But hey, Rudy Rudeen."

Angie gave a deep sigh, tried to place the accent. "Are you from West Virginia?"

"Close. Ohio. Crost the river from Wheeling."

"What are you doing out here?"

"Mountains," he said. "My brother-in-law's out here." Not "my sister." It was funny who people had. Cham and Pat, for instance, had each other. This man had his brother-in-law. Angie had Bill and Terri, to bring CDs with them on the night before her surgery and play her "Piece Of My Heart." Angie had a baby goddaughter, their child. She had Eric, almost a son.

"I've got a son-in-law I feel that way about," she said, though Eric was not her son-in-law and Wells hadn't said how he felt about his brother-in-law. "Your sister's husband, or your wife's brother?"

"Ex-wife's brother." He saw her look at his ring. "This keeps the ladies off."

This could be a joke or one of those unlikely truths. "Anyway, I wasn't going to faint," Angie said. "I got dizzy. I get that if I stand up too fast."

"You stay where you are," Wells said, with some authority.

Angie lay on the couch with her legs bundled in the red robe and the shawl Terri had crocheted for her. She pinched her cold legs, and drank the hot coffee she had made for herself and Wells. While she was pouring it in the half dark of the kitchen, Cham had come in, and stood there without switching on the bank of overhead lights, wringing her hands and talking under her breath. She had her khaki pants on and there were streaks, sweat or tears, in the oil on her face. When she saw Angie she jumped and stopped her mouth with her fist. "Oh, Cham, I'm sorry—" Angie began, but Cham stepped back from her and waved at the coffee maker, saying from behind her fingers, "I, I will do it."

"No, no, please, you get some sleep," Angie said. "Believe me I won't, I really won't let anything else happen. I mean it, Cham. I'm sorry." Cham rubbed at the streaks on her face. At the doorway she threw Angie a squinting look. "OK. So. You. You will watch. OK. OK."

The candles were burning low on the glass table but the sleeping bags were gone; Angie had banished the girls to Erika's room. "Let them fight it out," she said to Wells. "Hey, you, go to sleep." Across the room in the business alcove Jonah was playing a computer game, his face flickering blue.

When he didn't answer, Wells got to his feet. "Did you hear the lady?"

"Yes, *sir*," Jonah called back. "I'm going to sleep, *sir*."

After a minute Angie said, "You know, women won't let you go after a kid."

"Some will," Wells said.

"I'm sorry Cham got into it. Sorry she hit you. I didn't see that coming. But Cham had children." Angie had a vision of Cham running into flames, while soldiers went about some awful business. "Cham lost everything." She tried to think of some reparation that could be made when someone had lost everything. There was nothing. After all the marching and chanting from that war, there was nothing. What must they look like, all of them, to Cham? And she had worried that Cham didn't like her. Didn't like her. "Cham lost everything," she said again. "But she still takes care of her skin. She oils her face every night when she goes to bed. That's a good sign."

"Got herself an altar in there, just like back home in Saigon. Incense sticks, oranges, the whole works."

"Except not Saigon. She's Cambodian. You're telling me you went into her room?"

"I opened a couple doors. Went by the john the first time. This place is a hotel." Clearly he had figured out it wasn't Angie's place. "Lucky she can't swing, no arm on her. Anyway, the kid went after me, if you noticed. I let him off. I'm not going to beat up on a kid. I'll keep 'em away from her highness, though, I'll do my job. These kids can smell money."

"I don't think it's money he's after. And you just quit your job."

"If I had it after tonight. But you'd be surprised. Pappas knows the score. He's onto that little gal. Last time she run off she went clear to Bellingham on the bus. Met this fella there and they went to the doctor, if you know what I mean."

"Ah," Angie said.

"I know stuff he don't want to know, her dad. He can forget about watching that one, he's running the company but she's running the show."

"They grow up," Angie said sagely.

"Thirteen, fourteen—everything works. All systems go." He sat forward. "Uh-oh."

Angie followed his eyes. Erika was on the metal bridge and she was naked. With her arms outstretched and hands flat against the air she was treading slowly backward, holding the frieze of girls who followed her at bay. Meghan came first, soothing her, "Come on now, Rika, come on," but Erika was climbing onto the metal banister. When she got herself positioned she hooked her ankles and rocked.

Kirby Wells had the shawl whipped from Angie's legs and Jonah was out in the open staring up, knees bent, curved lips caught under his teeth as if he were going to shoot a basket. Ha! Angie thought, kicking to get her legs off the couch. See that? You'll find out! It's way more complicated than you think, with your fists and your kisses.

"You don' know!" Erika croaked. "How do *you* know? We were too going to Alaska! I was going. We were gonna see the Northern Lights!" She righted herself, grasped the rail with both hands. "I wanna, I wanna go!" She teetered on the rail. "We were too going!"

Angie got to the stairs but Wells was already at the top. With a heave, the way lumbermen threw bagged sawdust, he had Erika off the rail. "My dad!" Erika howled. "He's in Alaska! Get off me! And Jonah's! He's there. His real dad! You don' know! Tell 'em, Jonah! *Jonah!*"

Tamiko, holding her own cheeks in her hands like a flowerpot, leaned over the rail and raised her melodious voice. "Grandmother! Grandmother! She took pills!"

"What pills?" Wells had Erika wound tight in the shawl. "Spell it!"

"X-A-N-A-X. Two pills! From her mom's room! And—she drank wine, a lot of wine," Tamiko quavered as an afterthought. "It spilled all over her nightgown."

"How many pills? Get 'em!" With a knot of tassels, Wells doubled Erika over in the shawl while he stuck what looked like his whole forearm into her mouth. Obediently she retched, groaned, and vomited a stream that dropped in pink flags through the grate. Wells shook off his fingers and plunged them back in. "We got pills in this mess?" he snarled down to Angie. "Don't just stand there. Look."

"I don't see . . ."

"Get down and look. Two pills? Is that it?" He shook Erika, who flopped against him. "Answer me! That's all?"

"Tha'ss—all." Erika came to herself enough to hide her face in his jacket.

Tamiko was back with the pill bottle. "Here it is! I know it was two, I swear, I saw."

"Thanks. You're good, you can apply for my job." He called down to Angie, "She's all right, better than she looks. Two of those won't slow you down much. It's the wine." Another girl began to retch. "That's nothing. Copycat. They've all had a few too many, though, the little turkeys. Except this one here, the smart one." Tamiko stepped back, offended. "Don't worry," Wells called to Angie, "I did a couple years on the rescue squad."

Angie held on to the metal. Where was Cham? But Cham was shut away in the room with the altar. Cham had taken her at her word. I won't let anything happen, she had said. She wouldn't let Cham down; she would clean up the mess before Cham got a look at it. Then she thought, Pat's going to try to get the whole story out of me. All of it. Then she thought, if my heart stops now I'll get my chest ripped open by Kirby Wells of the rescue squad.

"Can't tell you what-all I shook outa kids," Wells said sleepily.

The girls were up. It was too late to go back to bed, it was frank morning and they were taking showers. Three of them were going back and forth along the walkway in a special, created quiet, carrying soft piles of enough towels for twenty bathers, coming down to get lotions out of their bags to offer Erika, who was showering for the second time. Meghan they softly cajoled through a closed door. "OK, here's the thing, you two have to make up. She will if you will."

A feeling of aloneness came over Angie, like the silence when a vacuum cleaner is turned off. Her legs were cold. The room, too, felt cold, and bare as the hall of a castle. One of the old castles. Not the newer ones, as she had seen for herself in Europe, taking the tour Pat had sent her on before Bill Diehl, but the small ruins, maybe from the Middle Ages—she had not held onto her brochures—that stood in the middle of nowhere with thick broken walls. The ones where women must have lived, with children if they were lucky, and few arrivals. Each one a kind of kingdom. A kingdom without a king, no matter how they gazed from the roof and waited, most of the time. The men would be out raiding.

Not any more, Pat would say.

Angie leaned back. "Did you ever hear the term 'pumphead'?" she asked Wells.

"Nope. Something to do with a bong?"

"Ha. It refers to somebody who was on the heart pump."

He was trying unsuccessfully to stick on the Band-Aid she had brought for his bitten hand. "You," he said. Glancing into the open neck of her robe he zipped his thumb down his chest.

"Give me that," Angie said. "Better see somebody for that. She broke the skin."

"You're a bossy lady."

"No, I'm not, actually."

"Lucky she got this one—see? Not my chord hand."

Funny how chord, the word chord, still went through Angie. She didn't listen to music. Her records slumped on the shelf; she had never even bought a CD. She had turned her back on music, outsmarting the traps laid by the past. Doing this gave her a stubborn satisfaction, a feeling of concealment, as though from a hiding place she could see people from those crowded days of travel and music and sleeping together but they could not see her.

Up and down the rungs went the girls' bare springing feet, their rings on the metal rails making a cross between a rasp and a chime. They took care not to wake Jonah, who sprawled on the couch in the computer alcove, flat morning light on his smooth ribs and tiny nipples and scabs, although they had peered at him long enough to memorize his openmouthed, frowning, half-slain condition and relay it to the two upstairs. They smelled of shampoo; they had pulled their hair back into rubber bands; their eyes shone.

Angie's eyelids were sore and she let them droop. She was not going to offer explanations to Pat. And Cham wouldn't either, she felt sure.

There was Pat's Xanax, after all. The Xanax had to be absorbing something. Cham must know about that. Maybe Cham looked after Pat that way, kept things from her, mothered her. Even though Pat had a mother. It was her father who had gone staggering away from her with his arm hooked over Angie's shoulders. "We'll be back," Angie had called to the neighbor, who hoisted the child up and made her wave. But Angie had come back alone.

The boy would still be in the house when Pat got home. That, Angie would let Erika account for. Erika would know what to leave out. She might not have any notion, anyway—if she had any memory of it—of what had possessed her to parade like that with her clothes off. Or maybe she would. Maybe Erika had worked out, already, that although it might appear otherwise, some things might never be hers. Or they might come to her not by any right but only by being gambled for up to her limit. More power to her, if she did. More power to her. Only don't give up, Angie thought. Don't give up. I saw you. And indeed, before she thought of a fall onto stone floor, or of pills, or that she was the one in charge of a granddaughter, all she had seen was a girl on a bridge, tall and naked and beautiful.

One night on the deck of the cruise ship, with Bill Diehl seasick below, she had felt a pause like that, at the wakeless speed the ship maintained in a narrow bay. She had been watching the sky turn a bold calm purple with the steep land outlined against it. She remembered the rail growing warm in her hands as the color in the sky deepened. Not for years had she been in this state, but she knew it right away. It wasn't weakness or age. It was something first made known to her at the timber carnival when she was a girl.

The thin new boy. The boy stubbed out his cigarette carefully to save it, and picked up his guitar, while she sat on cedar logs beside a bonfire and looked at him, suspended. And then . . . and then hardly any time later the doctor came in and told her the boy, now a man with caved-in cheeks, unconscious on a hospital bed, might or might not go on living.

She had been looking at Rudy's face, with its parched, invalid's beauty, all day. It was time to go to the neighbor's and pick up the baby—they called their little girl the baby, though she was four years old—but Angie just sat there rocking back and forth in the chair. The last time Rudy's eyes had opened they had stuck open for several minutes. Fever had burned off their expression. Her feeling was not even happiness at the news that he might not die, he might live. It was pure rocking, like a kitten swung in a cat's teeth. It was not conditional. He didn't live. It was in this sensation, and her surrender when it came, she thought, watching Kirby Wells as he began to snore, that she knew the girl who had sat on the logs was herself. She knew the girl, and the girl knew her. The boy sat down. His guitar gave out a bass, private note as he propped it. The girl went on looking into the fire and into her life, the life on the way to her. Lives, she knew now. A relay of lives. But the one who caught up with her was herself, passing on the same heart every time.

the ivy field

I t was Mary Catherine Ott. Below the woman's white bangs when she turned were the unmistakable eyes of the Otts. She was tall and wore a scarf around the padded shoulders of her coat, an expensive coat. "Mary Catherine?" I said. She put on a willing smile. Who was I? "It's Karen," I said.

"Karen!" she sang back, in the only tone possible, but after a pause, "Karen Lund!"

We wondered at the thirty-some years. I had stayed in Seattle but she had lived all over the place. We each had two children. As for her brothers and sisters, all was well. Although there had been divorces. "James?" I said.

"Oh, no, not James, he's been married forever. He's in Spokane. He's a vet, he always loved dogs. He walks fine, he runs." James had had polio. "His wife is a lawyer." A lawyer. A woman in a suit, walking with James . . . this I pictured so vividly, down to the sandy hair on James's arms, that as I saw it I realized, as you sometimes do when you're surprised like this, that the men with whom I had involved myself and twice even married had all had sandy hair and calm sad-dish natures like James's and had deserved kindness and it was too late to repair what I had done.

"What about Annie?" I said. Annie was married and had four children. Clark too, Clark, the never-toilet-trained, had four children. Natalie and Owen had had some of the divorces.

Mary Catherine did not put herself on either list, nor did I. "The divorces were very hard on our mother," she said. "You know how no one divorced in their day. But she got through it, and she's going strong. She still lives in the same house!"

Audrey. Audrey Ott. I heard my mother's voice say it. Sycamore tree and sagging screened porch flew up before me. And the ivy field. I did not say to her, *What about your father?*

She had not asked me about my own family—my parents or my sister Laura—but suddenly she said, "Did you ever learn to ride a bike?"

"Me?" I didn't think it was possible she had said that. "No, no. That was Laura. That wasn't me. It was Laura who couldn't ride a bike."

"Oh, yes, right, Laura."

"And the baby?" I said. "The baby who was born after we moved?"

"Paulette. So you moved away before that? How do you remember all this?" Did she, Mary Catherine, not remember?

"Does Paulette have four children, too?" Once I had said this I didn't like the tone, but it didn't seem to bother Mary Catherine.

"Oh, they've had no luck." We were outside the store, saying good-bye. I thought of getting her phone number. On the phone I would have been able to find things out without asking. When did anyone have to ask Mary Catherine? But she was saying very little, really. She mostly smiled, and held her leather purse strap with that musing patience, as if she had always been this tall, solid woman, well-off and settled in her mind, and bore no relation to the little girl who had striven with all those sisters and brothers in the noise of that grimy dark house, the girl who had longed to live in ours instead.

Her lined face had not gone soft in middle age but had taken on breadth and tightness, under the big staining freckles of her mother Audrey. A face oddly reminiscent of both parents. But attractive. Even striking, with the white hair. Certain eyes will do that, carry everything. I wished I had brushed my hair to give it height, and put on some lipstick. I wished I could produce out of myself something extra, some force of existence, to keep Mary Catherine from mar-veling on the way home, *To think! To think I admired Karen Lund, to think I yearned to be part of her family instead of mine! Yearned to be her!*

After our good-byes it developed that our cars were parked in the same lot, so we walked on together for two blocks in the cold spring air. It was then she thought to ask about my parents. "They're both living," I said. "Doing fine."

"My father died ten years ago," she said, and tears filled her eyes. That was when she looked at me for the first time as if she remem-bered me, knew me. She gave me a keen, prolonged look, as if she saw me think, *I bet he killed himself.* Little changes in the muscles of her face turned it almost mean. "His diabetes killed him," she said.

All the way home I thought of my mother and her sadness. I thought of Susie, my father's wife, saying on their last visit, "Your mother could have married again!" And my father, shaking his head with authority but speaking a bit wearily as he does now that his wife's energy has come to surpass his own, saying, "Not her. She never could. Not Billie, no, she does a thing once." He offers this comfort to his younger self. Still, Susie can see no obstacle to my mother's marrying, even now. "She's ageless," she will say generously. "If she'd just smile," she'll say, with her touching belief that it was losing my father that gave my mother the sober air we all know her to possess.

Susie is very like my father. She has nothing against my mother, having been married to him years longer than my mother was, and wishes her the happiness she wishes everyone.

· · ·

Soon after they moved in, Laura and I concluded in our pride that six Ott kids did not add up to any more than the two of us. You could climb the sycamore in our yard, crawl out over the driveway and look squarely into the bedroom where the boys slept and played and fought and were once in a great while—there were hardly any rules in their house to be broken—punished by being kept upstairs. On those nights the punished one, white face with the wide-set Ott eyes, would blindly look out the window, seeming, if indeed he knew we might be there, not to see us in the branches.

The three girls were not punished. This was not such an unusual practice in families then, at the end of the fifties.

Laura and I hoped to see the boys undressing and sometimes we did. But it was disappointing: bony legs and loose underpants like the clothespin bag and nothing more. There were shoes and clothes and bedcovers all over the floor, with the dog scrambling in and out of them. We could not see into the girls' bedroom across the hall. But we didn't need to, Mary Catherine was always at our house, in our bedroom. It was taken for granted that we would play there. She even spied in the tree with us. Her fat little sister Annie, who was in Laura's grade but was going to have to take a test for dumbbells, according to Mary Catherine, was allowed upstairs with us at our mother's insistence. But Annie's contributions to our games, and her possessions in the dim no-closet room she shared with Mary Catherine, had no importance.

Our kitchen window looked out on a hummock of dirt that never grew grass, called by our father the termite mound, and the rusted screen of the Otts' back porch, their clothesline, their woodpile with chair legs in it. In her own family, our mother had been the one to keep things tidy for the drunken neglectful parents who were the old, unbathed grandparents fifty miles away. We never saw them, though our phone rang very early one morning while it was still dark, and my mother gave groans that woke us up, and soon we saw their coffins. At two AM, leaving the Stop Inn at closing time, they drove onto the highway and up under a semi. Tractor trailers, we called them then.

I know now that my mother took care of her parents through this long decay, and even made excuses to them for not bringing us when she came. My father did not want us to see the chain smoking and staggering or hear the cusswords or smell the smells that we caught in my mother's clothes and hair now and then when we came home from school, that stood for our grandparents' house, their life.

From the sinking ship of that family he had rescued my mother, thrown a magic ring around her, the life her orderliness required. She did not impose her need for order on us, she was secretive about it, and didn't laugh if my father caught her setting books to right when she passed them, an inch forward or back, or stroking magazines into square piles. After dinner she pushed the chairs up to the table, not quite touching; she ironed sheets and stacked them with the folds forward, even though we had no linen closet then but only a shelf above her dresses.

Over the kitchen window were three prints in a row, of flying ducks. I don't know what happened to them, not that I would want them. If I see a duck print in an antique store a wave of sullenness comes over me, though my father defended these pictures of his, that had been in the law office of his father. One had a greenish-brown overcast sky. "There's something in that one," my mother said. "Some . . . oh, I don't look at it."

"She looks out upon the land of the Otts," my father chuckled.

"I do," she said.

James, Owen, and Clark. Mary Catherine, Annie, and Natalie. In the first of the three years we knew them, Natalie, whom my father called Natalie Wood, was a baby with heavy, wet diapers, Annie a first grader who could never quite understand or settle into a game. Mary Catherine was then eight, my age, the pretty one. She was the favorite of her mother, who would tell our mother, "I give in to that one, I know I do, because look at her." No one over there even whined about that, and if the Otts did not know there are no favorites in families, it might be, Laura and I thought, that they did not know anything at all.

Mrs. Ott was in the habit of coming over when the men were at work. Audrey Ott. My mother had only two friends, one of them in another state, but she gave them surnames when speaking of them to my father. It seemed to put a lid on them and then she served them. "Audrey Ott stopped by today." "Oh, I owe Audrey Ott a dollar ten for the milkman. Don't let me forget."

In the kitchen, and in the yard hanging up the wash before we got our dryer, she spent hours with Audrey Ott, who always arrived breathless and sticking the hair back into her ponytail as if she had swum over. She would say, "Billie! Let's quit for the day and go out

on the town." She would lean on the counter where the stew vegetables were laid out and watch my mother chop them with her little
black-handled knife. People didn't use the big knives they use today.
My mother cut vegetables so rapidly, in pieces all the same size, that
I always expected Audrey to stop talking and comment on her skill.
Being her daughter I thought I knew how she did it. It was a surprise
to me that if I cut things up they came out any old shape.

Audrey Ott alternated the same two Orlon sweaters, a green and
a brown, and snapped a thick rubber band around her hair when she
thought of it, without washing it, in our opinion, and had a wide face
of runny freckles and a wide rump that jutted out below her thin top
like a holder she had been set in. Mr. Ott was tall and bulky, big in the
rear like Audrey, with big dark cup-lidded eyes, set low and so wide
apart that it looked as if something might have been erased from between them. But he was supposed to be smart. He worked at Boeing
where our father worked.

Every child in the family had his big heavy eyeballs. I used to watch
Mary Catherine's from the side, as they roved to and fro over the
things in our room. It was true she was pretty, but being pretty, in
her, came close to being funny-looking, and then somehow overshot
it. This did not happen with Annie or Natalie, though my mother said
when they got older they would look like Mary Catherine.

Mr. Ott did not instruct or tease or in any way lead his family, or,
seemingly, take them anywhere, including the church for which the
others set off every Sunday before breakfast, bedraggled and hurrying.
You almost never heard his voice in the house. When you did it was
unexpectedly high, with a fretful sound in it. "Audrey? Audrey?"

He couldn't help his nature. So Audrey Ott said to my mother, who
repeated it, though ordinarily she did not seem to find the things
Audrey told her in the afternoon worth passing on, even if my father
took up the subject of the Otts at dinner.

Moping was what my father called it, but Mr. Ott was not a listless
or a sighing man. Something interested him in an intense way. Whatever it was it knotted his jaw muscles and made his glance, if it fell on
you, go straight down like a bird in a dive.

"Mary Catherine says her dad doesn't know our names!" Laura marveled.

"He may not know theirs," my father said from the next room. "Gil Ott is always minding the store," he would say, raising his eyebrow in the way we liked, "the store being himself. If he gets any gloomier they'll have to put windshield wipers on him."

No one said "depression." We didn't know the word, even my mother. We knew my father was never in a bad humor and did not believe in being down in the mouth or bored, or in mentioning it if you were. If we were sick he was in our room with plans for our being well the next day. He would bring in his *Brehm's Life of Animals*, or a volume of the Century Encyclopedia, so we could go through everything that began with A through C and forget our complaints.

Privately Laura and I drew up explanations for the bad luck of the Otts, every one, including the dog Mosquito. *They just don't know. Mosquito has never been trained.* Mosquito was tiny, a terrier of some kind, with splayed whiskers that made him look like one of those fish that suck the algae off aquarium sides. His joints were stiff and he bit. Often he had worms, from eating whatever he came across when he rooted in the ivy to find a place to lie down away from the Otts. When they found him he would come out snapping, pawing his fringed eyes. A car had hit him on our street, tearing his nose and dislocating his jaw so it stuck forward in an expression of fury. After she drove Audrey back from the vet, my mother said, "Mosquito's going to live. For once things went right for them."

"Yes and no," said my father.

Mosquito did not like to be petted or taken for walks. He was sensitive about the pads of his toes and could lick them for an hour at a time. He barked in his high, outraged register at cars, kids on bikes, flies on the windowpane, noises in the house at night.

Laura and I had no dog but we had rules for the treatment of animals. We instructed Mary Catherine, but not teasing animals was another doctrine mislaid or forgotten in their house. Mosquito was often trapped in Annie's doll carriage, being wheeled around panting. "He's carsick!" moaned Laura, who could not ride any distance in a car without throwing up, and could not even ride her new bike, to her bitter chagrin, because it made her dizzy. If James saw Mosquito in the carriage he would lift him out, under the arms, and cradle him away from Annie. For this, and for the long eyelashes that hid his opinions, we excused James from our dinnertime stories of the Otts, and even Mary Catherine left him out of her denunciations of her family.

Our house and the Otts' next door were on a street that was really a road, at one time a country road, my father said, with yards big enough to hold a horse and chickens. Some of the yards had tractor tires with flowers planted in them. We were in the broad valley south of Seattle, with the mountains in the near distance, close to the Boeing Company plant where the men worked, and behind our two houses was what we called the ivy field. It was a steep bank running up to dense holly trees that had marked the beginning of woods, though now there were houses you could see through the line of trees.

The ivy field was blanketed with a second crop of vines, morning glory, making it a lush, varied green from a distance. But it was dusty if you got into it, with things embedded in the vines: bottles, broken china, doll heads, and square gray sponges that had been newspaper, and pieces of stiff plaid shirt with the outlines of stems pressed into them. Cats and raccoons had made trails you could follow and broaden if you went in on your hands and knees through the anthills and cat leavings. Higher up you ran into fallen brown holly leaves that could stab you like thumbtacks, and thousands of dried-up holly berries that my father said were the toes of children who never found their way out. The smell inside the ivy was of many things dried and maybe edible, like pepper or tea.

For a while we played there with five of the Otts, Natalie being too little and bare, but eventually the ivy field came to belong to James and Owen, with Clark as guard because he was a crybaby who didn't go in under the vines, while we played at the edge, Laura, Mary Catherine, and I, and Annie if we couldn't escape her. Sometimes we would receive from James a password that allowed us to crawl in.

If you crawled in far enough, about halfway up to the holly trees, you dropped into a dusty cave in the slope where the vines went on uninterrupted above and the space seemed deliberately hollowed out for three or four to lie down in. There we played dead.

You had to get onto your back, feet down the bank, and be still, not even scratching. You could look up and see bits of sun running like mercury up the vines. At the same time we had made the provision that although dead, you could speak in a singsong voice and give reports of the place you had gone when you left your body.

"I wish my mom and dad would hurry up and die and get here!" Laura said, transported wholly into death and breaking, as she often did that year she was six, the rule that parents did not exist as part of any game.

"Not them!" Mary Catherine hissed, although she had been underfoot in our house trailing our mother all year, on the days she stayed home from school with her headaches.

Mary Catherine did not have headaches, Laura and I felt sure. She had the idea from her father and she wanted to be with our mother when we were not home. Around our mother, my father said, Mary Catherine was like a cat hoping to be stroked.

"I miss Mosquito," said Annie in the whine she thought was the dead voice, scrambling up so that her head hit the woven roof and showered us with seeds.

"Well, go get him then," said Mary Catherine, pushing Annie, knowing she would never crawl out alone. "He can be dead, too."

We had to stay there until the boys found us. When they did, they fell into the cave with their weapons, taking up all the room, jabbing us with sticks and knees and elbows. "We're dead," Mary Catherine protested angrily. Being found by her brothers, and by the unsmiling, intently playing James in particular, did not carry the queasy excitement for her that it did for Laura and me. But they drove us back along the slanting passageway and out into the sun where, once we were upright and squinting, captive, with dirt in our hair, they lost interest and went off to play basketball.

James was two years ahead of me in school when the Otts moved in, though he was to fall back. The third year after they came, when I was in the sixth grade, he got polio.

He just disappeared one day, into polio. Polio was vaguely related to what my father called the "conditions" at the Otts', which covered everything we could report of their shorted-out TV set, the scorched enamel of their stove, the failure of Owen and Clark to be properly toilet trained, their bent lawn mower that had run on its own up into the ivy, where the next spring all but the handlebars sank out of sight under the morning glory that wound itself onto the ivy.

"Oh, for heaven's sake," my mother said. "You girls are as prissy as a couple of parakeets. I'm going to write all of this down and read it to you when you have kids."

"Only please don't have six," my father said.

My mother said, "Audrey Ott does what she can with the situation."

"What situation?" we wanted to know.

"Mr. Ott," said my father with a wink.

But my father couldn't find anything to say when James got polio. During the school year he had put up a basket for James on our garage and taught him to shoot. James was out at the garage every morning before school and every afternoon when he got home. In no time he was better than my father. It was getting so he would call his orders out to us from under the basketball net, rather than lead the way into the ivy or be there barring us from it. "Go on in," he would say to me over his shoulder, which had changed shape. His upper arms showed muscle giving on muscle, sinking and locking in a way that offered a kind of rudeness to someone looking at them. "Go on in there, I don't care." But I didn't want to.

My father said, "That boy's going to play ball. This year. Hasn't got the height but he's accurate and he'll make the JV with his speed. The boy floats, Billie."

"I see that," my mother agreed. It was taken for granted that a man wanted a son.

After the basket went up Mr. Ott came out onto the porch and my father invited him to shoot with them. He put up his stiff hand to ward off the idea.

"Oh, Neil, he's heading down again, he's sad," my mother said. She always waved to Mr. Ott in the yard and sometimes sent my father over to help him with the lawn mower, before he aimed it at the ivy and let it go.

"There are the sad," my father said, "and there are the sad sacks."

Mr. Ott would be rubbing his little finger with his thumb, and then he would give the mower a heavy kick and wrench it over onto its side so that nuts popped or the gas cap came off and the gasoline ran into what grass was left in the yard. It was hard to say why these things were not funny when Mr. Ott did them.

My mother said, "If you men got together, Neil, Gil Ott could ride with you, and Audrey Ott could have the car once in a while." Once or twice when his car was not running Mr. Ott rode to work with my father, but this did not become a habit.

When James got polio, all the activity in the boys' room that we had watched from the tree came to an end. The boys went somewhere else in the house, where you couldn't see them, although their voices and the barking of Mosquito could still be heard. The doctors decreed a long period of quarantine, during which we were not allowed to play with the Otts. Any one of them could get polio and all of them probably carried it. During this time my mother's eyes followed us wherever we went. Every day she would look at our throats and feel our necks at the jawline and say with a tense look, "You don't feel achy anywhere?"

My father said, "Billie, you are going to have to face the fact that these girls are not going to pass away and leave you their money."

Mary Catherine waved whenever she passed a window, and stopped to twist her mouth into a scream, roll her eyes, and wind her hair in a strangling motion around her neck. Sometimes her voice on the phone would whisper, "It's awful over here."

"I know it is," I said. She belonged, we agreed, where there was no polio and for that matter none of Audrey's dried-up fish on Friday, no sister who couldn't learn to read and brothers whose smelly sheets had to be hauled out to the washing machine on the screened porch by Mary Catherine—a female responsibility that went with not needing punishment—and no father dumb with headache at the dinner table.

At Boeing Mr. Ott did something with chemicals that gave him headaches. When he had one of them he got a decayed look, like the fatigued bears we saw when we went up to the Woodland Park Zoo. He didn't go into his own bedroom and lie down on his own bed, and no wonder, everything in the house ended up there, he would have had to make room among the diapers and newspapers, and crumbs from eating toast in bed, and damp towels because the rods in the bathroom weren't fixed, and laundry, and Audrey Ott's old blue chenille robe with the hanging pocket.

He went into his boys' room and stretched out on one of the lower bunks. Laura and I looked in from the sycamore. You could see James's arm hanging off the bed while he read his comics, and Mr. Ott with his arm across his eyes in the other bunk that formed an L with James's.

Unlike us, with our sense of importance, Mary Catherine found nothing too private to tell. She told where the boys kept things they had stolen, how Owen and Clark both still wet the bed and the test showed Annie had a low IQ and Clark had ringworm on his penis because he played with it with his dirty little fingers. She told when her father worked for weeks on a letter to the newspaper about the Korean War. He had fought in it and had the idea no one understood things that had happened there. His letter was not published on Veterans Day, for which he had written it, and was not published in the ensuing weeks while the family waited. She told when her mother had diarrhea all night, and when she cried. Worst of all she told the story of a shooting witnessed by her father.

The husband of a secretary came in with a gun and shot his wife, and Mr. Ott, who was standing right there, didn't do a thing. Mary Catherine told how afraid he had been, so afraid he had had to drop into a chair with a pain in his chest.

"Hmm," said my father at dinner when Laura finished with the story.

"Well, I wonder if he shouldn't have made a citizen's arrest," said my mother in a voice that did not prevent Laura from starting to tell it all over again.

"This is a gal who drove her husband nuts," my father said. "I do know"—raising his glass of milk to my mother—"I'd want somebody other than Gil Ott to be there if you were going to get shot at."

"How about these girls?" my mother said.

"You mean you!" Laura shouted, pointing at him. Our father was not out in the open at Boeing the way Mary Catherine's father had been, he had an office.

"Well?" said my mother. "*Well?* Is she dead?"

"She's fit as a fiddle. All he did was wing her."

"Oh, is that all he did?" said my mother. "Well. Well then. She could just keep right on typing."

"Now, Billie," my father said.

The afternoon the police came, Mary Catherine was in our room. The quarantine was over; James was supposed to begin his recovery. "He can't pee, though. Mom's so worried she screamed and yelled at Dad and then she stayed up all night in the kitchen." How strange, Laura and I thought, to hear your parents speak of things they did not know what to do about, things that made them scream. "And when they make up—they always do that, make up—oh, oh, oh, that's even worse!"

Then James went into the hospital, where he stayed for weeks.

How strange, how possibly unfair, that there was happiness such as ours, and unhappiness such as theirs. Strange that Mr. and Mrs. Ott had married each other and produced six others, who would have been nowhere on earth otherwise, to live in that house among the broken appliances and strange, ignored repetitive prayers. How did one know how many children to have? What if you did not love them once you had them? Worse, what if one of them did not love you?

What if you didn't have any idea what anybody else thought of you, or realize that they saw you through the window when you got out of the car together and walked in holding on like a pair in a three-legged race, with your shoulders rubbing and your hips bumping together, or that they heard you not answering anybody except the baby, or knew you had sent all your kids out of the house at once, so that they ended up at our house all afternoon?

Strange that Mr. Ott should have as his daughter Mary Catherine, who came hushing and giggling to tell us when he got an Unsatisfactory at work. That James should be part of that house, and get polio, and disappear into his bedroom, James, tall and hard, able to twist your arm till you fell, able to grab the rim of the basket and make it clatter.

The luck was bad, in the Otts' house. Laura and I could feel it when we went through the front door, a fall in expectation, a penalty attached to being in the house. Diapers, bottles, coat hangers, and shoes piled in the baby carriage in the hall. Baby crying, loud warbling of the toilet that never stopped running. If Mr. Ott was home, a superficial quiet, broken by thumps of the younger boys' fighting upstairs. Mosquito dashing out if you left the door open. Mary Catherine yelling, "Catch him! And let's get out of here!"

The two policemen came up onto the Otts' porch and Audrey Ott opened the door. Mary Catherine gave a loud sigh. "I bet it's the bills. They have so many bills in that drawer that she says we could use them to burn the house down."

We knew this kitchen drawer, stuffed with papers and books of green stamps that kept it from shutting. "What good would that do?"

"Insurance," said Mary Catherine.

After a long time the policemen came out. They did not look our way. Although Mary Catherine had been glancing across the yard all afternoon, she did not go home to find out what had happened. And the next day she said nothing. We told our parents about the policemen. "That could be anything," said my mother.

There followed a month during which we often saw the two officers and strangers in suits calling on Audrey Ott during the daytime. When Audrey came over she and my mother closed the kitchen door. Eventually we stayed up and listened from the stairs to what our parents were saying, and we heard the word murder.

Two murders, actually. Early in the summer two women who worked at Boeing had disappeared, the same week. They had not been found but there was blood on something. Several times the word blood was said. We looked at each other. Something stuffed into a trash can had belonged to one of the women, and then a purse was found near the plant.

One of the women had worked in Mr. Ott's division. They had disappeared the week Mr. Ott put on the neck brace he had been wearing all summer. A man of his description had been seen in a car the color of the Otts', offering one, though not both, of the women a ride.

My parents went over and over this story.

"But Neil—"

"But Billie—"

I did not think of the two women—I thought of an act that completed Mr. Ott at last. It was a terrible act, to match his eyes and his awful secretive sadness. On the stairs with me Laura had started to giggle into her hands. "Stop it!" I whispered, yanking her hair so the barrette flew out and landed downstairs in the hall and our father came out into the hall to send us to bed. But he was making a face and he winked up at us, as if all the secret talking about the Otts were just a scheme between our parents, like where to hide the Christmas presents.

Later that week Mary Catherine said, "They never pay the bills." We were sitting with our Ginny dolls at the edge of the ivy field. Mosquito lay dipping his tiny tongue like a bit of balloon between his toes. Owen was camouflaged in the vines halfway up the hill, reduced without James to shooting the hard berries down at us. "Dad never pays," Mary Catherine repeated, unsnapping the long suckers of baby ivy that were always creeping out onto the grass. She glared at us. "They can put you in jail for that," she said finally.

"Did you see how red her face was?" Laura said later. "Oh what, oh what if she knew?"

Not long after that the policemen came to interview our mother. She took them into the kitchen and shut the door.

What did she think? If our father talked about it, it would seem that something else altogether was happening, something of much less importance, possibly even something we could laugh at. But our mother would have an opinion. And she would be right. But whether she would tell us what her real opinion was we did not know. She would not necessarily feel obliged to tell us the truth as she saw it. That was the thing about her that I had been working out. She would not necessarily think the truth belonged with us, she might even think it was for the Otts alone, or for herself if they included her.

I heard her say something, down in the basement. I don't know what she said to herself, doing the wash, in a deep, tired voice. As she came up the stairs I said, "Did Mr. Ott kill somebody?" She had a stack of folded sheets in her arms—we had a dryer by that time—and she put them carefully down on the kitchen table. "Sit down," she said. "Laura, come here a minute."

In the middle of the story our father came home from work. "Well, well, what have we here? Am I intruding on a female matter?"

I pressed on. "OK, do you think he killed them? He's so strange."

"And so are you. And so is Laura. And so am I," our mother said in a louder voice than usual.

"But we're . . . we're . . ."

"We're what?" she cried, with none of the pity she normally mixed in with any disfavor.

"OK." I took the offensive. "OK then, if he didn't do it why do they all think he did?"

"We don't know that they think that." We went on like this for some time. Finally my mother turned her back and picked up the laundry. "I think I've had enough of this subject," she said, "and it's none of our business, anyway." She sounded as if she were ready to cry. If he were innocent, why would she cry?

"None of our business? If he killed people—"

"Karen, I believe you are hoping he did," she said with her back to us.

"Time will tell. Either he did," said my father, lifting the lid of a pan on the stove, "or he didn't."

I thought, *If he thinks Mr. Ott did it, he should be afraid. Or maybe sad.*

My mother turned around. "And *you*. You think—whatever it is. You think whatever it is you think because he has a fat ass." This was a word that had not been used in our house. It had been buried with all the language of my drunken grandparents—with the very memory of them, of whom we had no picture, told no stories. "And if you don't want their kids over here, you be the one to tell them not to come."

The next day four men in overalls came with scythes and rakes and shovels and tore up the ivy field. All the years of layers that had fastened into the hill, with the morning glory wound onto the tough ivy, they hacked out and threw into wheelbarrows, which they heaved up and rocked down the hill and across the yard to their truck. The Otts' lawn mower appeared, humbled with rust.

"They have some sort of permit," my mother kept saying. She watched all day. Twice she said wearily, "I wonder how old that ivy would be."

The men raked the naked dirt and put the toys, scraps of cloth, chunks of newspaper, and everything else that fell out of the vines into burlap bags. They stabbed long sticks into the dirt and shoveled it here and there and then raked it neatly back, but it was still just a bank of gray dirt with a cave in the middle and a few low bushes, where the ivy field had been.

Mr. Ott came out. I looked over and he was on the steps of the screened porch watching, scraping his little finger with his thumb. His head stood stiffly on top of the neck brace and the rest of him sagged. He was home from work every day now, on a leave of absence, according to my mother. Why would they let him stand on the porch and watch? And Audrey had gone off to work, as if nothing were happening. Out of the blue she had a job at the Safeway.

What would it be like to be married to somebody who had, who might have, put bloody clothes in a bin and then come home to eat and go to the bathroom and sit on the couch with everybody else? What would it be like to be—worse than being his daughter, his daughters didn't pay any attention to him—his son? James. My skin went hot. After a long time, but before they finished with the raking, Mr. Ott went in.

In the evening I climbed up the sycamore tree while Laura was having her hair washed and set in bobby pins for her birthday party the next day. My mother had done Mary Catherine's first and sent her home. My father stood in the hall outside our room making faces. "What about Annie, are you going to do her, too?" he said, winking at us.

"And Natalie Wood!" crowed Laura.

"Mary Catherine needed her hair put up," my mother said. "Audrey Ott had her hands full."

The Otts' house was in darkness except for the boys' room. There they were, the whole family, in the boys' room, James in his bed with the crutches propped against it, Mary Catherine in her pin curls, Clark and Owen sitting on the top bunk with their legs dangling, and Annie, and even Natalie on the floor in her diaper, all listening to whoever was talking. It must have been Mr. Ott.

"He's telling them," I thought. He had on dark glasses and his neck brace. None of them, not even Mary Catherine, looked out at the tree where I was sitting. There they all were, and it gave me a shiver to see them all in one room, saying things that could not be heard. It made me wonder if Mary Catherine did not, after all, keep back something, if there might be something she didn't say, that belonged to the Otts as our jokes and stories and the wreck our grandparents were in and the things in our house belonged to our family and no other. But how could the Otts, in their mess and ignorance, with Mary Catherine spying on all they did wrong or never got done, everything they didn't do that had to be done to confer rightness, and the awful suspicion at the center of everything— how could they possess this thing? Yet there they were in James's room.

On the way down my hands let go before I was steady on the branch I usually jumped from. I teetered backward and landed on the gravel.

For a second I thought I might be dead, or close to dead, as I tried to get the first gasp of air. When I could breathe again I lay there bending and unbending my arm while the boys' lit-up window hung above me. There was the window of my own house showing the dining room light fixture on the ceiling. I began to resent my mistake, and to cry. After a while I got up, inspected my cuts, and limped to the door. I stood on one foot and looked in. If I had been lying with a broken neck they wouldn't know yet. Laura said, "Oh! Look at Karen! Eeuw, blood!" My mother took me upstairs and painted mercurochrome on my elbows and leg. Sitting on the edge of the bathtub I closed my eyes and deliberately swayed in her direction. When we came downstairs she went over to my father's chair and said in a low voice, "Neil, she's dizzy. She couldn't have fractured her skull, could she?"

"What's that?" said my father, cupping his ear with a grin.

"I'm asking you if you think she might have hurt herself," she said.

"Look at her. A little fall out of a tree? Nothing to a healthy eleven-year-old."

My mother stood where she was. Then she went as far as the doorway and turned back. "Is anything serious to you? Is anything? Some people's kids fall out of trees and get killed. Some people get murdered. Oh, go ahead and laugh. What makes you so sure? What makes you think nothing will happen to us? Do you think we're so wonderful? I'll bet you think some people deserve to fraction"—I remember in her haste she said "fraction"—"their skulls but not us? I'll bet you think people who die deserved it. If they have a horrible death they must deserve it. That's the way you think."

As far as I could remember nothing had ever been said about the way any one of us thought. As soon as she said it I saw that people think in ways, and from there I leapt to the opinion that my father's way was not, after all, mine. He could not think of an answer. In his chair he cocked his head and held out his hands to my mother.

She said, "I will not sit on your lap."

He had an idea, his eyes twinkled with it. "I know what. Let's call the doctor."

"No!" It was almost a shout. "Don't you *dare* get on the phone with him and laugh at me. No, leave me alone." But she didn't leave the doorway. For a long time she stood pushing at the rug with her foot. When he stood up she said, "Don't come over here." And then she said something else, very low. She said, "I can't stand you any more." I thought that was what she said. But maybe I heard wrong and it was only "I can't stand it any more."

My father pretended, and we all pretended, that she hadn't said any of this. He got up shedding his newspaper and went into the bathroom.

My father was right, there was nothing the matter with me. I tried to think of a way to undo that moment of pretending I might faint, that had led to these things being said. Laura ran back and forth, cooling off the washcloth my mother gave her to put on my forehead. With her small, cushiony fingers she pushed my bangs out of the way. I had my hair short and straight, now, like my mother's. I felt sorry for Laura, in her pin curls, on the eve of her ninth birthday. She seemed to know nothing. I saw that although she kept her schoolbooks in a neat line and could knit like my mother, as I could not, really Laura was like my father.

She didn't know what murder was, when it was more than a gunshot on TV, when it was women with their blouses soaked in blood. She didn't consider that people by the thousands were alive right that minute who would be dead in the next minute, while someone was still expecting them to come through the door, or no one expecting them because they were dead in cars like our grandparents, because of being drunk, and the phone ringing on and on in three houses to find the right daughter, the one who would wake her family with her sobs.

Laura never read about polio in the encyclopedia, or knew what really happened to nerves and muscles if you got it, what had happened to James. She knew nothing. I had passed beyond everything that concerned her.

In August the bodies were found. A week later they caught the murderer. It was not Mr. Ott, it was a big ugly man—even the paper quoted a neighbor saying "ugly"—with a similar car who did not work at Boeing. One of the women had lived in his building.

Mr. Ott did not kill anyone.

One day we saw Audrey, who didn't come over any more now that she worked at the Safeway, out digging in the old bare ivy field. My mother rushed out. "What are you doing, Audrey?" she said. "Are you planting?"

"I'm burying Mosquito," Audrey said. "I think something ruptured when Gil tripped over him."

"Oh, no," said my mother. She went close to Audrey. "Oh, Audrey. He was so old and brittle."

"He was barking at I don't know what and Gil tripped over him, coming off the bed. He had his shoes on, he was lying down with them on," said Audrey Ott, as if she had caught from Mary Catherine the requirement of leaving nothing out. "With the pregnancy I get sick thinking about it. But Billie, he didn't mean to. He was half asleep. He loved that dog. I don't know what to do for him. He feels so awful."

"I know that," said my mother. I knew it, too, when I heard her say it.

"It was the headache. And now he feels worse than ever," Audrey said, still talking in that odd, practical voice. "Billie, I don't know how that man is going to keep going. I don't know what's going to happen. But at least"—she started digging with the trowel again—"he has the baby to look forward to."

"He does," my mother said tenderly. "Oh, Audrey, I'm so sorry about everything."

"I know you are," said Audrey.

I said, "Me too."

"Girls, go on, go on," said my mother, flinging out her hand as if we were cats. "You don't need to be here."

"Oh, let them," said Audrey. "They always liked Mosquito." She threw her ponytail back and continued to dig the grave. "Mary Catherine was so careful. She brushed him, she wrapped him." He was wrapped in Audrey's chenille bathrobe. Owen and Mary Catherine and Clark filed out and stood there. "Annie won't come," Owen said. "She's in there. She won't stop crying."

"Well, that's all right," said my mother, as if she were part of it and had some authority to judge. Mary Catherine knelt and laid the blue package in the shallow hole. "I wish we had the ivy," she said as she turned the dirt in with her hands.

She and my mother were the ones who cried. "Oh, Audrey, are you really going to move now?" my mother said, with tears not in neat lines but all over her cheeks, and the skin around her mouth getting red.

"I don't think so," said Audrey. "It's close to work. And I think he can go back to his job. I don't know if he will. You know how he is. I just don't know, Billie."

"Oh Audrey," my mother said again. "At least you're not going to move. And the baby . . ."

At the end of the summer my father got a promotion and we were the ones who moved, up to Seattle where the company offices were. Audrey had no car so if my mother ever saw the baby she would have had to drive down to see Audrey. Most people took moving, in those days, in a less qualified way. You said good-bye, you moved; you did not expect the reprieve of visiting.

Laura and I were busy getting used to a new school, we forgot a baby was going to be born.

Our parents began to fight, to the extent that my father could fight when he saw no need for it. Our stories at the dinner table were not so lively; the ground at our new school was not yet firm enough for jokes. We egged my father on as he sank into a confusion of stories about his new office. My mother sat like a driver in the left lane waiting to turn. Laura and I strained to show her how to be interested, how to resume where we had left off early in the summer before there had been any murders. At night she sometimes stood in the doorway of my room or Laura's while we were doing our homework. She might have tried to say what she was getting ready to do. We shut our ears.

But she had done them anyway, my father had abased himself with tears, and Laura had screamed her wish to move away with him by the time I went up the steps of the high school and saw a way to blot them all out in loves of my own.

I know my mother never offered to take us to see Mary Catherine. I can't be sure whether we asked. Years later, in the apartment where she lived, I asked her about the Otts' baby and she said yes, she had seen her. A girl. "But with Audrey, I had to be close by, for us to be friends. We had to be living the same life."

That stopped me, at the time. The incomprehensible belief that we were leading the same life as the Otts.

"Audrey Ott," she said sadly.

Mr. Ott did not come out of the house for the burial of Mosquito. Probably he had gone up to James's room. Especially since his son was there so much of the time now, he liked to lie on the other bunk with his headache and his sadness, the kind that leads to the death of something, resembling some kinds of happiness in that way.

novel of rose

This would be the novel of Rose. First, two stone houses on adjacent hills, in the long pause after the war when everyone in Virginia was raising children. Five chimneys between them. Seven children, four parents, two dogs, the same cat seen in the grass and moving from window to window in both houses, old walnut trees dropping black fruit, locust trees in the fencerows, with groundhog tunnels in their roots. Innumerable empty shells of the real locust, the insect, a wheat-spun-to-glass color, clinging to bark and fencepost one particular year, the year Varden first unsparingly, despairingly loved Rose.

Anne and Sarah—the Montgomery girls. Their younger brothers Roger, known as Mont, and Varden. At the time Rose's family arrived, Varden Montgomery was seven.

Will, David, Rose. Two boys and a rose. The Chestons. Rose, also seven, was an Indian, a Tamil, the Chestons said, though as she grew everybody saw that at the same time she was so dark, she looked like Mary Cheston. She had the same gravelly voice her brothers had from their mother, as well. The Chestons had gone away to India and stayed years. They had gone with two children and come back with three. The novel of Rose would go into the trouble a Virginia grade school made about her color.

James Cheston was a doctor but not a rich one. With money from Mary Cheston's family they bought the house next to the Montgomerys, out of shouting distance but always seen as an offspring of the big old Montgomery place. In actuality it had been the original barn, a stone structure on the lower hill, accumulating dignity because of its years in county memory, and the time and labor that had gone into its conversion—the carving out of windows, for one thing, in stone walls two feet thick. And then it was a house, an immediate landmark, facing half away from the main house onto vistas of its own.

By the time the Chestons bought it the house itself was old, and grown shabby inside, with a remnant of rat society, descendants of the barn-raiders of the century before, still holding certain passages in the walls.

Seven children pounded up the steep front steps and landed against the screen door, where, if they yelled a password in time, they were safe. The screen hung ruined. If it was a Saturday and James Cheston was not out on a house call, he would speak quietly to the winner, who when she reappeared—for Rose, though the youngest, was the fastest—would tear unredeemed down the steps into the pack and down the hill.

At that time their ages ranged from seven to eleven, and for a year or two the older girls, Anne and Sarah Montgomery, played as wildly as any of them, wearing necklaces of locust shells they never would have touched had not Rose been the one who strung them.

They always played on the Chestons' hill. The Chestons were the newcomers but they held the power. Partly because of their foreignness, their greater indifference to risk, but more the result of their deep voices, they prevailed over the Montgomerys. Their courage, passed to each one like an allowance from the father, who after fighting in the war had gone into the hills of India to fight malaria, led them into proud dangers. It was nothing to them to climb out onto roofs and use the chimneys as base, squeeze into laundry chutes, excavate groundhog holes to make caves, creep up on the neighbor's

bull, play on tractors parked out of sight of either house. Their inno-
cence, another gift of the father, kept them from cruelty, from the
clever reprisals Mont Montgomery was known for at school. As it
was, Mont gave up some of his own ambitions in order to be with the
Chestons, though to his sisters he made fun of the Hindi patois they
could chatter in their odd, deep voices. "Abela-babela," the Montgomerys, except Varden, called it. In time Will Cheston, oldest of the
boys, held them all in a willing servitude. His rule developed without
any intention on his part, because like his father he was half shy when
not outdoors, where his daring carried him away.

The other factor in the ascendancy of the Chestons was Rose.

Like her mother and father, Rose had a sweet nature to go with
her beauty. At the thought of her, of something she had said, Varden
would stumble as easily as at the sight of her, streaking downhill with
the dogs to the fort in the locust trees. She always beat him. Her
speed and relentlessness in a race gave way to appeasement and little
gifts—dandelions and violets out of the grass—for him. But she gave
them to the others, too.

When Anne Montgomery faded into her teens, she tried to get her
sister Sarah and Rose indoors and upstairs, where on one occasion
Rose was induced to have her heavy hair put up in bobby pins.

By then Varden Montgomery was far gone. He hung in the doorway
when the dampened hair was being rolled into black coins. The effort
to make any movement casual set his face in a spasm. Now he was
ten, with no foreknowledge that his voice would not change until
he was fourteen. In his bed at night he tried to pitch it to the low
enchanting hoarseness of the Cheston boys, and Rose, Rose too—all
of them had the mother's soft growl. Varden loved the mother, too,
Mary Cheston, who seemed to know his feelings and even to expect
them, who gave off a faint scent his mother said was curry powder,
and whose eyebrows tapered like Rose's, though not so dark, in long
arches his mother told his sister Anne not to attempt on herself with
an eyebrow pencil.

Now Anne wore lipstick and kept to her room reading *Silver Screen*
with the cat in her lap, though she sat by the open window and looked

out when they were running. Now they were six, four boys and two girls. The fort was a castle in India. The boys and Sarah were defenders of the perimeter, Rose the queen.

In the novel of Rose, this would be the childhood in which some secret was embedded, to be unraveled in later life and serve as evidence that things proceed from a cause.

Varden Montgomery's love twisted his insides, he thrashed in his sheets to get at the root of it. A kiss, his shut lips on the open laughing ones of Rose, burned his inexpert mind at Scout campfires. Eventually he would surprise himself with success in sports, reach high school, Yale, and so on, and practice law like his father and brother Mont, though milder than either in a courtroom. He would marry and have two children.

Before his marriage he bought out his siblings to own the house where they had grown up and where the dog and cat were buried, and at his insistence the Chestons' dog. He did not live there, and in time he let it go and had a rough likeness of it built elsewhere out of lighter materials.

It was long before this that Will Cheston, seated at the dinner table, saw a tear drip from his father's jaw.

Mary Cheston went back to India, taking Rose.

Sarah Montgomery got a Fulbright to India and found Rose. The two of them came back and lived years together in New York. In the novel, these years would have the figure of a dance, a kind of reel. Rose would dance first with Sarah and then with others, and then, keeping to the nature of dance, with a final partner entering from the dark of the scenery.

Will Cheston died in Vietnam. Varden's children never knew their aunt Sarah, who stayed in New York, pursuing Rose for many years. Rose slowed her speed. A still point was coming. Resolution. The novel must end in a satisfaction of sorts. The ones who follow instead a logic of their own, succumb to it and end in the ground.

In India, Mary Cheston is speaking of her dead son Will to someone who listens with his hands clasped. The younger son, named David, the other brother of Rose: Did everyone forget him? What happened to him? And so on. The novel would have gone into this. Though the novel might not linger over the house in India as it did the ones in Virginia, in the novel we would see the man. He would be in some contrast to the soldier's mustache and doctor's kindness of James Cheston. What could he be like, to exceed these things? The novel would have told us. We will never know.

criminals

T he time came for Jean to meet Michael's friends. Like his
housemates, the friends, two women and a man, were his
own age, a dozen years younger than Jean who was forty,
something she knew was not going to matter to them because they
were easygoing about everything, while Jean kept coming back to the
fact that she had been a girl of thirteen when somebody was weighing
the newborn Michael, the size of a kitten as his mother always told
him, on the little scale for preemies.

She sat half awake at Michael's picnic table in the sun, waiting
for his friends to arrive. Dozens of tiny birds had swooped into the
forsythia and made it blink with bits of gray. They were the minute,
restless bushtits she had once watched in her own yard in summer, at
a time when she had paid attention to birds and looked them up in
guides, a time when she had had interests.

The table occupied a clearing in the yard, under a gnarled cherry
tree with a net over it. Mylar balloons printed with owls' eyes flew
from strings tied to the net, and higher up, wired onto the gutters of
the house, sat two large, real-looking plastic owls. All of this was to
protect Michael's cherries. The yard was full of lumber and sawhorses

because he was remodeling and had just finished ripping out the back steps, so going in and out of the house they had to use a ramp.

The three friends came through the gate, threw down their packs, and shook her hand. Before she knew it that part was over and they had opened beers from the cooler and straddled the picnic benches. They cut into Michael's bread and soon they were all, all but Jean, talking lazily in the sun. They were complaining about music. They didn't know all the songs the way they had even a few years ago, when there was a song for each of their occasions, each of their moods.

They seemed little more than children. Yet one of them—Jean could not remember which one—worked in the DA's office with Michael.

The conversation turned to song titles and Jean heard herself enter it. "I used to wonder why there's no song called 'I'm Pregnant.' A happy song."

There was a moment and then it caught. "A girl song! Or how about 'I've Got My Period,'" said one of the women, the one with the shining, light-brown braid. Lisa. She had swung her long leg over the bench and begun tearing wedges of bread off the loaf Michael had made, spreading cream cheese and cherry jam, talking with her mouth full. "Well, that's an important occasion. And for some of us it was a real cause for celebration. When it first came, I mean. And then of course many times afterward," she added, licking her fingers, "so I guess the song would be ambiguous. Michael, your jam is incredible."

"It's the cherries," said Michael. They all gazed up at the protected tree. "Starlings. They'd get 'em all." Everything you do, Jean thought, all this shoring up of house and yard every weekend, making jam, growing zucchini, for God's sake, all of it is orderly. It's all planned, it's careful, you write it down in those notebooks of yours. What for? Is it important? Why be so careful and ceremonious? Of course it was because he was a lawyer—or did he say "attorney," the way people his age liked to?—why be a lawyer at all at his age, and in the prosecutor's office, when it didn't suit him—surely when he had children he would not be good at punishing them—why try to do it, or any of the complicated, futile projects he engaged in, if not out of pride masquerading as modesty and simplicity? And yet he seemed modest, simple, kind.

By a silent agreement they did not have to work at any conventional understanding of each other, they had bypassed that. If they were seriously interested in each other, and it was not clear that they were, it was in some other way.

"But why not 'I'm Pregnant'?" Jean persisted, realizing as she said it that it sounded like an effort to turn things in her own direction. Neither of the women at the picnic table had yet been pregnant, as far as she knew. Or no children, anyway. No marriages. No deaths.

"Yeah," said Lisa thoughtfully. "Maybe a reggae. Hmm. There's 'Having Your Baby.'"

"That's different."

"What about the poor pregnant teenager?" said Steve. Already Jean didn't care for Steve because of his frequent soft, confident laughter, and her suspicion that he was the other prosecutor. "'I'm Pregnant' would be like 'oh God, what am I gonna do now?' It's kids that songs are for now, they don't write them for us." He ended with the soft laugh.

"Country songs, they do." Jean looked up because this was said by Michael.

"For you, maybe." Steve slapped Michael on the plaid flannel of his small, hard shoulder.

Michael had persuaded Jean to spend a weekend with him, then another. They did not sleep together. Why was he pursuing her? The question made her queasy. I am, she said to herself, like a can of something in the back of the refrigerator. Web and mold. But not mold, because I'm not alive. You don't know that, though, she thought, eyeing Michael, so you can't be blamed. Or if you said "dead," it would be a metaphor.

The sun was high. It was afternoon on Sunday, on his mowed grass with the neatly stacked lumber, netted tree, tomato plants and trellised peas, picnic table, all encircled by the high cedar fence he had built, with a row of hollyhocks growing up against it. In the spaces between forsythia bushes he had planted the tall flowers, soft, worn-looking blossoms with furred leaves. That was what he liked, that suggestion, in the countrified pink flowers, that nothing in the tiny field inside the fence had to do with what was outside it—the freeway they could hear gusting close by, the courtroom a few miles down it where he went in his gray suits. But Jean didn't want to be in a little field. She was waiting for the friends to go so she could say good-bye to Michael in some acceptable but abbreviated way and get back to her own unmowed, flowerless yard, her house. Her house! Her heart gave a throb of appetite and fear.

"Maybe you should move," Michael had said. At that time he hardly knew her, her friends pointed out. But he hadn't said, as those friends of hers, friends now half forgotten, had said, "What's in that house for you?"

She couldn't tell them, but she had told Michael. *His soul.* His soul is there. It hasn't gone, not yet. I can't leave. I don't like to be away this long, a whole weekend.

"OK, Jean," was all Michael would say to her wild look. Pity. She recognized his talent for graceful pity. A person could cry in the rather sharp hollow of his neck and shoulder, certainly; she had done so. But she would not again. Tears were not what they had been on that occasion. Tears had reverted that one time to their old purpose of cleansing and relief. Usually they were more like vomiting, they worked on the muscles, and now the few times they came, mostly in the car, she felt afterward as if she had fallen down the stairs.

"Have you considered seeing somebody?" This he threw out lightly, while he was making the bed. She had been standing at the new window the whole time he was putting the room in order because he was going to give his friends a tour of the house. She had picked up her things, there was no reason not to stand there a little longer and lean her head on the glass.

"Who, a counselor, a grief counselor?" She stopped him with her palms on his chest.

"Oh, right, I'm talking wellness." In the morning, climbing the hill in silence after he made her get out of bed and put on clothes and walk around the lake with him, they had seen it, the bumper sticker. "Visualize Wellness." Jean was out of shape and couldn't get her breath. The three-mile walk, the steep grade were nothing to Michael, a five-mile run barely raised a sweat, but when he walked with her he always stopped to give her a rest. This time he leaned on the car with the bumper sticker and screwed up his face. "I'm vi-sualizing. I think I'm getting it." He opened his eyes. "I'm not going to say what it is, though. Each person has to see Wellness for him or herself."

He never came closer than she wanted. Now he was letting her stand at the window in his bedroom. If she wanted to she could stand there all day without moving, just looking out and smelling the wood; he would not interfere. He merely said, "I would not make sugges-tions to a person unless"—he paused—"I really wanted her to be in OK shape so I could use her and cast her aside without any qualms. Because she's older. And us young guys don't have any conscience yet. That comes when you're forty."

"Well, maybe it does. And conscience is going to keep us together?"

"Oh, you want to keep together?"

"Oh, Michael." She did like using his name. It had been the name of her son's best friend. Was still his name. Michael. She could hear it being called down the stairwell in a voice. Out the window in a voice. *Hey! Michael!* "They'll be here and you won't have any lunch ready," she told him.

"I'm not giving them anything except bread. Bread with accom-paniments." But he had made the bread. There were men like this in Seattle still.

In the mornings his room was filled with dusty sunbeams, and when she lay trying not to wake up all the way she could feel sawdust in the sheets. Though he did not have to, Michael shared the house, like most people on his street, in his part of town just across the freeway from the university. Several houses on his street were starting to re-ceive new roofs and paint and to have their deep porches, which had been converted to front bedrooms, opened back up. He was taking part in all this, happily but with a certain fixedness, as if he had to invent the methods of renovation.

His housemates were away bicycling for the weekend. She had stood beside him to wave them off yesterday morning, with their bikes locked in frames on top of their van, two kids even younger than he, in those shiny black skintight pants everybody wore now to bike in, with small helmets and goggles, and tight mesh sleeveless T-shirts. They had shown her their slim packs of dried food. "Well, have fun," they said together, and smiled at the couple on the porch being left alone in the house, new lovers, seemingly. They were sincere, wishing Michael well, the one with his coppery beard and the other blond and open-faced. They were so direct, like Michael, that looking into their eyes Jean thought, I must stop lying all the time and just tell the truth, just say . . . nothing. That is the truth. Nothing nothing nothing nothing nothing.

Why do I pretend to be nice? she thought, shaking their strong hands. I had friends of my own and they let me be. Why am I standing here with friends of his, as if I were nobody? Because I'm nobody, she replied to herself, nobody and nothing. But she didn't mean it. She was something. Something high up and loosely put together, like a cliff nest of debris and bones and shed, hollow feathers.

Why would he have put his arms around a person like that when the car broke down?

They had met when her car stopped on the freeway. It was late at night, raining, after she finally went to see a movie. Her first in seven months. Coming out into the parking lot in the rain she could not have said what movie had played, but her head was aching with cha-grin at all the color, the woman's careless babbling, the foolishness, the man's inconsequentiality, the failure of anyone to account for the emotions being enacted. Children are born because of characters like you, she thought, born and made to live and made to go through whatever happens to them because you—*you*—

With a pounding in her head she drove onto the freeway.

The timing belt, Michael said later. The car just sank to a stop. She was a good driver; she had time to realize what was happening, change lanes, steer onto the narrow shoulder against the wall of the on-ramp, all before it came to a stop, like a top spinning its last and falling on its side. The rain droned on, the windshield wipers had not stopped. Of all the possible passers down the freeway at midnight—the murderer, the guy strung out on drugs who would force her to let him into her house where he would torture her—the man who walked into the red of her taillights with his arms out from his body to show no ill intent was Michael.

He came into her rearview mirror as a shape, outlined in rain by his own headlights.

While she was explaining, she let him get into the car out of the rain, because he was short. I'm taller, she thought, probably stronger. He can't hurt me. Though when she sagged against him she felt the muscles, like small sandbags.

His pleasantness in response to her tight voice explaining that she had never had any car trouble brought on one of the bad episodes. She cried for fifteen minutes. My son is dead! she said repeatedly, shouting almost, in the shut car. He was ten years old! Ten! And he, turned in his seat facing her with his arm on the dashboard, had drawn a black 10 with his finger on the fogged windshield. There was traffic, cars passing so close they shook hers with a *whump*. So this is hysteria, she thought. It was exactly like being drunk, the impossible load of wrath coming up from somewhere, the operatic gestures with hands on slimy face. And I, she whispered coldly, raising her head, when she got herself stopped, I was at the wheel.

Did he say, What happened? No, he must have said very little, but mysteriously conveyed his nonresistance to being told. Finally he put his arms around her. He was a hard, small man like a jockey. She accepted his offer of coffee at the International House of Pancakes.

On down the freeway to the University District he drove in his loud van, where in the dashboard lights she saw a pointed face with something impassive in it, abstracted, despite all the drama of her crying, which still seemed to echo around them. She looked into the back. No seats. Rope, boards, a gasoline can. He could tie me up and set fire to me, she thought, or lug me down the bank to the lake and roll me in. She looked again. No, there were bags of tied newspapers, bags of flattened cans. Recycling. Not a killer.

He said, "Don't worry, I'm not a killer."

She entered the House of Pancakes furtively, surprising even herself with the sight of her face, gnarled like a mop, in the dark glass of the door. But it didn't matter, because, blessedly, nothing mattered. It was the first time in months that these disfiguring tears had soothed her. She was released from all matters, in the steaming room with its brown and orange blinds half down like weary eyelids over the rivers of drips on the windows.

They sat down. He did not say anything sympathetic but explained again what he thought had happened to the car. Then he went to call the police, and later when she reached for the check he covered her hand with his.

"What is with you?" she heard herself say. "Are you a pervert?"

"Am I what?" he said softly, as if asking their joined hands.

"I mean, do you like suffering middle-aged hags?"

"Some," he said with a dignified smile.

Two of his friends were lawyers, Jean knew that, but most of them had nothing to do with his work; he had friends all over the city who sought him out. Why? Because of his unusual good nature? She ought to listen to the friends, look them in the eye, stop making statements. Of course he had told them about her, and they were prepared to like her. The fresh-faced Lisa, like a diligent little girl, was trying to appreciate everything she said from the perspective Lisa assumed her to have, of a bereaved person.

The sun shone, the birds in the weedy forsythia along the fence had begun a liquid chatter. This was a Sunday afternoon in life. And she was here. Whereas he, her son . . . had become a soul. The soul did not follow her when she went out, but stayed where it was. Where? If anyone tried to pin her down she could not say. But somewhere in the house. It might be in search of her, because on a Sunday, until recently, she had always been there. Looking for her, in its trapped, groggy, spirit way, in its insistent delaying in the world of things, each move it made for her sake, each wrench out of stillness having, she knew, pain in it beyond anything his years could have prepared him for. She saw it, his soul, not as vapor or smoke, not ghost, but more like something pulled in strands through an underwater lattice, a net, and the strands trying to reunite, and unable to, and pulsing, pulsing to her, through the element that held them back.

She must go home. It was that feeling, still familiar all these years after his babyhood, of a period of time like a length of rope, which, when you got to the end of it, pulled you. You had to be back in that one room, reach into the crib and draw up to you the bounty, the bounty of his requirements.

But she was here in a sunny back yard, with people treating her in a friendly way. She had no wish to know them. Yet no saving antipathy was coming to her, of the sort that had yanked her out of her seat at concerts when she first tried to listen to music—how was it she had never realized how she hated the jerking, sanctimonious concentration of chamber musicians?—and driven her to slam herself into booths where she had her rite of pressing herself against the wall and fixing her eyes on a white toilet until it became an unknown thing, a circle in a dark haze. She thought of her ex-husband at those times with sincere feeling, hating everyone but him. He, too, might be somewhere hiding in a booth.

But now, this much later, she was denied the ecstatic ill will that had been hers, like a dance she had made up. It failed her. Without that fury in her she had to sit and talk like a normal person, like anybody.

The chuckling Steve and the other woman, the dark-haired one whose name she had forgotten, had fallen silent after Lisa said in a thrilled voice, "Listen, the birds!" The dark woman closed her eyes and threw back her head. They didn't care that the tiny gray birds had just been chased away by starlings, or that the starlings produced a song like the opening and shutting of scissors.

"So how's your book coming?" Michael said to Steve. That jolted her. This silly boy, writing a book?

"It's getting there. It will actually appear on earth next March." Steve turned to Jean with his little idling-motor laugh and laid his hand on his chest. "My firstborn," he said, and as her being, her whole scalded being leapt in the air, she saw his eyes cloud and his smooth skin darken to the forehead with fright at having said that to her. *Firstborn.* She shut her lips and detached her eyes from his—even his lids had gone red—with a smile she knew was bizarre, humble.

Lisa said, "Oh my God, congratulations!" Jean got her breath and re-met Steve's half-shut eyes. She was willing to speak, but nothing came. Lisa said, "Now, it's about the jails?"

"About the parole system. How disorganized it is. Nothing having the desired effect. And—and so on and so on, all my deep thoughts on the subject. My master's thesis. Expanded."

"Well, you should know these things," Lisa said sweetly.

"Maybe," said the other woman. "But it all boils down to somebody's whim, who gets out and who doesn't."

"That's his point," said Lisa.

"You guys, you DAs, I don't know," the other woman said sleepily. "Bet you would have been public defenders in the eighties." Jean looked at her for the first time, thinking maybe she and Steve were lovers, and at the same time, for reasons she could not pin down, feeling sure all of a sudden that the girl beside her, Lisa, had been Michael's lover. Buttering bread with the same detached expression, the dark woman addressed herself to Jean. "His thesis won a prize, when it came out as an article."

Jean fixed an expression on her own face of readiness to hear about the parole system. Finally, when no one else took charge Steve leaned over and said to her, "I'm a parole officer. Juvenile."

"He's a cop," the woman said. So the lawyer was Lisa.

Maybe Jean could bring up Michael's remodeling. What . . . what was involved in stenciling a wood floor? But she could not find the energy to ask, and she turned to Michael and let him put his firm, small hand on hers. This softened the atmosphere, and the four friends resumed the conversation, excusing her from it.

After a long time, during which she fell by degrees into a familiar unthinking state, Michael said, "Listen, we'll have to call it a day. Jean has to get back."

"I do," she said. "I'm sorry. I should have gone sooner. But don't you leave, Michael, I'm fine. Please stay, don't leave your guests."

"Guests." Steve started up his laugh.

Michael said, "You don't have your car here." Lisa and the other woman and Steve stood up, as obliging as the housemates. Even now giving Jean latitude to be remote, or perhaps rude: was it rude to call them guests? Customs changed between generations. Things became funny. Things became stupid that had been normal. Her son had taught her that.

"But come in for a minute and see the upstairs. And take a look at this sander," Michael said. "It's a tractor." Steve and the dark woman stood up—she settled against him while she pulled her shoes on, so they were a couple—and followed Michael up the ramp into the house. Lisa stayed behind.

Lisa said, "I guess you must not like to drive now."

Personal. This girl, Jean felt it, had definitely been involved with Michael, and now she was his friend, a switch people he knew seemed to make without a lot of fuss. Now she wanted to be friendly and personal with Jean, cross the distance between the old girlfriend and the new, as well as the established chasm between the afflicted and the unscathed. Although Jean knew, she knew now, that people would always surprise you, most of them would have gone through something or other and not be intact themselves. It was a mistake to think the average person had absorbed no great blow, just because of smiles, the pushing of grocery carts, the driving of cars, remarriage. It was always a surprise, terrible, not kind, that this thing happened, this growth of membrane over a raw opening, and that the membrane thickened, the rawness grew more and more opaque, and slowly vanished, so that you couldn't tell by looking that a membrane was there, and then it really was not there, it was the skin itself, and the person would be proud of that. "It was bad for a while," the person would say. "You think it will never end."

All right. Suppose you ceased to judge what you had done, your speed and steering, your being on the road at all, with your son strapped beside you in the hopeless indenture of childhood, unable to say don't take me, not tonight, don't take me. Suppose you began to see it as something unavoidable. He with ten years' life in him and no more. Yourself giving birth, at his birth, to this night in which he is to be hurt unto death.

No, it must not sink into the thread of some hellish tapestry woven in aged, excusing greens and blacks. No, there must be repayment.

Yes. It must never end.

She knew she did not want to hear whatever it was Lisa might want to reveal about her own misfortunes. "I never liked driving," she told the girl curtly.

Michael had told them the details, she knew. It was a story they might have read in the papers. Jean knew people here and there might mention it even now, whether they had ever heard of her and her son or the other victims or not, especially on the peninsula where it happened, where some evil destiny had laid down a road, as if a road could simply be mined out of dark forest, and be traveled, black with rain, by weekenders driving to trailheads and campgrounds, forgetting the road was the den of machines of such weight, such speed—logging trucks with their tall prongs up when they were going in empty and down when they were coming out loaded with logs the circumference of their tires. And so it was not farfetched that a logging truck should appear on a curve, sliding sideways, drifting, with the illusion of slowness, on broad wings of spray, and lose its load. Hit its air brakes hard enough to heave the top logs off and torpedo the oncoming cars. The farfetched thing was that some few should open their eyes in the wet, black New World of the next minute: the truck driver, a teenager from a full station wagon. Jean.

Lisa began, "I only mention it because . . ."

"It's all right," Jean said, looking up and beginning the rueful smile that said the past, for all its confounding injury, was the past. "Michael has helped." You had to soothe people. It was the opposite of the popular idea that people did not want to remind you or to be reminded themselves. They did want to talk to you, touch you as Lisa was doing now, hand on her arm, and thereby touch the thing that had happened to you.

"I know you've done a lot for him. But nothing seems to convince him. He won't accept comfort. I guess that's it. I don't mean to butt in, but I'm so worried about him."

"About Michael?"

"He's leading such a hopeless life."

Michael came out onto the ramp. "Lisa, they're going to leave without you."

"I'm coming," Lisa said. She scooped jam onto her bread and turned. "Good-bye, Jean. I hope—we'll talk again, I hope."

When Michael came back, Jean considered him, his lean face with the symmetrical features that should have been handsome. But something was not in them. After a while she said slowly, "Tell me about your life."

"My life. Great. What did Lisa say?"

"She said you're leading such a hopeless life."

"Oh, she did? A hopeless life."

"I don't think it's fair, if that's true, that you haven't said anything about the hopelessness of your life."

"Wait a second. Do I look hopeless?"

"Don't just blow it off."

He studied her. "She means my past," he said, and shrugged.

"All right."

"So I don't have to tell you."

"No, you don't."

He put his hand on the table beside hers so his fingernails fit into the grooves of the wood. "I killed my father."

Jean did not move, but after a while she said, "I thought you said you weren't a killer."

"I am, though. So what do you think of me now?"

"Did you murder him?"

"Ah. She's quick. She asks the question."

"That must mean no."

"I didn't murder him if you mean first-degree murder. Premeditation. Or second-degree murder. Intent. No. I killed him, though."

"I wish you would just say what happened."

"It's a story I prefer not to go into."

"But lots of people know it."

"Some people. Some friends."

"Like Lisa. I bet she's more than a friend. But not me. All right. Why don't you take me home."

"I thought you wanted to talk." He took her hand from the table and opened it with his small, hard fingers. "Here's the story," he said, flattening her hand palm up on the table and holding it down with his fist. "I was wrestling my father and I had him down. We did that a lot. He liked to do it. Build me up. Because I was small. Premature. The size of a kitten. See?" He threw his shoulders back. "We had been wrestling for a long time, in the basement where my mom made us go. We had a mat. She didn't like it, because he was big. A big, muscular guy. And me—right? We got into one of those sessions where you just keep on and on. Longer than usual. I wouldn't stop. I had him down, I was not going to let him up. He let out a groan and I kept on. And by the time I stopped, right? and I decided to let go of him, let him up, by that time—he had died." He took his fist off her hand. The muscles of his lips had formed a slit smile. "First question, 'Of what?' Answer, 'Cardiac arrest.'"

"How old were you?"

"Second question. Let's see if you can just go right down the line with all the key questions and I'll answer and then you make the key statements. You, me, you, me." He beckoned her. "How old was I? I was fourteen."

"Why are you talking to me this way? I've never seen you this—"

"This unpleasant. Right. It's definitely the unpleasant side of me."

"I thought—"

"You thought I was just a nice guy. A boyish kind of a guy. The nicest guy you could have run into, under the circumstances." He had her hand back down on the ridged wood, hard enough to hurt. His forehead had popped out in sweat.

"Michael—"

"Wait a second. You haven't made the definitive statement."

"What is that?"

"Come on," he said, beckoning again.

"Michael, I'm tired and you're making me unhappy. I don't like this feeling you're giving me. I want to go home. I need to be there." For the first time she felt vaguely ashamed that Michael knew her the way he did, already knew things about her, knew why she had to get to her house.

"'It wasn't your fault.' You're supposed to say, 'It wasn't your fault.'"

Suddenly, as she inspected his dark eyes—brighter than she had seen them before, and smaller, as Steve's had been when he realized he had said *firstborn*—her nervousness fell away. Her fingers curled. She shut them on his and pressed back, hard. "Why would I say that?" she said.

He squinted at her.

"Why would I say that?" She leaned forward, his head filled her vision, she began to speak, right to the eyes and the twisted mouth. "When you did kill him. Why would I say you didn't? Is that what people say to you? It isn't your fault?"

"They do."

"They say that to me, too," she said.

She tore off a piece of bread. As she chewed, she thought she might be smiling as she had before, when Steve said *firstborn*, or as Michael had been smiling when he beckoned her with his hands. She couldn't be sure just what she might look like. Michael didn't turn away. He kept looking, nodding in the rhythm of the owl balloons above them. Their hands were hurting each other. Their faces were close. She swallowed the bread. Before this she had never smelled sweat on him. Under the owls' eyes they began to kiss each other, their teeth scraped, they were two people who would kill, and not go crying for mercy, they were criminals, both of them were, they went on kissing, they were criminals.